I0102738

Entertaining Tucson Highlights

Volume IV
Selections from Volumes I-III: 1950s through 1990s
Includes: Table of Contents & Indexes
& Features from All 3 Volumes

An *Entertainment Magazine*
Time Capsule Compilation

By Robert E. Zucker

BZB Publishing, Inc. Tucson, Arizona

Entertaining Tucson Highlights (Volume IV)
Index Volumes I-III: 1950s through 1990s
By Robert Edward Zucker

The fourth in a series of volumes. With selections from the *Newsreal*

ISBN-13: 978-1-939050-13-7
ISBN-10: 1-939050-13-8

First Edition: April 12th 2016

Published by
BZB Publishing, Inc.
P.O. Box 91317
Tucson, Arizona 85752-1317
520-623-3733

Email: publisher@emol.org

Web:
EntertainTucson.com
EMOL.org
EntertainmentMagazine.net

Printed in the United States of America by CreateSpace, an Amazon.com company.
Available for sale through Amazon.com and other outlets in print and digital formats.

ENTERTAINING TUCSON HIGHLIGHTS
The Condensed Version

Volumes I-III: 1950s through 1990s

This special "Highlights" edition of ENTERTAINING TUCSON combines portions of all three volumes, including the entire Indexes and Table of Contents, into a single condensed collector's edition.

The three-volume set of ENTERTAINING TUCSON ACROSS THE DECADES covers, in great detail, local Tucson entertainment from the 1950s through the end of the 1990s, as reported by several Tucson newspapers– *Entertainment Magazine, Tucson Teen* and the *Newsreal.* All three volumes– filling more than 700 pages– contain hundreds of original photographs, articles and interviews of popular Tucson musicians, actors and sports personalities over five decades. Extensive indexes of thousands of entertainers are in each edition.

Volume 1:
1950s through 1985
309 pages
Retail: $20.00
ISBN: 978-193050-06-9

Volume 2:
1986 through 1989
223 pages
Retail: $15.00
ISBN: 978-193050-07-6

Volume 3:
The 1990s
228 pages
Retail: $15.00
ISBN: 978-193050-09-0

Available to purchase online at Amazon.com (discounted) or BarnesandNoble.com
Purchase in Tucson at Antigone Books, Hotel Congress, Mostly Books, Summit Hut
and Oracle inn Steakhouse.
Call 520-623-3733 for more information.

Visit EntertainTucson.com for more samples and buy online.

Entertaining Tucson Highlights: Contents

ENTERTAINING TUCSON ACROSS THE DECADES..6

Contents of Each Volume 7
>   Table of Contents for Volume 1: 1950s through 1985 7
>   Table of Contents for Volume 2: 1986-1989 11
>   Table of Contents for Volume 3: The 1990s 15

The Compilation 20
>   *Youth Alternatives, Youth Awareness, Tucson Teen, Entertainment Magazine*..................21
>   *Mountain Newsreal & Newsreal* 22

ENTERTAINING TUCSON ACROSS THE DECADES 23

Volume 1: 1950s to 1985 23
>   Tucson's musical memories of the '50s 23
>   Sons of the Pioneers: Rooted in Tucson's history 25
>   Dean Armstrong: A Living Tucson Western Legend 26
>   The 1960s: A look back on Tucson's past 28
>   A Run-in with Tucson's Drive-In's 29
>   Lewallen Brothers: A blast from Tucson's Past..30
>   Tucson country music bands in the '70s 31
>   *Mountain Newsreal* makes its debut 31
>   Chuck Wagon & the Wheels: Keepin' spinnin' 32
>   Billy Templeton: the Elvis shtick 34
>   Disco fever heats Tucson teens 35
>   *Youth Alternatives* and *Youth Awareness Press*...35
>   Rockin' Tucson in the '80s 36
>   Tucson's 1982 Punk Rock Scene 39
>   Serf's up for Green on Red 40
>   Sandworms: Desert Sophistication 43
>   Statesboro Blues Band: Happy with the blues 46

Volume 2: 1986-1989 48
>   1985 Recap– the end of an era..48
>   January 1986: Local Tucson Music Column 50
>   The Fantastic Fanatiks First LP 50
>   Short Stories Gets New Drummer..50
>   John Sirkis Releases First LP 50
>   IF's New Tape 50
>   Statesboro's New Blues 50
>   Boogie Man Boogies 51
>   New Home for KXCI 51
>   HMS Preparing New Music 51
>   Global Goes NueVenue 51
>   April 1988...52

Local Musicians Recognized at Mardi Gras; Terry & Zeke's Arises Again; Gentle Ben's Gets the Boot 52

Tailor Made for Tucson 52

December 1988..53

Sidewinders to Sign Record Deal; Hellhound Fish Karma 53

Sunday Morning Bars Sport the Sports...53

Your Name in Lights...53

New Entry on the Club Scene – Rialto's 53

Reggae All Month 53

Bobby Taylor & Real Deal: Here's the Real Deal...54

Volume 3: 1990s **58**

1989: Tucson Nightlife Updates 58

Now Everyone's Wearing A Marshmallow Overcoat...60

March 1993 61

Tucson Bands Hold CD Release Parties 61

Tucson Blues Legend, Sam Taylor Dies at 74...62

Index: Volume 1 63

Index: Volume 2 74

Index: Volume 3 86

Publishers 99

Robert Zucker, Entertainment Magazine 99

Jon Rosen, *Newsreal* 99

To Purchase Copies..100

Titles from BZB Publishing, Inc. 100

ENTERTAINING TUCSON ACROSS THE DECADES

If you enjoyed Tucson's local entertainment anytime between the 1950s through the early 2000s, then you probably will be familiar with many of these people and places. Step back into time and live, or relive, Tucson's local culture, music and entertainment scene – evolving and revolving– over five decades.

The local entertainment scene in Tucson, Arizona during the 1950s through 1985 was vibrant– from the rock and roll of the **Dearly Beloved, Linda Ronstadt, Bob Meighan, Dean Armstrong**, **Pills, Giant Sandworms** and everything in between– thousands of Tucson entertainers over five decades.

Within these pages are the memories and the experiences of those people and places. These are the original articles and interviews published in several local newspapers which covered the Tucson entertainment scene. Follow their stories through the years. Read about the big breaks, record releases, hot performances and duds, break ups, tragedies, personal insights and struggles.

This book is in recognition to all of the Tucsonans who kept us entertained over those decades and to those reporters, staff and photographers who contributed their time to keep Tucson informed.

ENTERTAINING TUCSON ACROSS THE DECADES
Full Set (including this Volume IV)
Volume I: 1950s through 1985
Volume II: 1986 through 1989
Volume II: the 1990s
Volume IV: Indexes and Highlights

(Top Left to Right) **Nadine & the MoPhonics** (from 1986); **Statesboro Blues Band** (1984); **Dean Armstrong** (from 1991); **Los Lasers** (1985); **Jonny Sevin** (1981) Photo credits on inside pages.

Presented by

Entertainment Magazine

& Newsreal

"Entertaining Tucson" web site:
EntertainTucson.com

Contents of Each Volume

This volume contains the full Table of Contents and Indexes for each of three volumes of ENTERTAINING TUCSON ACROSS THE DECADES. Some of the articles from each of the three volumes are included in this volume. Additional articles and photographs can be viewed at EntertainTucson.com.

Table of Contents for Volume 1: 1950s through 1985

Entertaining Tucson Across the Decades..5

The Compilation 11

1950s: Rockin' & Cruisin' 15
Tucson's musical memories of the '50s 16
Sons of the Pioneers: Rooted in Tucson's history 18
Rex Allen: The legend of "Mr. Cowboy" 20
   Talking with Rex Allen 21
1950s-1960s: Tucson radio's misty memories 25
Shopping Tucson Downtown 26
Tucson's culture in fried chicken...27

1960s: Rock Evolves & Standards Endure..29
The 1960s: A look back on Tucson's past 30
A run-in with Tucson's Drive-In's 31
The Tucson Rodeo Parade..33
   History of the Tucson Rodeo Parade 33
1960s: KTKT's Battle of the Bands..34
The Vibrations: rockin' into the night 35
Dearly Beloved: The faces of the 60s 36
Linda Ronstadt: Tucson's "Girl Singer" 42
Dean Armstrong: A Tucson Legend 44
Lewallen Brothers: A blast from Tucson's Past 46
Frank Ace: An Ace up his sleeve...47
Up on Bourbon Street..48
Mickey Greco swings 50
Carl Guy: Guitarist turns actor 51
The acoustic ballad of Shep Cooke...52
Jimmy Greenspoon: Leading a Three Dog Life 54

1970s: Rock goes mainstream, disco flickers 55
Tucson music in the 1970s 56
Choo Choo's 58
Tucson country music bands in the '70s 59
   The *Mountain Newsreal* makes it's debut..59
Chuck Wagon & the Wheels: Keepin' those wheels spinnin' 60
John Hawk: The Hawk of the desert 62
Cass Preston keeps on swinging 63
John Denman swings with his quartet...64
Peggy Rose &: Company: A refresher course for "Swingers!" 65
Billy Templeton: the Elvis shtick 66
   Will the real Billy Templeton please stand up! 67
Where have all the Big Bands gone? Ask Cliff Juergens!...68
Disco fever heats Tucson teens 69

Teen dance launches new teen paper 70
Disco: A fad of the '70s 71
   Teen dances at the Gazebo...71
Cruising Speedway is a well-traveled tradition 74
Turning on to KTKT 77
The crew at KRQ 80
Disco fever spreads around Tucson...82
KTKT-FM: New 96 Rocks Airwaves 83
The Desert Springs Concert Event...84
   Desert Springs performances at the Pima County Fairgrounds 85
KHYT's disco machine 86
   Raffle's dazzles with lasers and DiscRock..87
Games Around Town: Video, pinball, pool and Flash 88
Sports: A new season with the Tucson Toros 89
Goodbye '70s, Hello 80s 90
Jim Anderson: Tucson icon...91

1980: Technology becomes personal **93**

Disco-vision, cable and home computers 94
What's on channel 375?...95
Rockin Tucson in the '80s 96
Video Games: Buzzes, whirls and pongs..99
Surge forward 100
"First Wave" concert splashed out 101

1981: Evolving Music Trends **103**

KTKT's new sound: Music changes trend..104
Cox gets nod for Tucson cable TV..105
Jonny Sevin: rising success...106
White Lightning strikes innocent audiences..107

1982: Revolving musicians **109**

Tucson Teens– some bands bite the dust 110
   Good news for local musicians 111
Pills: Return to Transition 112
Larry Miles: Spinning records for a living 114
Reporter Chuck Graham on work and music...115
Rick Allen: Radio as a career...116
September 1982: Local musicians release new tapes 117
TV at your fingertips 117
Leanne McCabe: singing her heart out...118
"Desert Tracks" Tucson's best– together on one local album 119
Tucson's 1982 Punk Rock Scene...120

1983: Alternative Music Scene Emerges **123**

LeAnne McCabe: Taking it to the Top...124
Young adult club opens..125
LFB: A sound looking for a name 126
February 1983: Short Music Notes..127
Uptones return "home"...128
Serf's up for Green on Red 130
Burroughs & Sandworms: Rock and roll on a budget 133
Teens in middle of Sundance West feud 134
Sandworms: Desert Sophistication 135
Lee Joseph: This man wants your tape! 138
KXCI to fill void 139
   Radio Free America..140
Confused is all right 142
(Phantom) Limbs ready for 'romance' 144
How to Stuff A Wild Bikini...147
Youth producing TV for the first time 148
Crosswind: Local trio kicks up dust 149
Slit: Underground Notes 150

Silent XChange: Local XChange 151
Los Lasers legend and myths 152
¿Que Onda? Where's the alternative music?? KXCI! 154

1984: Rock Reigns Hardcore Fledges **155**

Updating Tucson Music 156
January 1984: Jazz, blues, country punks 157
Statesboro Blues Band: Happy with the blues 158
Road Furniture: Born on the Highway 160
Shagnatty: A Twist of the Jah 161
Public Access Cable: A chat with Jan Lesher 162
Tucson's sounds abound 164
A Tost to the Blues 165
The Resistors: What are they resisting? 166
July 1984: New Music Column 168
September 1984: hardcore, new wave & other punk 169
The blues are alive and well! 170
Only "Only's," they say 171
Tucson's specialty music stores 172
Hard production work pays off in vinyl 173
   Rod rocks the TCC 174
Let's have the V-8's 176
   October 1984: Local bands try to get a break 177
Roc Lochner: Roc and roll 178
Roads to Moscow hits the road; Embers smolders 180
The progressive music scene in Tucson 181
Giant Sandworms reattack! 182
Progressive Music: Tucson keeps on rockin' 184
Tucson metal isn't dead– yet. 186
UPS: Useless Pieces of Shit 188
Overview for '84: Don't step on Tucson's blue suede shoes 190

1985: Entertaining Month by Month **193**

January 1985: Sandworms become Sandwurms 194
   More Tucson clubs close, bands prepare LPs 196
   Los Lasers stopped waiting 197
   It's the Aftermath that'll get you 199
February 1985: Tucson musicians rock WREX 201
   Chances burned to the ground 201
   T&Z to serve drinks, Chances bites the dust, Roxy and DanceTrax rises 202
   Tucson bands rock the clubs 202
March 1985: Local music lights up Spring Fling 206
   Spring sprouts local music news 207
   The heavy metal edge; Roc Lochner new release 209
   Etude prepares video 211
   New radio station on cable TV 212
   Rock Videos: Fad or Culture Shock? 213
   Connie Breeze: Breezin' down life's highway 215
   Tucson's Reggae History 217
   New Bands Heat Things Up 218
   Fred Espinoza: Lights, Camera... Stress 220
April 1985: *Magazine* is now *Entertainment Magazine* 222
   Saddle City Band stars with Michael Landon 222
   April 1985: Tucson's got all the jazz! 223
   Loser's Club debuts 223
   Nadine & the MoPhonics: Singing for success 224
   Local scene bursts with spring 226
   Ticket buying: made easier 228
   Wah-Deh Connection: Reggae Connection 228
   WREX closes, but the beat goes on 229
   Los Hamsters?! You got it! 230
May 1985: Local progressive music hops 231
   General Delivery: Delivering since 1985 232
   Tucson is jazzin' it up! 234

Roadrunner: Making music country-style 235
The Cattle are now on vinyl 236
June 1985: Jack's, Rockefeller's gone, Circus on 237
The Fanatiks: They're ironically fanatic 238
Not just another Buddy System 239
Other summer music 239
Adam Graham: The other half of O'Leary 240
Aces high on the go 242
Losers Club gain a winning reputation 243
Tucson has the comedy fever! 244
Diverse talents mold Sidewinders 245
July 1985: Tucson musicians beat the heat 246
Locals in the studios 247
HMS hums 247
Country rumbles: Bar hoppin' and Saddle City Stompin' 248
Comedy: Fun times on Tucson's stages 249
Gary Hood: Local comedian keeps his lines hot and his delivery cool 250
August 1985: Summer hot rocks fever 252
Street Pajama: On the Road Again 253
Tucson radio offers alternatives 255
Chuck Graham: Sorry Dave, Chuck was first 256
Black Sun shines through 258
Montreal is a rare Tucson breed 258
Nadine adds mo'Phonics 259
Tucson comedy clubs headlines Tucson's best 260
Armen Dirtadian: A golfer in sheik's clothing 261
Howard Morgan: Not just slight of the hand 264
October 1985: Hot blues cool jazz 265
Ronnie Mack: Pickin' in the autumn 265
Bands around town during fall '85 266
Nadine & MoPhonics 266
HMS 266
The Press 266
Twister 266
Neck Romance 266
Tucson comedy scene: Take my jokes, please! Karmel's melts. 267
November 1985: Comedy, clubs, variety and spice 268
No lack of blues 268
Keeping up with Tucson bands 269
Ronnie Mack: November Country Licks 270
December 1985: A Grab Bag of Comics 272
Country Cub hopping with Ronnie Mack 272
Tucson bands wrap up the holidays 274
TWIT is serious about TV 279
Kruiser Experience: Kruising for a bruising 281
Garry Shandling: keeping Johnny's seat warm 283

Entertaining Tucson Across the Decades: Volume II: 1986-early 2000s 287

Post-logue...**288**

Tucson City Map 290
Publishing Title Holdings 291
Publishers 292
Robert Zucker, *Entertainment Magazine* 292
Jon Rosen, *Newsreal* 292
Contributing Writers/Artists/Photographers 293
Illustrations/Credits 294
Photo Captions 295

Index..**299**

Table of Contents for Volume 2: 1986-1989

Tucson Nightlife Across The Decades 3
The Story of the Entertainment Magazine..10

1985 Recap 11

1986... 13

January 1986..**13**
    Garry Shandling: Keeping Johnny's Seat Warm 13
    January: Country Stalking The Great South Side Of Tucson 16
    January: Local Tucson Music Column 18
February 1986..**20**
    Tucson Bands Crank It Out...20
    February: Kickin' Up Those Tucson Rodeo Licks 22
    Tucson Laughs With The New Comedy Zone 23
March 1986..**24**
    Ed On The Air: Working For The Fun Of It 24
    Tucson Bands Rock 26
April 1986..**30**
May 1986..**31**
    Rotating Nightclubs, The Distant And More 31
June 1986...**33**
    Summer Sounds Winding Down 33
July 1986..**36**
    Entertainment Magazine Relocates And Expands 36
August 1986...**38**
September 1986..**39**
    Fall Brings New TV, Events And Music 39
October 1986..**40**
    Tucson Music Is On The Loose! 40
November 1986...**42**
    Tucson's Top Talent! 42
December 1986...**44**
    Local Sounds Ring In The Holidays 44
    December After Hours And Band Updates 45

1987... 47

January 1987..**47**
    Tucson Bands Earning Respect Of Club Owners 47
    January Sounds Around Tucson 48
    Boogie Animals: Better Than Party Animals...49
February 1987..**51**
    Rodeo Time In The Old Pueblo 51
    All The Fixin's – The Best Country Food In Tucson 53
    Getting A Fastbreak 54
    Nemesis: Avenging Rockers 55

The Bullies: Bully-ing Around 55
Audrey St. Clair: Her Heart Goes Out To Vicki Lynne 56
Waking Up To Tucson's Nightlife 57
March 1987 .... **58**
No More Ed In The Morning 58
April 1987 .... **59**
Speedways Are Rolling Along 59
All Of The Stars Gather In The Deserts' Tucson Classics 60
May 1987 .... **61**
Short Stories Offer: Use Me 61
Electrifying Short Circuit 62
RFA On Break 62
Bluesman Sam Taylor Joins Statesboro Blues Band 63
Sharon Hodges: A Comedian To Watch 64
Get Some American Pie, It's Hot! 64
Backstreet Boogie Is Back On Stage 65
The Sidewinders Show Their Good Side 65
June 1987 .... **66**
Tucson's Summer Country Nightlife 66
Charles Bowden: 'On Top Of Frog Mountain' 67
Tucson Comedy: Howl Like A Mad Dog 68
The Comedy Of Genesis 68
July 1987 .... **69**
Will The Trolley Make Tracks For $5,000? 69
The Cattle Rustled Onto 45 70
Rick 'Shadow' Joes: Dance in the Shadows 70
Ross Nickerson Fills Bluegrass Void 71
Musicians Boycott Arizona 71
August 1987 .... **72**
Happy 212th Birthday, Old Pueblo! 72
Daniel Steenken: Ex-Chemist Is Catalyst 72
Cool Jazz In Tucson's Hot Sun 73
Necromancer: Rising From The Dead 75
So, May I Introduce For You... Billy Shears Band 76
September 1987 .... **77**
Autocatz 77
Summit Studios: Tucson's Recording Industry Grows Up 78
Las Cruces Romps The Room 79
Rough Is Smooth 80
October 1987 .... **81**
It's Time To Meet Yourself, Tucson 81
Arizona Opera 'Menu' Feeds Varied Tastes 81
Highbeam Blues Band Makes Some Changes 83
Tucson Nightlife: A Primer For The Recently Spontaneous 84
November 1987 .... **86**
Valley Of The Moon Shines Over Tucson 86
Sam Smiley Is Serious About Acting 87
Tucson Has Brain Damage 88
Aftermath: Metal With A New Approach 88
December 1987 .... **90**
Rockin' With Rockefeller 90

1988 91

January 1988 .... **91**
Atrophy: Ahead Of The Contenders 91

February 1988 ....**93**
   Tucson Rodeo And Parade 93
March 1988 ....**94**
   The 2nd Tucson Mardi Gras; 1st Music Awards 94
April 1988 ....**97**
   Local Musicians Recognized At Mardi Gras; Terry & Zeke's Arises Again; Gentle Ben's Gets The Boot 97
   Tailor Made For Tucson 97
May 1988 ....**99**
   Stalking The Great Wild Tucson Nightlife 99
   Arthur/Brand Band Makes A Grand Stand 101
   Glombecki Playing Around Town...102
   Craig Lavelle: Choral Director Branches Into Local Music 105
June 1988 ....**106**
   Tucson's Sizzlin' Summer Nightlife 106
   There's A New Tucson In Town 107
   More Ways To Tickle The Funny Bone In The Desert 108
   Robert Apel: Falling Down Got Him Up 108
   A Run-In With Drive-In's 109
July 1988 ....**110**
   Community Media Celebrates 2nd Year 110
   Christmas & Halloween In July??? 110
   Local Rockin' 'n' Rollin' 110
   Metal Banging Bands 111
   ATC Announces 1988-89 Season 111
August 1988 ....**112**
   Tucson's Nightlife is Rockin' And A Rollin'..112
   Western Music Has Its Distinctions – Not The Same As Country Music 113
   Titan Valley Aims Its Warhead, Captures 1st Place At Telluride 113
September 1988 ....**114**
   Vince Frighetti: Keeping Tucson's Beat 114
   Xavier Marquez: One Of Tucson's Premier Guitarists 115
   Tucson Rockers Insane Jane 116
   Twister Rocks Tucson 117
   911: Between A Rock And A Hard Place 118
   Tucson's Scene Comes Alive With Students' Return 119
   There Is New Age Music In Tucson! 119
October 1988 ....**120**
   Tucson Bands Head Into The Fall 120
   LRQ: Roadhouse Fuses Jazz 121
   The Host: Shooting For "Another World" 122
   Local Country Pickers: A Tide Turns In Tucson 123
   Twister Keeps Rocking Tucson 123
November 1988 ....**124**
   Tucson's Year of Musical Change...124
   In Hot Pursuit Of Live Dance Music..125
   Restless Rockers 126
   White Rabbit: Straight From Wonderland 127
   Necromancer Takes The Stage 128
   Fiddling For Charity And Fun 128
   Robert Bernhardt: Tucson Symphony Both Diverse And Exciting 129
December 1988 ....**130**
   Revivers Keep The Oldies Alive 131
   Joe Myers: A Surprising Talent...132
   Liz Fletcher: "It's Up To Me To Make It Happen" 133
   Tucson's Trolley Awaits!...134
   Bygone Yuletides 135

1989 136

January 1989 136
Tucson RROC's – Rock 'n' Roll Cable TV Show 136
The Naturals: Acting Naturally 137

February 1989 138
Local Western, Bluegrass, Country Rock 138
Duncan Sitt: Local New Age Country Rock 138
Surge To The Top 139
Managing A Nightclub Is More Than "hanging out at the bar" 140

March 1989 144
Tucson's Musical Memories Roll On: The Nifty '50s 144
A Man Called Sam (Taylor) 144
Taking A Chance On Romance 146
LifeForce Enlightens 147
Marshmallows Not Soft On Music 148
Sons Of Western Plains To Tour Arizona 148

April 1989 149
The Local Alternative Music Scene 149
KXCI: An Evolution In Radio 150

May 1989 151
Ken Lofton: Little Big Man– Kenny Conquer? 151
Tucson's Nightlife Changes Corners 152
The Chambers Put Their Brand On Western Music 153
In Pursuit of Tucson's Hot Pursuit 154
In Your Face, In Your Mind 155

June 1989 157
EM's New Look, Format, Circulation Up 157
The Fall From Grace 157
Battle Of The Bands At The Garden 158
XL Strives To Be Tucson's Band 158
Local New Age: Soundings Of The Planet 159
Bobby Taylor & Real Deal: Here's A Real Deal For You 160
John Denman Swings With His Quartet 164
The Lewallen Brothers: A Blast From Tucson's Past 165

July 1989 166
The Cadillacs: Back On The Road Again 166
T.J. Canyon Band: Down A Country Road 167
Cass Preston Keeps On Swinging 168
Al Perry: Brahman Bull In A Cattle Field 169
Cynthia Stacey: A New Age For Tucson's Spirituality 171
Signature On Tucson: Sam Taylor 173
Pollo Elastico To Tour Cooler Areas; TW&T Showcases 173

August 1989 174
"It's The Garry Shandling Interview. " 174
Entertainment Magazine Thanks Readers 176
Local Tape Reviews 176
The Talents Of Ted Moreno 177
A Top Hat And Marshmallow Overcoat 177
Mickey Greco Still Swings 178
Peggy Rose &: Company: A Refresher Course For "Swingers!" 179
Joey "The Kid" Medina: Tucson Boasts Its Own Set Of Gloves 180

September 1989 182
Tucson's Nightlife Comes Back To Life 182
The Statesboro Blues Band: Blues For Yesterday, Today & Tomorrow 183
Tucson Comedy: Keeping Tucson In Stitches 185
Everyone Entertains At Porter's House 186

Table of Contents for Volume 3: The 1990s

Tucson Nightlife Across The Decades 3
The Story of the Entertainment Magazine 9

1990 10

January 1990 10
November Guest: The Poetry Band 10
Fridkin: In Another Galaxy 11
The Paid Pyper of Tucson 12
March 1990 13
A Brand New Bag: Hackensack 13
Romeo, Oh, Broken Romeo 14
April 1990 15
Night Crossings: Crossing Paths In The Night 16
Ray Whittaker And Gary Favron 16
Votang Curries Favor In Tucson 17
May 1990 18
You're A Good Man, Armen Dirtadian 18
TSO: Bernhardt Stays In Tucson 19
Tucson Nightlife Updates 20
Mondo Guano: "It's Like Soup!" 21
A Pair Of Crystall's 23
June 1990 24
Fireworks Festival At TCC! 24
An Ace Up His Sleeve 25
What's Filming At "Old Tucson" 27
Tucson's Local Standards 27
July 1990 28
Good Vibrations: Recalling A Simpler, Solid Rock Era With A Tucson Band 28
Now Everyone's Wearing A Marshmallow Overcoat..29
Street Gypsy: Some Serious Plans For Musical Success 30
August 1990 32
Vicki Tapp: Musical Ambition Began In Ajo 32
September 1990 33
Linda Ronstadt: Tucson's "Girl Singer" 33
Bobby Mahon: Pickin' And A Grinnin' 36
Local Rockin' Scene Downtown 37
Local Jazzers Obsessive Jazz 37
October 1990 38
Where Is Tucson's Entertainment? 38
Local Kicking And Swinging At The Clubs 39
Giant Sand: Hitting The Beaches 40
Marshmallow Overcoat: Taking Off To Higher Ground 40
Jaime's Revenge: Revenge In Tucson 41
November 1990 42
Western Music Festival: Bringing The West Back Into Western Music 42

Chuck Wagon and the Wheels: Keepin' Those Wheels Spinnin' 42
Acoustic Music Alive And Well In Tucson 44
Bobby Taylor & Real Deal 45
Eat To The Beat At The UA Cellar: A Treat For Bands And Fans 46
Nostalgia Tucson Rock– The Vibrations 5 46
Undercurrent Carries Low Max 48
Arizona Theatre Co. Now State Theatre Of Arizona 48
December 1990 ....**50**
Tucson Compilation Tape Now In The "Ruff" 50
Sons Of The Pioneers: 57th Winter Season 51
Yuletides Of YesterYear 52

1991 53

January 1991 ....**53**
EM On TV: "Tucson NightLife" In Production 53
EM On Audio: Compilation Tape Nears Release 53
Overcoat Releasing 4th LP 53
Dean Armstrong: A Living Tucson Western Legend 54
February 1991 ....**56**
Tucson Rodeo: New Twists To An Old Tradition 56
Tucson Gem & Mineral Show: A Polished Milestone 57
Festival In The Sun Shines In Tucson 57
Sam Taylor Has The Ingredients 58
March 1991 ....**60**
Robyn Austin: Singing With A Determination 60
Margie Rye With Exile 61
April 1991 ....**62**
Neon Prophet: Turbo Reggae 63
Adding Special FX 63
Broken Romeo: No Broken Hearts Here 64
Users Of The Wicked Gravity: Industrious Users 64
May 1991 ....**65**
Landon's Spirit Fills The Tucson Classics 65
Tucson-Arizona Boys Chorus: Singing for Peace 65
OPJB: Up On Bourbon Street In The '60s 66
Sidewinders/Sandrubies: Winding Up With A New Name 69
Cynthia Stacey Celebrating A Second Release 71
General Delivery: Not Your Average Oldies Band 72
Billy Shears Band: The One And Only… 74
Musical Band Names– Sand Rubies And Overcoat 75
June 1991 ....**76**
"Desert Reign, The Mother Of All Compilations" CD Release Now Available 76
Chambers Sing On Comstock Records 77
Jimmy Greenspoon: Leading A Three Dog Life 77
Underneath The Overcoat 78
July 1991 ....**80**
The Ballad Of Shep Cooke 80
Molly Who… You Ask 81
August 1991 ....**82**
Tucson: Happy 216th! 82
Tucson's Country Music Scene: Kicking Up The Dust...83
Betty Stress: This Band Is Under Stress 84
September 1991 ....**86**
Rex Allen Days In Willcox 86
Dave King: Time To Move On 87
Brian Berggoetz: Inspired By Hendrix 87

Betty And The Bebops...88
Don Reeve: Wild Spirit...89
Alternative Music: A Musical Oasis Amidst The Sand...........................90
October 1991...**92**
Tucson Meet Yourself Shows Tucson's Ethnic Diversity........................92
Local Musicians Rock..92
The Shooters: Capturing Tucson With Music...93
Western Electric: Alternative Country..95
Desert Reign: Enthusiasm Gets Group Started.....................................96
Fall From Grace: Dark, Aggressive Music..97
Tucson Alternative Music: What's Under Those Desert Rocks?............99
Twister: A Unique Twist...100
November 1991...**101**
Western Music Festival...101
Musical Life On The Eastside..101
Ramones Go To Europe; Fall From Grace And Some Pulse.................103
Blue Lizards: Happy To Have The Blues...103
December 1991...**105**
22nd Annual 4th Avenue Winter Street Fair...105
Tucson Boys Chorus Visit White House..105
Swing Shift: Working The Country Shift...105
The Chambers: Western Tradition..106
More Kidd Squidd...107
Cynthia Stacey: A Little Bit Of Alchemy...108
One Blood: One Love, One Heart, One Blood.......................................109

1992.. **111**

January 1992...**111**
J.C. Skinner: A Corvette With Gas..111
Karaoke: Singing Your Heart Out..113
Rappin' it Up: Alternative Club Scene Stirring Up................................114
February 1992...**115**
"Lollipop Music" Not For 1·2·1..115
March 1992...**116**
Keeping Up With The Overcoats..116
April 1992...**118**
The County Fair Is Back In Town!..118
Spring Fling: Put Fling Into Your Spring...118
Bridges Hosts Classics; Landon To Be Honored..................................118
San Xavier Mission Turns 300..119
May 1992..**120**
Bobby Taylor: Real Deal Hoping For A Big Deal...................................120
Zebbhi Niyah: Reggae Gives The Word..122
June 1992...**123**
Keeping Up With Tucson Musicians CD's..123
July 1992..**124**
Hector Rodriguez: Not Just Another Musician......................................124
August 1992...**126**
San Agustin Celebration: Tucson's Oldest Festival Returns................126
September 1992..**127**
Chased By The Roadhouse Hounds..127
Night Watch On Spotlight...128
October 1992..**129**
Tucson Entertainment In The Fall...129
November 1992...**132**
Western Music Festival Even Larger This Year.....................................132

December 1992 133
    The Thin Men: A Slim Lead..133
    Threshing Floor: Threshing Around...133
    Rex Allen Weds...133

1993... 134

January 1993 134
    Janos Widler: Talent Who Creates Art On Plates 134
    Rockin' TG Fridays; Back From Berlin! 136
February 1993 137
    Bob Kessler Of Jeromes 137
    Tucson Music Scene Blooming 138
    Bill Tester's Bushwacker 139
March 1993 140
    Tucson Bands Hold CD Release Parties 140
    John Jacob: A Tucson Native Serving Hearty Food For 47 Years 141
April 1993 143
    Sand Rubies: Keeping Heads Above The Sand 143
    U & The Risk, Rubies, Tantrum Spotlight April's Music 144
May 1993 146
    Al & The Cattle, U & The Risk, Flys & Dollhouse 146
    Taylor And Brooks: Tucson Duo Has New York On Their Mind 147
June 1993 149
    Drew Vactor, The Tack Room...149
    Mollys Duo, UFO On The Road 151
July 1993 153
    Tucson's Trolley Is Back On Line 153
    Tucson Toros: 25 Years And Batting Strong 154
August 1993 156
    La Fiesta de San Agustin: Sunday, August 29 156
    Founder's Day Portrayed In Play: August 20-21 156
    Rediscover Tucson's Rich History: August 17-29th 157
    Cattle On The Prowl 157
    Gentle Ben's Brews Great Beers Locally 158
September 1993 161
    Plastic Museum Waxes Battle Of The Bands 161
October 1993 163
    Meet Yourself, Tucson...163
November 1993 164
    Si, Grimble & NORML 164
December 1993 165
    Rappin' It Up For The Holidays 165

1994... 166

January 1994 166
    New Clubs Break Into The Scene 166
February 1994 167
    Crist Has The Heat On Tucson...167
    Music Scene On Tap And On Plastic 168
March 1994 169
    Ace Scores Again 169
April 1994 170
    Tucson Toros Take Charge! PCL Champs!...170

Rappin' It Up: Ockham, Jargo, Clampetts, Gunga Din 171
May 1994 ....**173**
Bobby Taylor Speaks Out: Clubs And Musicians Need To Work Together 173
June 1994 ....**175**
Rappin' It Up: Awards, Media & CS's 175
July 1994 ....**176**
The Undone Redone– No More Gunga Din 176
August 1994 ....**177**
Tucson TV honored 177
September 1994 ....**178**
The Cadillacs: Keeping The Roots Of Rock Alive 178
October 1994 ....**179**
Music Awards, Bobby & More Cattle 179
New City Ordinance Poses New Questions 180
Last Print Edition Of EM, EMOL.org Goes Online 181
Tucson's Legend Sam Taylor: Taylor made to sing the blues 182

1995 and on…... 185

"Rapping It Up" 185
The Blue Light Blues Band 186
New Neon Prophet CD 188
George Howard And The Roadhouse House Hounds 189
Funky Bonz: A Lot Of Funk 191
Ockham's Razor 192
Plastic Museum "Full Frontal Nudity" 193
Michael Gulezian: Acoustic radiance 194
Al Perry's New CD, "Losin' Hand" 195
U.P.S.'s Paul Young dies 195
Giant Sand New Bootleg Release 196
Gerry Glombecki: poet with a song 198
Sam Taylor: Back Home Again 202
Tucson Blues Legend, Sam Taylor Dies At 74 204

Tucson Map **205**
Tucson Nightclubs **206**
In Remembrance **212**
Publishing Title Holdings **213**
Author Robert Zucker **214**

Index 215

The Compilation

Between 1974 and 1994 several local tabloid newspapers reported on the Tucson, Arizona entertainment scene. Although these papers are no longer published, their archives have been preserved and collected into a compilation of articles and images that historically record Tucson's culture.

This content is compiled from selected images and articles previously published in:

- *Youth Alternatives*
- *Youth Awareness Press*
- *Tucson Teen*
- *The Magazine*
- *Entertainment Magazine*
- *EMOL.org*
- *Newsreal*

The first volume of ENTERTAINING TUCSON ACROSS THE DECADES spans between the 1950s until the end of 1985. The second volume features 1986 through 1989. The third volume features the 1990s.

Since these articles and advertisements were published at least 30 years ago, the schedules, addresses and events are no longer current.

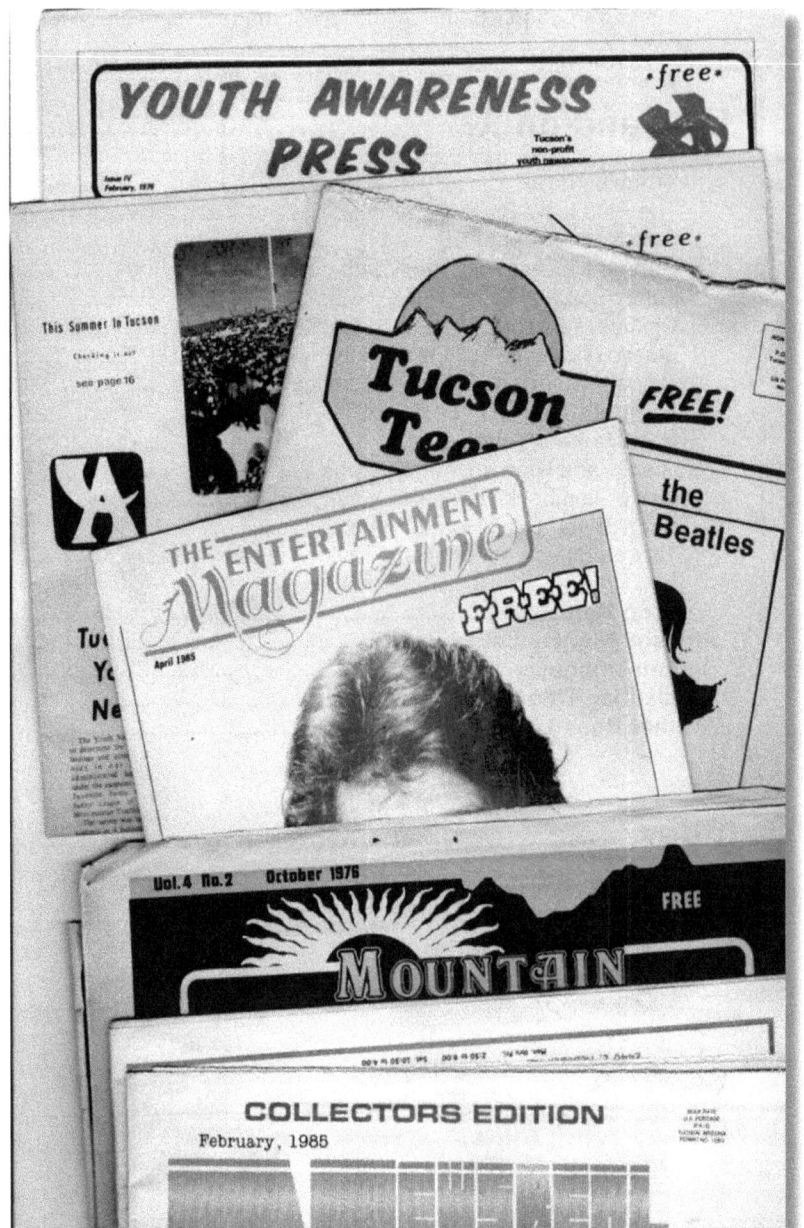

Covers of the *Youth Awareness Press, Tucson Teen, Youth Alternatives, Entertainment Magazine* and *Newsreal* newspapers.

Youth Alternatives, Youth Awareness, Tucson Teen, Entertainment Magazine

The first newspaper published for youth in Tucson was the *Youth Alternatives* (summer and fall 1978). An experimental project funded by grants later became titled *Youth Awareness Press* (December 1979 through December 1980). The newspapers provided Tucson youth an opportunity to gain journalism skills and learn how to publish a newspaper.

The *Tucson Teen* newspaper continued the concept of a youth newspaper beginning in June 1981 through September 1990. The monthly tabloids were published through the **Tucson YWCA** until 1981 when **Southwest Alternatives Institute, Inc.,** a non-profit organization, became the publication sponsor. A sister publication for the wider Tucson community called *The Magazine* published from September 1982 until it became titled *Entertainment Magazine* in April 1985.

In January 1995, the *Entertainment Magazine* became one of the first Arizona newspapers to go online as **EMOL.org** (*Entertainment Magazine* On Line). **BZB Publishing Inc.** acquired publishing rights in 2006.

Robert Zucker, the author and the founder of all of the publications, spent over a decade teaching at the **University of Arizona** (1992-2005), and **Pima Community College** (1998-2005).

Entertainment Magazine Web Site: http://emol.org

Photos: (left to right) First editions of *Youth Alternatives, Youth Awareness Press, Tucson Teen, Magazine, Entertainment Magazine.*

Mountain Newsreal & Newsreal

The ***Mountain Newsreal*** started in 1974 as a monthly alternative culture tabloid by **Jonathan L** and evolved into the popular music magazine, ***Newsreal.***

Jonathan L is an American radio presenter, programmer, and international entertainment media publisher.

His radio career began in Tucson, Arizona in 1982 at **KLPX**-FM with a show "**Virgin Vinyl**" which predates Alternative radio. He left Tucson in 1986 to start up alternative radio station KEYX-FM.

Jonathan L organized his first large music festival for alternative station KUKQ in Phoenix, Arizona in 1989, years before the launch of festivals like Lollapalooza and the KROQ Weenie Roasts. For this reason, he is often called the "Father of all radio festivals."

In 2005, he returned form Los Angeles to create "Lopsided World of L" which ran on Saturday mornings and Sunday evenings on KUPD-FM until he moved to Germany in 2010. The "Lopsided World of L" is now produced and presented internationally every week by Jonathan L from his flat in Berlin, Germany.

Lopsided World of Jonathan L Web Site: http://www.jlradio.com/

Photos: First edition of *Mountain Newsreal*, 1974 and last edition of *Newsreal*, October 1985.

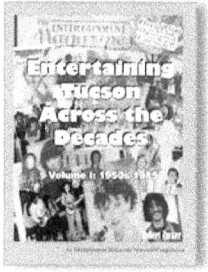

ENTERTAINING TUCSON ACROSS THE DECADES

Volume 1: 1950s to 1985

Tucson's musical memories of the '50s

By Michael Hamilton [1]

Hey Daddy-O! Let's hearken back once again to when today's baby boomers– those born between 1946 and 1964– were assembling their first mini-crystal sets and searching for their first station with "rock and roll" rhythms. It was a chance to dig the world of cars, cliques and class, with this new mod music in the background. This was the 1950s in Tucson, Arizona.

The newest fad– customizing cars in California– set the pace for a few local car clubs. Tucson's **"Banshees"** beamed proudly with vehicles sporting fender skirts, flipper hubcaps and continental kits. The twin aerials brought in radio signals from a society of high fidelity, both fraternal and familial. Yah, man, Ike smiled, Khrushchev rattled his rockets, but all else was well!

From '53 to '63, the nation cruised as smooth as a finely tuned engine. Life was lived for the daily fun of it like an adventure rather than a venture as it is today. Young lads had fun pegging the five local stations on their brother's car radio before he went on the "big date" that evening. She looked neat with his class ring hung on a chain around her neck, as they smooched (in front of people). He looked cagey in his flashy car club jacket as they roared down the lane with the open pipes purring.

Kids sure wanted to be 16 in a hurry to cruise about– even in an Edsel! Vroom! But, kids just rode their bikes and settled for a "transistor" sister radio hanging from the handlebars listening to **KTKT-990 AM** [2] – Tucson's top rock and roll radio station. This reporter reminisces each time he sees a '50s logo, be it cars, soda pop, or petrol! *Like wow man!*

Pop art Americana comes to Tucson in the '50s. The sweet, colorful echoes of heartfelt "Fabulous Fifties" music sprung to life in the form of the **Sonic Drive-in** restaurant, on West Grant Road east of the Interstate. Baby boomers, who once cruised the four **Johnnie's Drive-In's**, then **Ritchie's** on 22nd Street, with great pride, will reminisce with much fervor once again here, as the spontaneity of youthful life whiles on and idles by ...

This classy red arid white striped burger eatery by day becomes a "Sea of Neon," Jewel of Illumination," "In the Still of the Night" and under "A Thousand Stars in the Sky." Golden oldies ooze through the atmosphere from radios of a line of parked cars nosed into nostalgia. One needs merely to push the menu button and order from the past... **Elvis, Fabian, Dionne, Bobby Rydell**. Sadly, there are no skating carhops.

Lighthearted frolic has given way to liability, still "Only You" can watch the sprightly lasses disperse the fast food, as they display their darling derring-do, while the drive-thru lane "rumbles" on with "busyness." Even today's teens and preteens will 'dig' the "bob-shoobob" tunes of yesteryear, in this super Sonic place of fun. Look for the classic car out front.

---

[1] **Michael Hamilton** is a long time Tucson musician who performed with the Vibrations, a popular local rock and roll band of the 1960s.
[2] **KTKT**, Tucson's fifth radio station, went on the air in 1946. Popular disc jockey, Frank Kalil, was hired in the mid-50s to play the new "rock and roll" music format. Tucson's first FM station was KTKT-FM (99.5). Source: "Remembering Tucson Radio...From the Beginning! By Russ Jackson.

As the "Nifty Fifties" came to a close, lazy contemplative weekends in our amiable, affable town were celebrated by folks in myriad ways. Some viewers watched "**Dean Armstrong**'s Country Music Store" on **KOPO-TV**, Channel 13.

Dean occasionally featured the perennial national craze for square dancing. Dancers also promenaded at **Old Tucson** each Sunday, or at nearby ranches. There were a dozen colorful clubs and even more callers. **KTKT**, the Old Pueblo's mainstay station, highlighted its "Swinging Seven" rock and roll DJs. One recalls **Jerry Stowgram** and **Dave Nelson** 'swinging through,' among others.

Yes, we even had fun high-jinx crafted by mobile transmitter announcers at shopping centers then, too! **Radio 99** (KTKT) also sanctioned The **Miss Tucson Trailer Court** contest in the late '50s.

Then, they really revved things up by sponsoring the **Speed Sport** dragster at the **Tucson Strip**. This was located on what is now Golf Links Rd. on the Davis-Monthan Air Force Base. City folk also reveled in **PhD Richardson's** radio-editorials. Noted, too, were daily ditties, such as "Sleep well tonight, your Air National Guard is awake."

Ah, Tucson in the '50s…

Grabe's Record Center, from 1951 *Tucsonian*, Tucson Senior High School yearbook.

Jeri Denslow
Dick Anklam
Henrietta Martz
and Ann Hall
at

GRABE'S
RECORD CENTER

26 E. Congress St.

Photo of a brand new 1953 Chevy, by Bertram Zucker, 1953.

This story was compiled from articles published in the March 1989 edition of Entertainment Magazine, page 5; June 1989 Entertainment Magazine, page 23; and April 1989 Entertainment Magazine. Page 13.

Sons of the Pioneers: Rooted in Tucson's history

By Nick Nicholas [3]
December 1990 – Entertainment Magazine. Page 5

Sons of the Pioneers, the legendary group, founded by Roy Rogers along with former Tucsonan, Bob Nolan and Tim Spencer as the Pioneer Trio in 1933, is well into its fifty-seventh year (as of 1990) entertaining millions with a great musical tradition.

The Sons of Pioneers has included such past notable members as Hugh and Karl Farr, Pat Brady, Lloyd Perryman, Ken Curtis, Shug Fisher, Tommy Doss, Roy Lanham and present trail boss Dale Warren.

This world famous group, whose popularity is greater today than ever has been making Tucson its winter headquarters since their 50th anniversary year in 1983 appearing at the **Triple C Chuckwagon**, serving up western-style entertainment five nights a week, Tuesdays through Saturdays.

Trail boss, **Dale Warren**, in his 39th year (as of 1990) with the Sons of the Pioneers possesses a superb singing voice. He began his musical career in his home state of Kentucky. As a young boy, he would be standing on a box to play the bass fiddle and singing into the microphone with his parents famous group, **Uncle Henry's Original Kentucky Mountaineers**.

In 1953, he was recommended as a replacement for **Ken Curtis** (Festus of "Gunsmoke" TV series) who himself had replaced original Pioneer member Tim Spencer. Warren, well aware of both past and present feelings among Western music fans wherever the Pioneers perform, has managed to preserve the traditional classic western musical style of the group while adding new instruments with a touch of big band sound designed to please fans of all age groups.

As part of their stage performance the Pioneers also include salutes to the silver screen cowboys and their sidekicks and especially, to the godfather of the group, Roy Rogers and former Pioneers who have been a part of the group across the years by means of a multi-media slide show. Known as "The Aristocrats of the Range," Sons of the Pioneers are on the Advisory Board of the **Western Music Association**. Members of both the Country and Western Music Hall of Fame and have been acclaimed as an American Institution by the Smithsonian Institution. Their class recording of "Cool Water" is in the Grammy Hall of Fame. The Sons of the Pioneers have preserved the western musical heritage from their summer home in Branson, Missouri and their winter home in Tucson through their relentless efforts while creating innovations in western swing music that brings thousands to their feet.

---

[3] **Nick Nicholas**, a Tucson musician, had his own radio program, "Western Music Caravan," on KXCI-FM 91.7 Community Radio each Sunday afternoon from 2:00PM to 3:00PM. The show featured all time western music artists.

Dean Armstrong: A Living Tucson Western Legend

By Nick Nicholas
January 1991– Entertainment Magazine, page 17

Dean Armstrong (3rd from left) with his band in an outdoor performance. January-February 1991, *Entertainment Magazine*, page 5.

What more can be said which has already been said many times over for 10 these many years about a well-known and loved Tucson performer with a warm and generous personality as well as a graceful magnificent voice?

Well, for starters, just ask the countless thousands whom **Dean Armstrong** [4] and his now legendary **Arizona Dance Hands** have entertained with their brand of Country/Western and good time music for well over forty years now and which many think has been just short of forever.

Born in Illinois and after having served in the army during World War II, Armstrong came to Tucson for a brief visit in 1946 and immediately fell in love with the area's Western mystique, its people and, most of all, the beautiful music of the West and the cowboy. In 1948 he formed his first group, a house band for a popular dance hall and nightclub on the Benson Highway and soon after began a radio show from the club. This led to Dean's own weekly show on **KOLD-TV** Channel 13 that continued for more than twenty years. Armstrong also worked for Channel 13 as an advertising executive for many years and continues in that capacity, having switched in recent years to **KGVY-AM** radio where he sells radio advertising in addition to his musical appearances.

In 1963, Dean and his Arizona Dance Hands, by now sounding as polished and professional as any of the day's best Western bands, were hired as the house band for the world famous **Li'l Abner's Steak House** where they perform to this day every Friday and Saturday night at 8501 N. Silverbelle Road.

However, much of Dean Armstrong's unselfish efforts these days are devoted to singing and playing for residents of Tucson's health care centers, crippled children's homes and patients at the **Veterans' Memorial Hospital**. These combined appearances exceed 150 in number yearly as Dean continues to dedicate himself to bringing his brand of good-time music into the lives of the reclusive and disabled residents.

The Arizona Dance Hands are still primarily made up of its original members– Armstrong on guitar and vocals, **Edsel Smith** on fiddle, a member of the Cowboy Fiddlers Hall of Fame, **Bob O'Haire** on string bass, **Toni Clark** vocals and Fender bass, **Rosemary Koshmideron** vocals and accordion, **Earl Mock** vocals and lead guitar and **Paul**

---

[4] Dean Armstrong passed away on March 6, 2011.

26

Humphrey on drums. Also, original member **Lavernne Davis**, who now resides in the Phoenix area, returns to perform with the group for special occasions such as the **Pioneer Days Celebration** and the annual **Western Music Festival**.

Dean Armstrong (left) and Billy Burkes photo, Entertainment Magazine, 1991.

Billy Burkes, [5] the beloved steel guitarist joined Armstrong's outfit in 1955 and along with fiddler Ed Smith formed both a professional and personal friendship among the three of them that lasted until Burkes' death two years ago.

Burkes made a name for himself a good twenty years prior to joining up with Armstrong recording with the legendary **Jimmie Rodgers** where he made more records with "The Father of Country Music" than anyone else. Billy Burkes' beautiful steel guitar sounds coupled with his joyful glance and happy grin brought much musical happiness into the lives of those who listened and danced to his sounds.

Some of Dean Armstrong's "personally rewarding" credits over the years include performing for 31 years at the **Tucson Rodeo Breakfast**, 32 years at the **Old Time Fiddler's Contest**, playing for the Grand Opening of the **Tucson Community Center** in 1973 and its expansion in 1989 and benefits for worthy organizations such as the **Arizona Kidney Foundation** and the **Tucson Girls Ranch**.

He has been recently honored with a listing in the 1989-90 22nd edition of "**Who's Who in the West**," which limits honors to individuals who have demonstrated outstanding achievement in their own fields of endeavor and who have contributed significantly to the betterment of contemporary society. Dean Armstrong and The Arizona Dance Hands are professional members of the **Western Music Association**. They have performed on the "Today Show" on NBC, "Nashville Now" on the Nashville Network and will appear in the soon-to-be-released movie, "Kid."

In talking to this classy Western gentleman whose voice remains undiminished by time, it's easy to see how his satisfying smile and charming Western personality brings an immediate happy response from audiences everywhere who enjoy his brand of goodtime music. It is these and other great qualities which account for the fact that Armstrong has built one of Tucson's longest-running and most popular entertainment careers which continues to endure be it on radio or television, at a dance, fair, barbecue, hayride or festival. His brand of Western music blends into the Tucson scene like mesquite, adobe, a silver and turquoise belt, or faded jeans.

It's been a great forty years of so for both Tucson and Dean Armstrong and the Arizona Dance Hands. It's been a happy trail for the legion of fans that have hummed, sung, whistled and danced to their music for all those years.

It was wonderful then...and by cracky...it still is.

---
[5] Billy Burkes passed away in 1989.

The 1960s: A look back on Tucson's past

By Michael Hamilton
January 1989 – Entertainment Magazine. Page 18 and
September 1989 – Entertainment Magazine. Page 19

As we enter the new decade with high aspirations, let's think back once again to the time when pop music played such an important part in the lives of baby boomers, when they first became teenagers. In Tucson, the local scene was taking hold.

This reporter played tenor sax for The **Vibrations**. Our lead guitar struck rapid-fire notes, like traces of flamenco .... **Buddy Holly** had a tremendous influence upon our style of playing in this '61 through '65 era. In Sierra Vista, we once played off an early remote desert generator ... our volume covered its noisemaking! Now that's entertainment!

Cruising Speedway (let's make that speeding Cruiseway) was just as popular then as nowadays. We had our car radios pegged to **KTKT-99 AM** and **KFIF-1550 AM**, rocking all the way. The gang made the big circuitous route around town which included: **Frank Kalil's Teen Town** on the north side, the **HIHO Club** on the east, and **Sunset Rollerama** on the south central side, near the **Cactus Drive-In Theatre**. They were all non-alcoholic clubs for teens back then.

We were proud of our "cool cars" then, too! We noted that many of the singing groups were automotive namesakes: The **Lark**s, The **Edsels**, The **Continentals**, **Little Anthony and the Imperials**... We cruised the four **Johnnie's Burger Shoppes** and, when inside, pumped nickels in the mini-table jukeboxes.

We dug the barbershop harmony of the rock group **Pendletones**, who later became the **Beach Boys**. Rock chords and rhythms were somewhat simplistic compared to today's tunes, but we had just as much fun. Brushing aside the glossy gossamers off mind's memory, one recalls rising for high school to the radio alarm clock and the **Guy Williams** program of the city flagship rocker station **KTKT**.

Car photo by Byron McClure, August 1979, *Youth Awareness Press.*

A Run-in with Tucson's Drive-In's

By Michael Hamilton
June 1988 – Entertainment Magazine. Page 17

Tucson is known in some cinema circles as quite a movie-going town. Indeed, the price of admission makes one think that local cinema fans have paid for part of those giant new letters in H.O.L.L.Y.W.O.O.D.! As searchlights rove outside the indoor theatres, let's pay tribute to several of Tucson's Drive-In's– some gone, some refurbished, and some still the same (editor's note: the last Tucson Drive-In, the DeAnza, closed in 2009).

Condominiums now rise over the ground where the **Prince Drive-In** [6] gave us "Tammy" and "PT 109." Northbound cars on Campbell Avenue would often stop to view the showings until landscaping was installed. Gusts of wind felled one screen, yielding a strange sight, like that of white dominoes, lying scattered on the ground ...

The **Biltmore Drive-In** [7] (the defunct **Miracle**) on Oracle Road gave us "Charades" and "The Day the Earth Stood Still." Films here were projected after kids vacated the amusement rides below the tall screen at twilight. Now, only the tumbleweeds are threatened by encroaching apartment complexes. The **Apache Drive-In** [8] added two screen years ago and was famed for the $3 a carload entry ticket (others were trunkload). Once a single plane-and-truss sculpture in the deserted desert, the threes screens are now surrounded by a gathering of Tucson's new industrial growth.

But the most fun of all lay just beyond the mid-60s marquee of the **Midway Drive-In** [9] that has since yielded to commerce. The white uniformed attendants took our dollars and my date and I chose a space on a special terraced row between two monaural speakers, known to be working. No doubt it was humorous to watch this scramble for favorite spots in the last row.

Thinking about those good old days brings back memories of lip-reading back-row patrons, lightly pompous Universal Newsreels, and "squelching Cupids," attendants with red-nibbed flashlights whose job it was to interrupt any activity which did not involve directing your whole attention at the screen.

The July 4th holiday evening was about 80 degrees (my friends in the east couldn't believe that our drive-ins were also open in the winter). I'd tell them we had two feet of sunshine on the ground. Some jazz music started playing discovered our first "Pink Panther" cartoon complimented by our homegrown "Roadrunner" caricature (Beep! Beep!) Yep, truly the funniest one-word vocabulary around!

The screen dimmed. Floodlights flooded. My date waited loyally in the car while I went to the snack bar for some sarsaparilla and "red hots." Curiously, all Drive-In eateries seem to be grubby on purpose. Here was an example of a 1949 "adobe abode," laced with hard cement which had oozed out of the brick joints. Inside? Instant California prices! The precursor of today's inflation, but few foresaw it.

A look around noted a line of teens, bikers, cowboys and standard Americans. So, back to my car I strolled with my unbalanced divided box of beverages and goodies, even as the rolling topography beneath me was uneven. Tilt! Whew! Almost. ... I located my wheels amid the usual sprinkling of '57 Chevies, Corvettes and a few "T" bucket roadsters. Getting into my car while avoiding the speaker wire cause me to chip the car paint on the post ... damned "doorknick city." My date said her classmate just had her friend call at the theatre so she could have her name paged over the speakers. Oh, those nocturnal shenanigans ... Those truly were the days-the "sizzling sixties." Many drive-ins have been driven out, but the soul or "The Last Picture Show" remains... [10]

---

[6] The **Prince Drive-In Theater** was located at 2015 E. Prince on the Northeast corner of the intersection of Prince Road and Campbell Avenue. It opened in 1953 and closed around 1979. Two workmen were killed when a 57-foot movie screen collapsed during construction ("*Arizona Daily Star*," January 11, 1953).
[7] The **Biltmore Drive-In**, located at 600 W. Glenn at Miracle Mile, opened in the early 1950s. Its named was changed to the Miracle Mile Drive-In in 1963 and closed in 1978. (driveinmemories.com)
[8] The **Apache Drive-In**, located at 1600 E. Benson Highway opened in May 1955 and closed in 1994. (driveinmemories.com)
[9] The **Midway Drive-In**, 4500 E. Speedway, was built in 1948 and closed in 1979. (cinematreasures.org)
[10] At one time, Tucson had 10 different Drive-In theaters. All are now closed. The **DeAnza**, located just south of 22nd Street at 1401 N. Alvernon, opened in 1977 and was the last to close on October 3, 2009. (Source: driveinmemories.com)

Lewallen Brothers: A blast from Tucson's Past

The Lewallen Brothers, June 1989,
Entertainment Magazine. Page 23

By Dan Starr
June 1989 – Entertainment Magazine. Page 23

I waited 18 years to see The **Lewallen Brothers**. At first, I was too young to get into the clubs during their reign as Tucson's most famous band back there in the late '60s. Then, when the drinking age was lowered, I found myself too wrapped up in college when one of the brothers had died and the group was disbanded.

For new Tucsonans, let me fill you in. The Lewallen Brothers actually are all brothers, with the exception of father, **Cal Lewallen**, founder and bassist. They are all Tucson natives. Their band played all over the city from the late 1950s to 1980, quite a feat for any band!

They were in their heyday in the late 1960s and moved into "the big time" with national tours and major dates playing with **Paul Revere & The Raiders, The Turtles, The Yardbirds, The Lovin' Spoonful**, and **Chuck Berry** himself.

In 1968, they placed second in a nationwide "Battle of the Bands" produced by **Dick Cla**rk, and then appeared in Dick's Television Special "Happenin' '68." They also recorded on the same label as **Ritchie Valens** and The **Bobby Fuller Four**. After the death of their brother in 1981, the family stepped away from the spotlight. Their name faded in the memories of old-timers like me, and it's a safe bet that the majority of live music fans in this transient city have never heard of them.

The Lewallen Brothers are back, this time as a trio, and considering the wave of interest in '50s and '60s music now sweeping the Old Pueblo, they're probably headed right back to the top. The group is father **Cal** on bass guitar, brother **Tim** on drums and brother **Keith** on lead guitar.

The Lewallen Brothers appearance is an attempt to cash in on the success of the '50s and '60s music craze. But, the Lewallen Brothers are not a nostalgia band. They are the real-thing. They are playing music they learned when it first appeared on the Top 40. They lived the era, not re-lived it. This gives them a grip on how that music is delivered that is simply impossible to obtain in any other way. They played the tunes on the equipment those tunes were written for, sang the lyrics with three-part harmony that is a trademark of that age of music.

30

Tucson country music bands in the '70s

By Charley Yates [11]
October 1990 – Entertainment Magazine. Page 5

The first entertainer to bring the Las Vegas style country variety show to Tucson was **Roy Clayborne** in 1971. He talked to the crowd. When he walked right off the stage, the crowd went wild. He would do a full show with a follow spotlight, costumes, and a real good band. Roy drew large crowds with his magnetic personality. This dynamic entertainer used comedy, impressive impersonations of many well-known country music stars and motion picture stars, and even stars from the old time rock and roll era. He could really motivate an audience into a frenzy.

As the highest paid entertainer to do a long-term show in Tucson, he made quite an impression that shall be remembered for years to come. However, other bands said that there is no sense in doing a show because no one will pay attention any way. Others followed, such as **Frank and Woody**, **Jean Chastain**, **Kelly Koplin**, The **Original Jacks** and The **Lewallen Brothers**.

But, **Billy Templeton** drew larger crowds than any local entertainer in a 20-year period. He did it with his Elvis snow. So far, no other entertainer has broken his record. Billy drew over 20,000 people into the **Corona De Tucson** Race Track. People jammed the bleachers and aisles and overflowed onto the grounds. Wherever a person could stand or sit, they could see the show in the center of the track.

One of Tucson's local highlights was one hot June in 1972 at **Copper State Recording Company** during the mix downs for the first "Country Sounds of Tucson" album. This is the same studio where **Linda Ronstadt** made her first demo. **Larry Allen**, **Gary Allen** and this reporter arrived at the studio early that morning. **Johnny Leonard**, **Kenny Durrell**, **Gary Skinner**, **Rick Skinner** and **Mike Ramsey** were waiting at the **Sambo's Restaurant** across the street, having breakfast and coffee. **Rocky West** came in to find out who was going to put the guitar parts on his songs. Everyone pointed a finger at **Charley Yates** (me!). Other musicians started filtering in, **Leo Dominguez**, **Mike Atar**, **JoAnna Leroy,** just to mention a few, who wanted to witness this historic event.

Mountain Newsreal makes its debut

The *Mountain Newsreal*, Tucson's monthly newspaper of popular culture, was first published in May 1974 by **Jon** (**Jonathan L**) and **Joan Rosen**. The tabloid later became known as the *Newsreal* and focused on music– both local and national. The *Newsreal* continued to publish through October 1985.

---

[11] **Charley Yates** is a local country entertainer who has performed in Tucson since 1967.

Chuck Wagon & the Wheels: Keepin' spinnin'

By Tim Martin
November 1990 – Entertainment Magazine

Chuck Wagon & the Wheels are a premier country/western band, but every fan knows they can knock out some pretty mean rock and roll, too. Formed in 1977, Chuck Wagon & the Wheels became familiar to Tucsonans in the late '70s and early '80s for their satirical music when they called the **Stumble Inn** [12] their home.

Chuck Wagon & the Wheels, Wagon Track Records. November 1990, *Entertainment Magazine.*

Best known for their "Country Swings Disco Sucks," these guys hit #1 on the "Dr. Demento Show's Funny 5 Countdown" in 1980, closely followed by "The Gas Song (Let's Drop the Neutron)."

Unfortunately, this was released during the Iranian hostage crisis, and wasn't looked upon as funny. Maybe the time has come now to get some airplay.

After 13 years, five albums, six singles, international airplay, domestic and European tours, and a few changes in the lineup, this band can still get a crowd rowdy, whistling and screaming the names of favorites such as "My Girl Passed Out in Her Food," and "We Ran Out of Gas on the Road to Love." Popular in California and Colorado, they have opened for such names as Jerry Jeff Walker and have been compared to Asleep at the Wheel.

---

[12] The **Stumble Inn** was later called **Mudbugg's** nightclub. It is now called The **Rock** at 136 N. Park Avenue at 9th Street.

Performing on a small, low stage spanning the back wall of **Tiny's Saloon**, [13] it seemed to this reporter, like walking into a roadhouse. The only thing missing was the chicken wire in the front of the stage. But as it turned out, this was not the case. It is a nice comfortable place to meet friends.

The band plays music from such divergent groups as Ted Nugent, the Rolling Stones, and does a great impression of Willy Nelson with Chuck reverently holding his nose to achieve just the right nasal quality.

Chuck "Wagon" Maultsby, a Tucsonan since the mid-60s, began his career in various rock bands, and landed a contract from Capitol Records in 1969. He changed format in the mid-70s and got into country/western. He is founder, singer, songwriter, and producer owning **Wagon Tracks Records**. His favorite song is "Carolinda," but it was never a big seller. Chuck has won one music award for "Sales over 100." It is a disc of bubble gum music.

Chuck is married to a raven-haired beauty named **Sharon**, and has two sons from a previous marriage. Chuck and Sharon are both professional leatherworkers. Chuck's goal is "to have just one Top 40 hit before I die. I'd be happy with #39."

Backing Chuck on the steel pedal guitar is **Neil Harry**, a member since 1978, when he left the **Dusty Chaps** band. He played on two albums produced by Capitol Records for them. Neil is a steel guitar instructor and recording session performer.

Bass player and vocalist, **Randy Cochran**, is from Tulsa, Oklahoma. Once a staff musician for Leon Russell's Shelter Recording Studios, he came to Tucson as a member of the Grain of Salt band from Denver. He now works as a civilian at Davis Monthan Air Force Base.

On lead guitar, native Tucsonan **Jay Quiros** has become a "second to none picker and harmony singer," says Chuck. Jay is also a songwriter, and has helped with the **KWFM** radio compilation album.

Doug Parmenter is on drums. As a graduate of the Musician's Institute of L.A., is highly successful studio musician, and has played with many country and rock bands.

This version of the band has been together for a little more than three years.

Kristi Bird, of the *Flagstaff Lumberjack* has described this band perhaps better than anyone. She says, "The music of Chuck Wagon and the Wheels is more humorous than crude, creating a party atmosphere for dancers, drinkers and 'hell-raisers'."

She certainly is right, some of the songs she must be alluding to include "Red Hot Women Ice Cold Beer," "How Can I Love You If You Won't Lay Down!" and "One Less Jogger on the Road."

There is good news for fans of Chuck Wagon and the Wheels. There is going to be a new album. "The Best and Worst of Chuck Wagon and the Wheels" will be released near the middle of November (1990).

---

[13] **Tiny's Saloon**, 4900 W. Ajo Highway.

Billy Templeton: The Elvis shtick

By Robert Zucker
1990 - Entertainment Magazine

'70s rock and roller, **Billy Templeton** moved to Tucson, Arizona in 1970 from Chattanooga, Tennessee. From his base in Tucson, Templeton began to perform professionally all around the Southwest for any event he could. He is best known for doing an incredible "Tribute to Elvis Vegas Show."

Templeton and his band's talents are not limited there however, as he has gained a wide respect for his guitar playing in the tradition of James Burton, Albert Lee, Roy Buchanan and the likes of these talented musicians.

Billy Templeton

The **Billy Templeton Band** has worked with many other groups and individuals since he arrived here. In 1972, Templeton won the Tucson **Battle of the Bands** as a guitarist and bandleader.

From 1973-1976, he performed with the **Larry Allen Trio** as singer and guitarist. He also did stunt work with **Old Tucson Gunfighters** in 1974 and made a television appearance for the "Country Sounds of Tucson" in 1975. His first 45-RPM single was recorded in 1976. A year later, Billy recorded "A Tribute to Elvis Album," as an Elvis impersonator.

The Billy Templeton Band consists of four players for the most part– guitar, piano, bass, drums. Templeton likes to incorporate showmanship along with the music to form a better entertainment package. The music they play is "high energy" for rock and roll, Blues and Top 40. The Country music they play has a list that contains more than 600 songs. He has performed in many of Tucson's top spots, including **Manny's**, **Music Box Lounge**, **Panama Pete's**, **Boot Hill**, the **Hilton Hotel**, and the **Sheraton Hotel Resort**, among others.

In the 1980s, Templeton expanded his Elvis shtick and worked on his own show called "A Tribute to Elvis As Elvis" and broke a ten-year record attendance at Tucson's **Corona de Tucson Race Track** for his "A Tribute to Elvis Show." A year later, he took his tour across Arizona. He won the 1984 Battle of the Bands competition for performing "A Tribute to Elvis" and was named "Most Professional Act" and "Best Show."

From there, Templeton went to perform in Las Vegas Hotels as an Elvis Presley act. He returned to Tucson in 1985 to do "A Tribute to Elvis Show" at the **Tucson Community Center**. From 1986-88, Templeton worked in various bands for musicians such as Crystal Gale, Freddie Weller and Johnny Rodriguez.

Billy Templeton photo, 1990.

Disco Fever Heats Tucson Teens

By Hilary Bass and Veronica Rivera
Autumn 1978 – Youth Alternatives. Page 11

Once disco was limited to people 19 years and older, but no longer! Many of Tucson's finest nightclubs have set aside one or two nights a week for teens to get into the disco scene. Now, it's for anyone who likes to get down to any kind of music, from rock to disco, live bands or the Top 40.

The manager of **Bogarts**, **Joe Bono** says, "There is a lot we can do to keep teens interested. If they can't dance, we will teach them." Bogarts is offering free dance lessons on Thursday nights from 7:00PM to 9:00PM. If Bogarts is not convenient for you to take lessons, there's always the **El Dorado Disco**, which is offering dance lessons on Tuesday from 7:00PM to 8:00PM. **Steve Somerman**, banquet manager of the **Ramada Tucson Resort** has arranged a Ramada Trans Disco Club.

Many of the discos have regular customers. At Bogarts, "There's a different group of people every week," Joe Bono told us. But, the situation at **After The Gold Rush** is different. According to **Sean O'Hayre** "The same 120 come every week. Now, we get 700 people. But there's a regular group." The Ramada Tucson Resort's Trans Disco has grown from 113 teens to 911 teens since the disco started, Somerman added. The El Dorado disco gets 100 to 200 teens, and usually it's the same 200, but that may vary.

O'Hayre, part owner and manager of After The Gold Rush, says that to keep teens dancing "We want to have another **Community Food Bank** night and maybe a dance contest."

If you want to dance to the beat of Macho Man, Boogie Oogie Oogie or San Francisco, you know the places that you can get on the Groove line.

Photo: High school disco dancers during the February 1979 weekend teen dances at **Gazebo Restaurant and Nightclub**. The dances raised funds for the *Youth Awareness Press* and provided youth with their own teen nightclub near the University of Arizona. *Youth Awareness Press* archives.

Youth Alternatives and *Youth Awareness Press*

The first newspaper for Tucson youth, *Youth Alternatives*, published two editions in 1978 and as *Youth Awareness Press* (YAP) from the winter of 1978 through 1981. The newspaper then published as *Tucson Teen* from the summer of 1981 through the autumn of 1990. Each month, up to 20,000 free copies were distributed into public schools, libraries and hundreds of businesses. The publications were created by **Robert Zucker.**

Rockin' Tucson in the '80s

By Constance Commonplace
February 8, 1985 - Newsreal

I returned to Tucson in July '79, from a two-year desert break in Boston. Music in Bean Town was already at a rapid boil in terms of the "new wave" thing, and it was hard to leave knowing what hard rock and country comforts awaited my now aurally expanded ears, but the call of the cactus was too great.

The musical climate was calm with an electric edge to it– kind of like the end of winter with snatches of spring no longer at the wishful thinking level - almost there, but not yet. People were looking a tad different and when I went to **Pearl's Hurricane Bar**. I knew it was just a matter of time before this ripple would rip through town like a tidal wave.

The **Pedestrians**, **Suspects** and **Z-Nine** were playing. **Dissonance** became the bottom layer upon which songs were built.

Black was the only color you were caught dead in and those hippie locks of the '70s were shorn. The sleepy, creative, energy hanging around the Old Pueblo was replaced by a youthful zeal and was raising its fists, making a joyful noise.

It was late '79/early '80 when things began to jell. Bands were forming and developing consistent styles. Remember **Romeo and the New Deal** on 36th Street? Bands were labeled as New Wave, in **Night Train** club listings, so those die-hard rockers would know what they were getting into.

There was loads of animosity on 4th Avenue between the wavers and hippies in those early days. **Tumbleweeds** was staging bands like **Channel 88**, **Memory Product** and the **Serfers**.

By June '80, **Pearl's Hurricane Bar** was booking blues, the **New Deal** had gone Hispanic, and **Tumbleweeds** was bulging at its threadbare seams with "new music!" **White Pages** was playing regularly with various out-of-town punks. The summer of '80 was no time for those kind of blues as the air was filled with the music of The **Pills**, **Giant Sandworms**, The **Erotics** and **Ménage a Trois**. One end of this new era was the closing of **Pearl's Hurricane** in July.

October was a month of major changes. On September 29th at the **Contractions** and **Pills** concert, it was announced that **Tumbleweeds** would close. The **Serfers** left for L.A. to find fame, and sometime during this period **Memory Product** had been signed with **Subterranean**. **Loudness One** is formed and brings a unique concept to Tucson entertainment.

The Christmas season begins on a sad note as Tucson mourns the death of John Lennon with the rest of the world. **Tumbles** opens where Tumbleweeds once was and continues its new music format. **Ménage a Trios** becomes the **Phantom Limbs**, while other Tucson bands are moving to Phoenix and beyond. In the new year, the **Assassinators** and **Suzie Caruze** are new acts in town.

I would like to mention something about promoters and this spot seems as good as any. Incredibly good acts continue to be brought into town by **Feyline** and **Evening Star Productions**. ESP filled **Dooley's** with some of the top touring acts.

Jonny Sevin performing at Reid Park Bandshell, circa 1985. *Newsreal.*

The spring brings us **Jonny Sevin**, a band that had Tucson music lovers at a fever pitch just knowing they were practicing at Broadway and Columbus. **Tumbles** does just that and closes its doors.

In May, just as the shortage of venues becomes oppressively apparent, **Club Europa** opens on North Stone Avenue. Although great acts are being booked, the scene seems to have taken itself on vacation to another part of the world. The **Giant Sandworms** are sending tapes from the Big Apple, **J7** is in the studio with **Bill Cashman** recording on his **Art Attack Records** label. Frequenters of the **Pawnbroker**, club for the elite dealers in town, start roaming **Yanks**, home to the ever-popular **Bob Meighan Band**. The fall of '81 is actually quite boring except for the opening of the **Backstage** that was formerly Tumbles.

In early September, **Green on Red**, from L.A. (who were the **Serfers** when they left Tucson) played at the Backstage and gave a sweet and sour performance. The FM radio stations are as bland as cold oatmeal and lacking in texture– it's like they sent our ears to Siberia. The **Chromatics** and **Les Seldoms** are finding it difficult to be different in this musically unsettling time. People are becoming apathetic and not supporting music as they had in the past. As '81 slips away, so does the direction of Tucson's music scene, and one more club bites the proverbial dust, **Club Europa** closes.

Trout Unlimited forms with ex-members of the Serfers and the Chromatics, they have abandoned the wave and put out no frills rock and roll. R&B gets a boost with the Salt and Pepper band and Straight Up. All around groovy musician **Lee Joseph** produces two cassettes of his own weird brand of tunes on his **Iconoclast** label. The **Pills** have returned from N.Y. and add **Barry Smith** of **Loudness One** to the line-up. And, radio closes the door further on originality– **Bob Cook's Bezerko Lounge** is off the air.

37

On March 27, 1982, **Whistling Shrimp Records** hosted a Smash-a-thon to boycott the corporation influence in radio programming. **Chances** Night Club gives Tuesday a new lift with recorded new music and live acts on Sunday. **Jonny Sevin** is changing personnel and **Ned Sutton** puts together some new **Rabbits**.

Photo: Ned Sutton
(2nd from right, top row) and the Rabbits. *Newsreal*, February 1985.

Spring '82 has a new club featuring country-rock. **Nino's** opens on First Avenue. **Jonathan L** and **Bob Bish** get an hour to air new releases on **KLPX**. **Lee Joseph** is at it again with a compilation tape including: **Pink Dancing Elephant, Conflict, Jacket Weather, Stainless Steel Kimono, Urban Guerillas, Cowgirls, Les Seldoms** and **The Chromatics**. **Virgin Vinyl** begins on KLPX. Downtown, **Moda Modeling Studio** features live new music.

Photo: Chris Burroughs and the Nationals

The next six months are pretty unearth-shattering. Eighty Go Ninety, Chris Burroughs and the Nationals and Clean Dog make musical entrances on the scene. Nino's starts booking new music. A major loss to the music scene of Tucson occurs in August when DJ Bob Cook is shot and killed in a church parking lot.

'83 has Dooley's changing its name to the Stray Cat. Stainless Steel Kimono becomes The Freds and Evening Star Productions [14] is booking at Cowboy's. The Night Train becomes the Midnight Express and it seems that nothing stays the same.

As we enter '85, three clubs have been felled by fire– The **Stray Cat**, the **Backstage** and **Chances**. **Rainer (Ptacek)** and **Naked Prey** are making an impression at **Jack's Pub**. **Gentlemen After Dark** (formerly the **Pills**) had hooked up with Alice Copper, gone to L.A., and have since returned wagging their tails behind them.

Photo: The Chromatics

Major acts being book in town are at an all time low, but **Evening Star Productions** keeps trying to keep us musically informed. Radio has plummeted to its most nauseating level of garbage as **KWFM** turns to adult contemporary to raise ratings and **KLPX** isn't sure what it wants to do. **Los Lasers** have put out a fine little album and other locals will soon be following suit.

Maybe it's me, but it feels like the mid-70s again, with a lack of innovation from the music-makers of Tucson. Fortunately, I remain optimistic and sense this period as one of transition, a calm before the musical storm, so to speak, for if Tucson's musical history repeats itself ... the beat will go on and the song will not remain the same.

Photos from *Newsreal*, February 8-March 18, 1985.

---

[14] **Danny Zelisko** has been bringing shows to Arizona since 1974. He founded and ran Evening Star Productions up until 2001 when he sold his company. Zelisko returned to Phoenix to present more shows, including at the Celebrity Theatre, and hosts a weekly radio show, "Phoenix Finest Rock," every Thursday night at 8:00PM and heard locally on 93.9 FM or on the internet at www.KWSS.org

Tucson's 1982 Punk Rock Scene

By H. "Slitboy" Salmon
January 14-February 11, 1983 - Newsreal

Change is good, and so is growth and Tucson's punk underground showed signs of both. It was a year that started off real wide– the scene was disjointed and so diversified. Some bands were real serious, they'd left town to do well, and Tucson was behind them. That is, until most came back with unhappy confessions that were in stride as real life lessons.

But all of a sudden the bar scene was aching for some people to scrape off the mold that was caking on the teen-punk thrills for which their stages were made 'cuz the year started off with a scene that was jaded.

But don't get me wrong, it wasn't that bad. It's just that Tucson's nightlife has always had a tendency to be kinda slow– the scene needed more kids in order to grow! '82 (the early part) was working with the ghost of some "new wave" fun that had once been the most about 2-3 years ago, when it all started here, that was all in yesteryear.

We were groping for direction, we wanted some action we had three different bands, and three different factions!

(And the bands I'm talking about are the bands that have played most of their gigs at "that bar" on 4th Avenue!) They were **Sin of Detachment**, the **Seldoms** and **Conflict**– the latter being Tucson's token punk outfit and the former being more dirge-like and not as fast. They both released tapes on **Iconoclast International.** The label was young at the time and still forming, but the fires of inspiration they indeed were warming, for if they did anything, they focused our attention on the small-time garage bands who usually go without mention. And, just for background, between January and May there was the short-lived **Trout Unlimited** and **S.S.K**.

Jonny Sevin were briefly the big band but soon turned out to be a flash in the pan, the **Limbs** came back from San Francisco, and "new wave nights" were happening at discos, and that sounds kinda gross - you could hope for more, when not too long after Tucson goes hardcore! It was the hardcore uprising that provided the glue, it was fast and exciting (though it wasn't that new) and bands began thrashing toward one common vision: a world without supervision!

But the end of the summer is when the real fun began because Tucson sported three hardcore bands. There was **E.S.S**, **Civil Death** and **Conflict** and a great new faction of bands: psychedelic!

And, of course, there're the bands that are arty like **Clean Dog**, **Chromatics**, and **Yard Trauma** party (!) (Y'see the art school faction has always been around. It's just that they're the most underground!)

And there are also the new bands the scene's got in store, like the **Hecklers** and the **Corporate Whores.** The last four months have been the ones of most celebration while the previous eight were the ones of preparation! The scene's now got fanzines, some radio, some indie cassettes and visits from Black Flag, and Dream Syndicate, the Circle Jerks, the Necros, and Channel 3, and isn't it sickening reading all this in poetry? You might think that it's all just ego inflating when actually it's myself that I'm really nauseating– I like to make all of these gross generalizations, but enough of this song-song-like masturbation let's just hope that for the New Year the underground scene will shift into high-gear, that the punks will grow and the word will spread, that there'll be lots of great shows– enough said?

Serf's up for Green on Red

Green on Red
Tucson's loss ▭ LA's gain

Green On Red. April, 1983 – *Newsreal* Cover photo.

February 11-March 11, 1983 – Newsreal. Page 10

Having evolved from the seeds germinated a year ago, the **Serfers** are now in their toddler stage and about to break into a run toward a successful musical future … is where we left off in August, 1980. They ran to L.A., changed the name from Serfers to **Green on Red** and after doing some roller coaster rides through reality, the band seems headed toward musical recognition.

"Recognition" seems more appropriate than "successful" because even though their debut 12 inch EP has been favorably reviewed in *Creem, Bam* and the *LA Times*. **Jack Waterson** (**GoR** bass player) is still on the bus at 8:15 to do warehouse work 'til 5:00. "Success" on the other hand seems to mean one can skip the 9 to 5 slide and cruise on the revenue generated by the creative endeavor and, according to Jack, the band hasn't reached that phase– yet.

Early Green On Red return to Tucson. *Newsreal* photo, February 8, 1985, Page 29.

Early Green on Red return to Tucson.

Musically, it was a magical period for Tucson with a communal, innovative energy abounding in **Pearl's Hurricane Bar** and **Tumbleweeds**, but for the Serfers the sequence was coming full circle and burnout was setting in. Days were spent drinking beer and seeking smoke 'til stage time.

"We had kind of gotten down to the very depths of humanity living gig-to-gig… REAL, distraught. You reach a point when Halloween has gotta end," reflects Jack in a recent phone conversation. There were many doubts, but the intuitive feeling of the band was to move on and make music for a larger audience and although at times the obstacles seemed insurmountable, Jack (speaking for the band) says, "We're all glad we did it."

When they first arrived in L.A., Jack, **Chris Cacavas** (keyboard/vocals), **Dan Stuart** (guitar/vocals), and **Van** (drummer), lived in a studio apartment on Vine with some mice and a few other people. Only Dan was working. Van left L.A. on the same day **Darby Crash** OD'ed and **John Lennon** was shot, leaving a trio of Serfers behind. They didn't play music for a year.

In February of '81 a friend of theirs gave them money and told them to do a record. At that point **Green on Red** had no drummer, so they recruited **Alex Mac Nicol** for the sessions and he eventually became the permanent fourth member. Jack looks at the record project as a learning period, "you're aware of what only experience can teach you. You see all the truths ... and you see all the lies, and you know when somebody's trying to give you the knife."

They knew it wasn't worth playing gigs without "the ace up our sleeves," which was vinyl. In L.A., "very few bands become well-known without having a record behind them." The 12-inch EP was released in June. In the period between February and June they played as a trio and became "solid as hell." They also met "Comet Man" in the hall of their apartment building.

He was a black, funk bass player who played a left hand bass with his right hand and it was "like he was trippin' when he played, his eyes would roll back in his head and sometimes he drooled. He used to tell us the only problem we had was we didn't have any soul. So he kinda gave us soul lessons."

They hung-out with Comet Man for about a month and then moved from the studio into a house. Alex began getting them music jobs that they played for free. In mid-August they landed an X gig and played with Lydia Lunch the following night.

It looked as if the band was finally beginning to roll. But, by November the band made no progress and Alex became

41

disheartened and left for New York. The sputtering stops and starts left the remaining members in a sad state. They didn't interact with their instruments and they had little to say to one another.

Alex returned from the Apple and although they hadn't practiced at all, they came and played in Tucson (February 1982) and were "flipped-out" by how good it sounded to them. Sometime after, they put out a demo tape and on May first they played in L.A., meeting members of the Dream Syndicate, which became a turning point for GoR.

They decided to have a barbeque and invited Dream Syndicate and members of other bands they had grown to respect. A communal feeling began to develop, as those Sunday parties became regular events. During one of those gatherings, GoR played their tape for Steve Wynn of Dream Syndicate and he decided to put out GoR's first album on his Down There label.

The gigs just started happening and they began playing an incredible amount of dates. They recently did six shows in four days, while doing their day jobs in between...crazed! Musically, Jack describes the band as an "electro-folk-combo" and they are as rebellious as ever. As in the **Serfers** days, they are still "revolting against everything we see as normal."

Dan Stuart sees the seeping of societal desperation from the urban landscape, then, lyrically etches his impressions onto a background of neo- psychedelic and the naive urgency of the folk era. Dan's voice lyrically conveys raw reality juxtaposed with Chris' sweet, almost lilting harmonies. Chris renders his organ riffs with Doors-esque textures while Jack and Alex provide precise rhythmic support.

Having suffered and squirmed through the head-reeling realities of rock, Green on Red is now headed onto the L.A. freeway toward musical "success." They are working on a second 1-inch EP to be produced by Steve Wynn and have several labels quite interested in them. Word is, these former desert rats will be bringing their anxiety ridden dance music to Tucson sometime next month– a party NOT to be missed!

A Limited Pressing 4-Song EP from Giant Sandworms and Chris Burroughs and the Nationals, "An Evening at Wildcat House," Sunday, May 1, 1983. The *Magazine/Entertainment Magazine* archives.

Sandworms: Desert Sophistication

Giant Sandworms members Scott Garber and Howe Gelb.
Magazine cover photo by Lydia L. Young, December 1984. Not pictured: Billy Sed and Dave Seger.

By Constance Commonplace
July 15-August 12, 1983 – Newsreal. Page 10

It's summer. The heat of the day can be assessed before ever opening a blind in the morning by sensing the quiet of the outdoors. A silence, broken only by the mating songs of the cicadas whose life span is so short they can't afford the luxury of waiting 'til the sun goes down.

'Yeah, but it's a dry heat,' is a true enough statement to an east coaster used to the moisture making-humidity. But, no matter how dry, at 101 degrees Tucsonans still sweat. We may moan about the cultural drought existing in our environment as our energy is being zapped by the sun– yet, we stay.

So why are we here? There seems to be an attraction about Tucson that seeps in and never quite leaves the bloodstream. Perhaps it's a matter of learning to survive on so little– like the saguaro growing in grains of intensely hot sand, getting minimal amounts of water yet greening and stretching their arms toward the sun. It is not all so bleak as we sip margaritas and tequila relaxing in our cultivated mañana attitudes or experiencing the wonder of a

desert night with gnomes and UFOs dancing in the silhouette of mountains under spectacularly starry skies.

Tucson is a healthy incubating environment that allows us to stretch out and take risks. We are surrounded by an inexplicable energy that somehow nourishes the spirit– something magically magnetic that keeps sucking us back from wherever it is we go when we say we're finally getting out of this bloody town. Ask the Sandworms– for it is from this Sonoran desert that **the Giant Sandworms** were spawned and ran from only to return.

It has been three years this August (1983) since **Rainer Ptacek**[15] invited his friend **Howe Gelb** to return to the desert and make music. "My first picture of the city's music scene was in June (1980). The **Pills** were playing on a Monday night and I went down with Rainer to see what was going on. We had left and come back as everybody was leaving the place. This car rolls around, does a u-turn and a guy gets out of the back rear window with a semiautomatic and starts opening up on the crowd. It was then we knew that people weren't happy with what was going on and needed something new," wryly recalls Gelb.

A few days later, drummer **Billy Sed** went to Howe and Rainer for a jam bringing guitarist **David Seger** along. Seger and Sed had been playing together for six years in this desert town. They tried to loosen up with the old standard, "Louie, Louie," and just couldn't do it. The next attempt was "Me and My Rocker" which "was awful, but there was a magic there."

The band (which was not yet the Sandworms) definitely had some beginning of a 'sound' yet was rather amorphous. Rainer's influence was felt in the rhythm and blues aura conveyed in some of the covers played by the band. There was no one arranger for the music. "Somebody would say what flavor they thought they wanted, but everyone would interpret that flavor differently," explained Howe. Somewhere along the way Rainer left the band and the remaining trio decided to make the musical move to New York. "We wanted to see what was going on," cites Howe, "which meant leaving the desert, making us very sad."

The cross-country trip was "wild" by their own description communicating via walkie-talkies and running out of money and gas. Settling in a rural New Jersey town close to the city limits, they practiced in what was once the lion house of the Ringling Brothers/Barnum and Bailey circus. The owner turned-out to be a bit of a maniac– "he had a nasty habit of shooting at werewolves and vampires in his house"– the Worms made the city move. Dredging through New York's outrageously priced apartments for two weeks while crashing on various friends' floors they met Larry, a red-haired Irishman who said with a bit of a brogue, "It's a great little place, you guys."

In a recent *Rolling Stone* article, reference was made to Toilet, a renowned scoring place on the Lower East Side. It was in a cubbyhole occupying the fifth floor of this building on Avenue B that the Sandworms called home. Once settled, they immediately began hitting the clubs and tried to find a place to play music. Appropriately enough, they connect with a Mexican man who rented practice space for a fee that seemed to vary with his mood but averaging about ten dollars an hour. Many of the popular neighborhood bands played there– popularity being determined by neighborhood demand and the amount of time put into the music. The Sandworms were not a popular band but began accumulating the necessary hours to become contenders for the coveted title of best band on Avenue B. Dropping off tapes and making continuous club cans consumed much of their time. Meanwhile...

Scott Garber, who currently plays bass with the Giant Sandworms, was not a Toilet resident (didn't even know the Sandworms existed), was doing the same dance with a more visually oriented beat. A landscape photographer from Rochester, New York, Garber was in the city hustling his portfolio around art galleries. Seems the thing was more S&M oriented. Success was contingent on who you knew and Garber never met the right ones. He wanted to photograph...the desert. So, Scott ran to the desert while the trio of Sandworms were running around the city he was running from.

The Sandworms played a few of the lesser known clubs and were told they had a "western sound," a definition they never quite understood. The first time they played "Mad City" (a popular Sandworm song) in CBGBs the person at the board added echoes on the drum and vocals– it was a major awakening of what Sandworm music could become. They experienced an incredible high and felt that the dream freeway may be clearing a lane for them.

---

[15] **Rainer Ptacek** passed away on November 17, 1997 from a brain tumor discovered in early 1996. He was born on June 7, 1951 in East Berlin.

Reality and time tends to pale the techno-color quality of dreams and after months of slum living– the dream was over. Howe was in Atlantic City gambling, David was an x-ray technician in Jersey, and Billy was doing the city slide of trying to get by. At their various locations they learned they were booked at CBGB's for that night. Howe who was the farthest away arrived first with ten minutes before they were due on stage. Mishaps and breakdowns had to be dealt with and while they were setting up, Billy and David were ragging at each other. It was not a great gig. Though they persevered through the sequence of obstacles– the Giant Sandworms heard the call of the desert. David and Billy left the city slums and saw saguaros forty-two hours later. Howe stayed a bit longer selling Indian artifacts and pots in an American Indian art gallery and met someone who had connections at **Trax**– a coveted club date– but it was too late. Truly, it was a matter of just not the right time for Sandworm success.

Early photo of Giant Sand, sans Rainer, in New York before returning to the Old Pueblo. February 1985, *Newsreal*. Page 29.

Back in the desert the guys took a summer sabbatical ... from each other. The city scene had frayed some wires weakening the connections. Howe played with **Ned Sutton** in the Black Hills (South Dakota). Billy and David continued to play together.

Around July, Scott was introduced to David and the three began jamming on a regular basis. He was interested in joining the band as bassist that would allow David to get back to his preferred guitar. The only thing left was to talk to Howe about it when he returned from playing with Ned. "I remember the first time I met Howe," Scott conveys, "It was like the decision had come into town." Scott became a Sandworm.

Retrospectively, Howe feels the effects of the city on their music, "exorcised all of our demons toward each other and because of that we can perform and create together a lot better." The music that left the desert had become sophisticated, with crisp edges and a city strut enriched by a fourth member. Scott holds down the backbeat freeing Howe to interact with David and to play his keyboard more often. The band's original music has no real game plan. Each tune has a structure that each member builds his own sound around: Howe, the great experimenter; shy David, popster who lets his lyrics convey his message; Euro-techno is Scott's addition; and Billy is Mr. Soul himself.

The idea of an identity caused a bit of discussion as they felt they don't have one. Scott felt that the urban experience has been ingrained in their music, "the whole idea of cacophony, of everything happening at once is very much like the way the city is. For every city block there are at least five stories going on; someone trying to pick your pocket, people in business suits and folks with no arms or legs– all aspects of life occurring at the same time."

There have been four stages of evolution since the inception of the band and with Scott having been with the band for almost a year, Gelb feels they are moving into a fifth. No matter what phase of progression, the Giant Sandworms is one of the most exciting bands around. Each performance is fresh because they are free to interpret the song for that moment and the delivery conveys commitment to their craft. A Giant Sandworm's gig leaves you dripping with dance sweat and the satisfaction of being able to say, "I can feel the passion."

Statesboro Blues Band: Happy with the blues

Photo of Statesboro Blues Band from L-R: Patrick McAndrew, Bruce Tost, Brooks Keenan, George Howard, Bob Benedon, *The Magazine*, January, 1984.

By Mary Simon
March 1984 - The Magazine. Page 19

Editor's note: Last month, the Statesboro Blues Band was introduced in the ¿Que Onda? column which spotlights local music. This month completes a full profile on the band.

The *Magazine* has been dogging the footsteps notes of the five members of the **Statesboro Blues Band** for nigh on to a month and a half and can report that they do indeed have the right amount of funk.

When first seen at the home of harp and keyboard player **Brooks Keenan**, the men in the band were worried about set structure– that is which songs should be included in a particular set and in what order.

Guitarist **Patrick McAndrew** asks, "Aren't we pandering to the audience including (commercial) hit like this?" They had just finished a truly elevating rendition of Jack Wilson's "Your Love (Is Lifting Me Higher)" and were considering what to continue with next.

Professional concern is not wasted on the audiences the SBB performs to **Terry & Zeke's**. As a friend with me commented, "So, this is where all those people go." Those people are the hardcore dancers, jazz and music lovers who populate a good entertainment establishment. They did not look like they would take much pandering.

But, any band with exuberant talent and expertise of the men in this band are probably only equaled only by the **Tucson Symphony Orchestra**.

Comprising the rest of the band are **George Howard** on drums and most vocals; **Bob Benedon** on bass and **Bruce Tost** the omnipresent saxophone player whose loomy presence dominates proceedings.

Howard, from Asbury Park, N.J. is a professional photographer. He says he got burned out working in the finance department of banks for 10-15 years. He has played with Benedon and McAndrew in the **Subterranean Blues Band**, a group that opened for such national acts as the Fabulous Thunderbirds, Roy Buchanan and John Cougar.

Howard does an admirable job combining vocals with percussion that any drummer will attest is a hard job. On B.B. King's "The Thrill is Gone" for example, Howard gives an unique twist drawing the lyric out just a couple of belts longer than "Thrill" listeners might expect. It is appreciable

Indeed, the beat is the message. "I'm real interested in keeping the beat steady and uncomplicated" says Howard. "Maybe that sounds too simple but when I see people dancing I just want to keep it going.

Keenan who contributes to some of the original material ("Midnight Kitchen") is an architectural engineer with a local consulting firm. With a penchant for three-piece suits this unassuming baby-faced keyboardist can give the audience a real goose with his jazz-blues harp playing. Several solos had the Terry & Zeke's crowd hooting while they were hoofing.

Keenan sums up the group's philosophy: "What we're aiming for is playing some of the nation's blues festivals. There's one in New Orleans in April, for example. That's really what we want to do continue to play locally and go to a few festivals."

Playing locally is what the SBB is all about. They are the house band at **Terry & Zeke's**. The club seems designed for them. Owner **Terry Glassman** says he put a couch near the club's dance floor to induce a feeling of home and the band members agree. "It's like playing in our living room."

It must be. We've never seen veteran sax man **Bruce Tost** quite so comfortable. Weaving a knitted cap down to his ever-brooding eyes. Tost actually danced his saxophone into the audience and up to a table or two during their performance.

Seeing Tost let loose is a treat. You've heard him for years as he puts it, "In every idiom from jazz to gospel." He seems to dominate many sets on Sunday nights at the **Marriott Hotel** where Tucson's jazz musicians gather to jam. "Dr. Sax," who shows great facility on all four saxophones, holds an M.A. from Illinois State University (where he also taught.) He is employed as music teacher in **Tucson Unified School District**.

Bob Benedon helping Howard keeps the steady beat displays a frantic marionette approach to bass playing. From Wisconsin, Benedon finds the blues a spiritual medium he has been chasing off and on since the early seventies.

Patrick McAndrew [16] is a teacher. Political science is his medium in Marana and at **Pima Community College**. His music contributions can be found on three albums by **Dusty Chaps**, as well as on movie and on television soundtracks. Like Keenan, Howard and Benedon, he also played with the **Subterranean Blues Band**. But like his band brothers, he is a familiar face to Tucson audiences. He writes ("Working Man's Blues") and props up the band with quicksilver licks that pack a lot of sound. Music, he feels, "is a generational thing."

The Blues has transcended the generations and Statesboro Blues Band in their new living room off Speedway is proving that Tucson has an appetite for this all American art form.

---

[16] **Patrick "Pat" McAndrew** passed away on December 28, 2008 at the age of 61 from a heart attack.

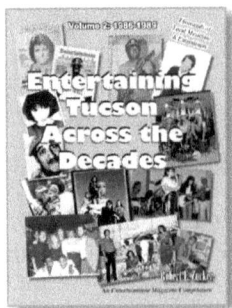

ENTERTAINING TUCSON ACROSS THE DECADES

Volume 2: 1986-1989

1985 Recap– the end of an era

Michael Landon [17] appeared on the cover of the first edition of the ***Entertainment Magazine*** in April 1985. When he attended the annual **Tucson Celebrity Classics Tennis Tournament**. In 1985, Tucson had only 376,195 residents. By the end of the 20th Century, it grew to 486,699 people living within the Tucson city limits. [18] This influx of new Tucsonans not only brought new businesses, but also, new entertainment venues and entertainers.

As 1984 ended, so did **Rockefeller**– Tucson's number one hard rock venue. **Mark Newman** [19] took over the old **Outlaw** nightclub on West Lester (which also closed) and renamed it the **Roxy.** The Roxy gave local rock bands a larger place to play and showcase up-and-coming bands. An all ages club opened in February 1985 on North Oracle called **DanceTrax** with recorded music. Country music enthusiasts got a big change with the moving of the **Outlaw** from West Lester location to midtown at 5822 E. Speedway.

Chances Nightclub after arson fire, *Entertainment Magazine* archives, January 1985.

The charred hull of **Chances Night Club**, 6542 E. Tanque Verde Road, was condemned hours after an arson fire ripped through the building on Thursday, January 11, 1985. The bar opened in November 1978.

There is a change in spelling from **Giant Sandworms** to the **Giant Sandwurms**. According to **Howe Gelb**, the change reflects the new concept direction of the band. He said the Giant Sandwurms were working on their new material and looking for a drummer. They moved to Los Angeles and recorded as **Giant Sand**. Garber said the name was changed to end the affiliation with the movie.

Al Perry and the Cattle began recording a six song EP at the **Sound Factory Recording Studio** on January 2nd. Perry said it would be released by February (1985). **Jeff Keenan** said the **Phantom Limbs** are scheduled

---

[17] Michael Landon passed away on July 1, 1991 from pancreatic cancer.
[18] "Tucson Update – Population," City of Tucson Housing and Community Development, 2015.
[19] Mark R. Newman passed away on October 24, 2012 at age 55. Newman also operated Mudbuggs, Head East and Head West Smoke Shops in Tucson.

to record a second record in San Francisco during February.

KBLE-FM, Tucson's first cable radio station went on line in early March 1985. Locally owned and operated, KBLE-FM was available to basic subscribers of **Cox Cable** through the audio portion of a yet to be assigned channel.

The Saddle City Band with Michel Landon (center). From right to left: **Mike Sullivan**, **Mike Holloway**, Landon, Rick Nuttall and **Bill Cashman**, the band's producer. Photo courtesy of **Art Attack Records**, March 1985. *Entertainment Magazine* archives.

In April, the **Saddle City Band** appeared a second time on NBC-TV's highly rated and very successful TV series "Highway to Heaven," starring **Michael Landon** and **Victor French**.

Unfortunately, for local music, especially the punk and metal bands and fans, the months old **WREX** nightclub closed down in April.

By the summer, **Jack's Pub** closed its doors to live music. At the **Maverick**, **John E. Mann** continued as the house band. **Lil Abner's Steak House** was perfect for dinner and the music of **Dean Armstrong**. **Street Pajama**'s release, "Beast de Resistance," came out on vinyl at the end of July 1985. For the past six months at **KXCI** (91.7) and for nearly 2½ years at **96 Rock's** Sunday nights with the **KLPX Virgin Vinyl** show radio alternatives opened the airwaves to new, local and "non-commercial" music.

By the fall, **Marc Levinson** and his partner **Howard Stern** planned to reopen the **Comedy Zone**, which was discontinued when **Karmel's** closed. The newly reopened Comedy Zone later relocated to **Terry & Zeke's Friendly Tavern** on East Speedway. **Terry Glassman** says they are trying a new concept. **Tequila Mockingbird**, at **El Con Mall**, continues its Comedy Night.

In November, the **Tucson Fire Department** (TFD) closed **Splinter Brothers Warehouse** and ordered all patrons to immediately evacuate because the 13-year old building didn't meet current fire code standards. At 10:00 pm, about a half dozen members of the TFD filtered into the crowd and ordered the building to be evacuated during the show after citing a number of fire code violations. At about the same time, **Brooklyn's Night Club** was also being checked by TFD. When a TFD officer overhead someone at Splinter Brother's determinedly say, "We're going on," he called for police back up to avoid any incident. The 100 people were ushered to the exits as the TFD and **Tucson Police Department** made sure the show wasn't going to go on. Disgruntled patrons question the ethics of shutting the building town in the middle of the performance. It was an incident that could have been avoided.

January 1986: Local Tucson Music Column

By Angie Lumia
January 1986– Entertainment Magazine

The Fantastic Fanatiks First LP

Fanatiks, a contemporary rock hip, will release their first album "Here There Be Tigers" early next month. The album is on a new independent record label in town, **Karl Records**. "Tigers" is a six-song album with five months of writing, rehearsing and recording behind it. The Fanatiks are **Rob Paulus** on guitar/violin, **Steve Merski** on keyboards, **Dave Nahan** on bass, and **Miguel Monroy** on percussion. According to bassist Nahan, "All the have commercial potential, a strong melody and a solid dance beat. "Tigers" was recorded at **Westwood Studios**. "Although it has taken us a while to get done, the excellent capabilities of Westwood and our producer, **Roger King**, have made it all worth the wait," says bassist Nahan. February 13th (1986) marks the Fanatiks one-year anniversary. Over that year, they've played their brand of original music in all major clubs in Tucson, as well as in Bisbee, Wilcox, and benefits including those for MDA, Ethiopia and Mexico. They hope to distribute "Tigers" locally and regionally.

Short Stories Gets New Drummer

Short Stories recently got a new drummer, **Ernie Mendoza**. They did their first show with Mendoza last month at **Brooklyn's**. And their songs were well done and well received. Short Stories original Reggae and rock is energetic and very danceable. Their originals are attention getting. This month, Short Stories will perform at Brooklyn's on the 10th with the **Fanatiks**, and on the 23rd and 30th with a guest appearance. Short Stories will leave Tucson when they get four sets together. They plan to hit clubs that cater to original music.

John Sirkis Releases First LP

John Sirkis, part time Tucson resident (when not in Colorado), has just released his first LP. In sound and appearance, Sirkis is reminiscent of the folk singers that flourished throughout the 1960's. His is a music with a "good time flavor" to it– from standard folksy love songs to an upbeat number about the street fair in Texas. Sirkis is assisted on this LP by, among others, **Scott Cossu** of the **Windham Hill** label.

IF's New Tape

IF is described as a blend of funk, Reggae, new wave British American rock and most accurately, "human dance music," will be performing at **Gentle Ben's** on January 19th and 26th and at **NueVenue** on January 25th. Later this month they will be back in the **Sound Factory** to work on a new tape. Their current tape, put out in October, is available at **Discount Records** and **First Strike Studios**.

Statesboro's New Blues

The **Statesboro Blues Band** recently released "Working Man Blues." The tape is available at the **Blues Company**, **Only Oldies**, **First Strike Studios**, **Loco Records & Tapes** and all **Zip's Records** locations or from the band at **Terry & Zeke's**. They will be at **Keaton's** on January 31st (1986).

Boogie Man Boogies

On stage, the third weekend of every month at the **Chicago Bar**, is the **Boogie Man Blues Band** featuring **Harmonica Mike**.

New Home for KXCI

The **Foundation for Creative Broadcasting**, Inc., license holder for **Community Radio** at 91.7 FM has permanent site for **KXCI**, 220 S. 4th Avenue, in the historic **Armory Park Neighborhood**. The property has a two-story brick home built in 1904 and house both studios and offices for KXCI.

HMS Preparing New Music

HMS also is taking this month off. They'll be using the time to write new material. Their drummer, **John Booth**, is also playing with **Friendly Warning** while their keyboard player, **Phil Stevens**, is also playing keyboards with HMS. Their long awaited video "Riding Palomino," will definitely be completed this month. HMS's tape, "Untitled Wish," is available at **Al Bums** and their first tape, "Never Shoe A Dead Horse," is also available at Al Bum's.

Global Goes NueVenue

The **NueVenue** is the new name of the **Global Village Nightclub** for young people under 21 years old. The club, located at the **Tucson Y.W.C.A.**, 304 E. University Blvd., west of the **University of Arizona**, continues to feature live and recorded music showcasing youth bands in a 6,000 square foot hall. For bands who want to gain exposure and play on a stage in a large hall, the NueVenue provides Open Stage. Special events nights like Psychedelia Face-Painting Nights with **Affirmative**, Christian Dance Nights, $1 Cover Nights and a multi-daylong band benefit are just some of the upcoming events. Besides bringing nightclub bands to the under-21 crowd, showcasing high school bands, arrangements are being made to feature more outside groups.

NueVenue club for teenagers, operated by *Entertainment Magazine*. From *Entertainment Magazine*, January 1986.

51

April 1988

Cover Interview: James DePavia

Local Musicians Recognized at Mardi Gras; Terry & Zeke's Arises Again; Gentle Ben's Gets the Boot

April 1988 – Entertainment Magazine. Page 7

Tucson musicians were awarded plaques from *Entertainment Magazine* during the 2nd Annual **Tucson Mardi Gras** held at **Rillito Downs** March 25-27, 1988. **Dave Pratt**, **KUPD** morning man and leader of the **Sex Machine Band**, made the presentations during his Friday night performance.

Awards went to **Rockefeller**, the **Porter House Singers** and a special plaque for each one of the more than 30 Tucson bands that participated. The **Nostros Teamwork Program** made the awards.

When the phoenix arises out of the ashes, it gains new momentum. This seems to be the case with one of Tucson's former blues nightspot– **Terry & Zeke's** now called **Terry & Zeke's Again**. **Terry Glassman**, owner of the only blues nightspot in Tucson that offered blues seven nights a week re-opens the same location to feature more than just the blues. Terry & Zeke's now boasts of a remodeled club– with an improved stage and lighting, new ventilation and a CD juke box. "This won't be just a blues club," he explains, "We will include a variety of other popular music." Glassman mentions that he is still looking for a new location but will stay at the present spot on E. Speedway near Columbus until he finds the right investor.

A long-time college favorite bar, **Gentle Ben's**, on North Tyndall Avenue, is about to hit the ashes when the wrecking ball brings down the building to make way for the **University Commons Dorm** on the block surrounded by Euclid Avenue, University Blvd. and Tyndall. Where is Gentle Ben to hibernate after the end of April? Not too far, he is expected to be mausoleum-ed inside the new building around the corner on University Blvd. once it arises.

Jon Miller, owner of the popular **Tucson Garden** plans to expand his schedule to include Country music. **Boon Docks** now features blues on Sundays.

Tailor Made for Tucson

By Katherine von Holtzer
April 1988 – Entertainment Magazine. Page 13

Tailor Made, a local mainstream rock group with an engaging stage presence as well as an engaging physical presence, made a return appearance recently in the **University of Arizona Cellar** and the **UA Student Union**, performing some of their own original tunes along with popular hits from the '70s and early '80s.

This energetic, tight-knit band consists of **Jimmy Mac**, guitar and keyboard, **Troy Wisehart**, bass, and **Craig Harris**, drums. All three are "showmen." With Mac as the lead singer, and strong vocal backing from **Wisehart**, the band held the audience captive with such original tunes' as "Ride the Time," "No Harm," "Women in Red," "Absence of Color," and "The Lesson" to name a few. After two encores, with the audience shouting "more, more," the band closed with "Walk All Over You," and "The Jack."

December 1988

Cover Interview: Adam Baldwin

Sidewinders to Sign Record Deal; Hellhound Fish Karma

Tucson's rockers, the **Sidewinders**, are about to sign a recording contract with **RCA Records** and the band's independent label, **Mammoth Records**. RCA will handle distribution, promotion, marketing and publicity for the band. Mammoth will deliver the finished masters to RCA. The Sidewinders released their first album, "¡Cuacha!" early this year on **San Jacinto Records**, a small independent label. The Sidewinders include singer and guitarist **David Slutes**, lead guitarist **Richard Hopkins**, bass player **Mark Perrodin**, drummer **Diane Padilla** and singer **Andrea Curtis-Olson**.

"Hellhound on My Leg," is a new 45 available by **Fish Karma** through **Addled Records** in Tucson. The record contains songs such as "I had a Dream," "Big Daddy," "Swap Meet Women," and "God is a Groovy Guy." Fish Karma is on vocals and guitar with the **Cattle**, **Al Perry** (guitar and keyboards), **Dave Roads** (bass), and **Julia Mueller** on drums.

Sunday Morning Bars Sport the Sports

Tucson bars can now be open during Sunday mornings due to a unanimous decision by the **Tucson City Council** last month to allow bars to open at 1:00 am on Sunday mornings. They will not be allowed to serve liquor until noon, though. "Sports bars," which cater to sports enthusiasts with large screen and multiple TV's and satellite dishes were unable to open their doors to show Sunday morning sporting events because of a city code which prohibits bars from opening until noon on Sunday. **Jack Ivans**, owner of **Daddy Jack's Sport-A-Rama**, led the petition drive for bar owners. Bars outside city limits are able to open 6:00 am on Sundays and many sports bars were losing those customers. Bar owners are also trying to get the state law changed to be able to start serving liquor at 1:00 am on Sundays.

Your Name in Lights

Did you always want your name up in lights? Well, **Boon Docks Lounge** is offering you that chance. You can let all of Tucson know about your next special event (birthday, job, whatever...). If you call ahead and bring in six or more people, **Bill** and **Celia Katzel**, the owners, will let all of North 1st Avenue know about it on their marquee. And there's more. You'll get Boon Docks t-shirts, champagne and a serenade by the band and a photo of the occasion!

New Entry on the Club Scene – Rialto's

The grand opening of Tucson's newest club, **Rialto's** was held late last month. You can dance to some of the hottest DJ sounds around in the **Plaza at Williams Center** on Broadway & Craycroft. Rialto's is also a restaurant offering lunch and dinner from 11:00 am to 1:00 am from Monday through Saturday.

Reggae All Month

Abel and Allen presents a Reggae revue at **Graffiti's** every Saturday night. From Woodstock, New York. Abel and Allen have performed with many big name groups such as the **Meditations**, the **Wailers**, the **Ramones**, the **Clash**, and others. The group began 12 years ago when **Tony Allen** appeared with **Cedric Brook**'s Jazz group United Africa. Allen plays bass and is lead singer, **Sonia Abel** is lead singer, DJ **Rick Tarantelli** is on drums, **Ralph Frazier** is on guitar, **Willie Victoria** on lead guitar and **John Browne** on keyboards.

Bobby Taylor & Real Deal: Here's the Real Deal

Bobby Taylor, June 1989, *Entertainment Magazine*. Page 19

By Beverly Craft
June 1989 – Entertainment Magazine.
Page 18

If you are a fan of the Motown sound, or you just appreciate creative and inspiring vocals, then there's a new band in town you won't want to miss. They're called **Real Deal**.

This dynamic soul band is the creation of singer **Bobby Taylor**, [20] the son of bluesman **Sam Taylor**. Music is the Taylor family business and Bobby has inherited more than his fair share of talent.

From his father, an accomplished singer, songwriter and musician, be has acquired his charisma and his ability to reach deep inside himself and fill his songs with heartrending emotion. He has received from his mother, **Beatrice**, a gifted gospel singer, a voice with such range that he can reach notes so high it is difficult to believe they are being produced naturally. Bobby was introduced to music when he was a small child. He would listen to his father rehearse in the family living room.

"My brothers and sisters and I would listen to Dad sing. Then we would go into the bedroom and try to sing the songs ourselves," Bobby recalled in a recent interview. It was Bobby's sister, **Sandra**, who took the first step into show business.

"I never thought Sandra was that good until I heard her on tape. Then one night I went to see her perform at a club that had a reputation for being rowdy. I watched her control the audience with her singing and I was so impressed that I decided right then and there that music was for me."

Bobby sang with several different groups in his hometown of New York and in L.A. When his father moved to Tucson in 1987, Bobby divided his time between here and New York. While in Tucson, he sang with the **Blue Lizards** and his own band **Bobby and The All Stars**. He liked it here, but business kept calling him back to New York.

---

[20] Bobby Taylor died of a heart attack on June 20, 1997 while playing basketball.

(left to right standing) Karen Brooks, David Muñiz, Mitzi Cowell, Danny, Sonia Thomas and David. In front: Jacques Taylor, and Bobby Taylor. Photo by Pierre. May, 1989. *Entertainment Magazine* archive.

Bobby had won the 1986-87 Amateur of the Year Award at the **Apollo Theater**, a prestigious accomplishment that carried a great amount of press coverage and landed a recording contract with **Capitol Records**.

Bobby went to New York fun of hope and cut an album of Motown covers for Capitol. A bad business decision, however, put everything on hold. He returned to Tucson discouraged and depressed. He decided he just wanted to perform with his dad, but Sam convinced him he needed to form his own band. "My dad told me, 'It's alright. You just have to start over. Just remember, I'm behind you.' It was because of his encouragement that I formed the **Real Deal**. I just started looking around until I found the musicians I wanted."

For one member, he didn't have to look far. **Jacques Taylor**, Bobby's cousin, moved to Tucson about six months ago and had been singing occasional back up for Sam. "We used to sing together when we were kids, and he has such outstanding stage presence that I just had to have him in the band."

Jacques, who is also from New York, has been performing in rap groups for the past ten years. He has worked with **Kool-MoeDee**, D.J. **Marley Marl** and **Grand Master Flash**, to name a few. Singing back up is not exactly the

same, but the transition has been fairly easy since all of his rap tunes were harmonized.

Karen Brooks is another vocalist in the group. A native of Flagstaff, she moved here four years ago. She sang previously with **Champaign Pyramid** and **Bourbon Street Jazz Band**, but her real roots are in gospel.

Mitzi Cowell plays guitar. Mitzi is a former member of the **All Stars** and **Feline**. On bass is **Dan Muñiz**, a noted Jazz musician who also plays with The **Brotherhood**. The keyboard player is **David Bynes**, who formerly played for **Small Paul**, among others. An accomplished musician, David also plays harp. On drums is **Dan Lynch**. This is Dan's first real gig, but he has been jamming for quite awhile.

"I carefully picked these people for my band," says Bobby. "They are the ones I wanted. We had a gig within our first week of getting together and we've been working ever since. Right now, we're doing mostly covers, but we plan to start doing some original tunes very soon. We also plan to do some recording. I think we're good now, but we just plan on getting better." With all that Taylor talent, I think he's right.

It's among every musician's worst nightmare. Your gig is booked and for the past three weeks the band has been revving up for the day to come– only it never does. The day before the show you get a call notifying you that you've been cancelled.

Or even more horrifying, as one local rock musician recounted, is to show up at the venue mid-afternoon to set up equipment and see a notice posted on the door that states they will be closed the next few days due to an emergency. Still another said he refuses to play at a certain restaurant because the management was more concerned about how many drinks and meals were sold and basically viewed the band as an inconvenience, although the crowd enjoyed them. One club changed ownership and did not honor the shows the previous owner booked.

Bands that are getting cancelled with little or no notice are an annoying occurrence. Taylor feels some local club owners should handle this task in a more professional manner. Speaking as a musician whose band currently plays out six nights of the week, Taylor is well versed with the local club scene.

"A club will schedule you for a Friday or Saturday and they'll call you Thursday and cancel you out," explained Taylor. "That's totally unfair because musicians can't do anything about it. I think that the only solution is that musicians should stick together."

Taylor also feels that a written contract that covers both the band and club should be a standard procedure "because bands also cancel out." Granted, some club owners do not want to sign a contract and that pretty much leaves the group vulnerable to the whims of the manager.

"That's my point. I think it should be mandatory that there should be some kind of agreement so both parties are covered," he emphasized. "Musicians always get the bad end of the deal. A club owner can get another band to make their money. But the band is out in the cold. They have bills to pay and club owners don't respect that. I think that's a disgrace."

Losing a gig, granted, is part of being in the music business, but the manner in which the information is conveyed leaves a lot to be desired. Some club owners view running an establishment more as a hobby instead of a business, let along zeroing in on the music aspect of it.

Likewise, some musicians sorely lack professionalism, but the majority of them are serious, learning the ropes, recording, performing, working day jobs, and yes, trying to pay the bills.

A good rule is to stick with those venues the group feels comfortable. Also, musicians networking among each other could help in avoiding unpleasant situations as well.

"If you're going to book a band, I think you should stick with the choice," said Taylor. "Everyone should be entitled to a two-week notice (if plans have changed)."

In all, in some clubs problems do exist. However, if both parties use common courtesy, common sense and respect–well, it's a start.

"We've got so many club owners and promoters that don't even know what the hell they're doing. You can get disgusted, discouraged. I mean, it's hard to discourage me. But musicians, especially when you're first starting, when you get turned down, it's hard to get that confidence up."

Tequila Mockingbird and **Obsessions Night Club** advertisements, June 1989. *Entertainment Magazine*. Page 19.

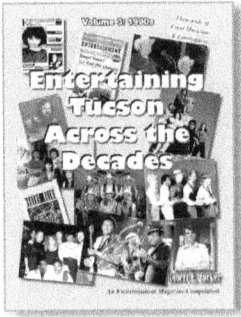

ENTERTAINING TUCSON ACROSS THE DECADES

Volume 3: 1990s

1989: Tucson Nightlife Updates

Compiled by Peggy Rose, Heather Marshall and DeeJaye Kemp
May 1990– Entertainment Magazine, pages 4, 6 and 10

Sam Taylor is playing the blues loud and clear all over Tucson. On Monday and Tuesday nights, he is at the **Pacific Beach Club**, at the **Chicago Bar** on Fridays and Saturdays, and **Westward Look** on Sunday, May 27th. Sam sports a great horn section, exciting and driving arrangements. The drummer, **Reno**, is awesome and **Arvin** and **Dave** round out the rhythm section with the talent you would expect from a Sam Taylor organization.

If you are one of the brunch aficionados, you might like to know that brunch at the **Westward Look Resort** is not only excellent, but is also offering a soft, very tasty Jazz background every Sunday in the **Gold Room** starting at 12:00 pm. **Hal Pyper** keeps you gently entertained with his subtle flute, clarinet and saxophone backed by his own recorded music.

If you stick around until five, you can catch current Jazz in the **Lookout Lounge** at the **Westward Look**. They offer Jazz each and every Sunday. Two special shows this month include the **Pat McCauley** Scholarship Benefit Concert on May 13th as a tribute to one of Tucson's most renowned guitarists/instructors, a Memorial Weekend Jazz Sunday Blowout on May 27th with **Sam Taylor**, and several other fine local bands.

The local rock/alternative scene keeps rearranging as clubs re-format their entertainment. Many seem to be headed toward recorded music over live bands. But, as the schedule below indicates, there is still plenty of live rock to be found.

Tucson's alternative rock band, **Marshmallow Overcoat**, celebrates the release of their 3rd LP "Beverly Pepper" and a CD compilation of six other vinyl releases dating back to the group inception. They plan a concert at **Mudbuggs** on Saturday, May 5th. This will be their only Tucson appearance in 1990. This summer takes the Overcoat to both coasts and Europe. Other Record Release Parties include **River Roses** on Thursday, May 10th and The **Host** will hold a Record Release party at Mudbuggs on May 18th. The **Statesboro Blues Band**, a longtime favorite, also is releasing an LP this month.

Workshop Music and Sound on Oracle Road is providing a venue for new talent to get some first class exposure. The **New Artist Concert Series** is being presented on alternate Saturdays. The creative force behind this idea is **Charlie Van Dusen**, manager of Workshop's Oracle store. Charlie, a member of The **Brain Damage Orchestra**, saw a need in the community for new artists to launch their musical talents Workshop is providing the forum, sound equipment and media support– the ingredients lacking that new artists critically need.

You'll be pleased to know that live music is alive on the eastside at **Jin's Sneak Joint**, which is becoming one of the fastest growing eastside clubs. **Bobby Taylor**, son of **Sam Taylor**, appears May 26-27th.

Tucson has a wide range of Country and Western music clubs by the mere fact of its locale. For the country and/or Western fans that means a plethora of bands and places. There is a difference between Country and Western music.

At the **Round Up Saloon** on Benson Highway, the featured **Round Up Band** and the **Marty Allen Band** play seven nights a week and a couple of afternoons also. The Round Up features good food, spirits and a good dancing

atmosphere.

On Tucson's far west side, over the Tucson Mountains, on Kinney Road, near Tucson Estates, you can find two favorite spots. **Tovi's Hoof & Horn** features the **Southbound Group** with **Dan Goodberry** at the helm. The restaurant also features smorgasbord style. A stones throw down the road is the **Road Runner**, a long time frontrunner with the **T.J. Canyon Band**. Both clubs feature good grub and dancing. The **Desert Canyon Rose Band** keeps the patrons of **Tiny's Saloon** happy on Ajo Way near Kinney Road. They are famous for their big, big Thursday Burger.

Hidden among the rockers, Country kickers and Jazzers, swing/big band and the standards are still playing strong. Try the **Baron's** restaurant on Sunday and Monday nights. Sunday starting at 8:30 pm, its the **Mickey Greco** quartet featuring **Peggy Rose**, vocalist. On Monday evening starting at 8:30 pm, it's the **Cass Preston Quartet**. The rest of the week, its **Hot Pursuit** plays top 40. At **Faye Anne's Memory Lane**, Pantano near Broadway, you'll find live nostalgic music five nights a week. They feature various groups including Cass Preston throughout the week. **Peggy Rose** appears on weekends. Dancing starts at 8:30 pm.

Then you might want to try the elegance of **Loew's Ventaña Canyon Resort**'s Lounge where **Frederick** holds sway along with his drummer, **Janet** and **Cass Preston** on trumpet and vocals Thursdays through Saturdays. The entertainment starts at 10:00 pm on Thursdays and 9:00 pm Fridays and Saturdays with dancing.

Another old standby for swing and Dixie is still going strong at **Gus & Andy's Steakhouse** on Oracle Rd**. John Denman** [21] is our English import, featured on clarinet and when symphony or recording commitments appear, **Len Ferrone** [22] ably holds it all together. Len sings and plays bass along with **Mary Jane** and others at the piano, **Pete Swan** at the drums, and a parade of horns and vocalists week after week. Len sings many a favorite himself when he is not graciously inviting others to do so. You can never be sure of what wonderful musical treasure you might miss if you stay away from Gus & Andy's too long. Friday and Saturday, 8:30 pm to 12:30 am with dancing.

Even if you are not a Green Valley resident, you might want to venture out to the **Arizona Family Restaurant** on a Friday night to hear one of Tucson's favorite vocalists, **Peggy Rose**. She is introducing her new presentation of singing all the old favorites to recorded music and is performing in **Easy Street Lounge** at the **Arizona Family Restaurant** at 8:00 pm.

If your an elk, stay away from the woods but do wander into the **Elks Lodge** on River Road where **Clint Harrison** will ply his trade through July, Thursday through Sunday. Excellent music for listening or dancing. Versatility laced with humor. Clint comes to Tucson from the Midwest and is packing them in. Lois, his pretty wife, lends her vocal talent and is a positive addition.

Toxic Ranch Records, May 1990, *Entertainment Magazine*, page 4.

---

[21] John Denman died on November 6, 2001.
[22] Len W. Ferrone passed away on September 4, 2007.

Now Everyone's Wearing A Marshmallow Overcoat

Marshmallow Overcoat, LP "Beverly Pepper." Skyclad and Get Hip Records.

By Joe Chemoux
July 1990– Entertainment Magazine, page 4

The national success of **Marshmallow Overcoat** shows that Tucson bands do have a chance to gain the vinyl spotlight.

Their most recent release on **Get Hip/Skyclad Records** is "Beverly Pepper" and a Best of CD anthology, "1986-1990." A new video clip is forthcoming, along with a compilation video containing many of the band's award winning clips of concert footage.

The Overcoat consist of Tucsonans **Timothy Gassen** on vocals, **Mark Panico** on guitar, **Scott Gassen** on drums, **Dan Magee** on bass, and **Debra Dickey** on keyboards.

The group began in the summer of 1986, when vocalist "**Randy Love**" assembled some friends to cut some 1960's-inspired "garage demos." A debut 45 was released when Love's long-time friend, **Lee Joseph**, **Dionysus Records'** president, heard the tapes. This started the group's growing international reputation with their unique combination of fuzz guitar, swirling keyboards and a driving beat. Timothy, who uses "Randy Love" as a stage name, contributes the bulk of original compositions. He also produces the Overcoat recordings. **Dan Magee** at **DB Studios** and **Steve English** at the **Sound Factory** engineered this recent release. Their music has been described as everything from "modern psychedelia" to "punk-pop" to "folk garage."

The 1988 effort, "The Inner Groove," gained praise and airplay across the globe, with heavy response in Italy, Spain, France, Germany, Sweden, England and, of course, the United States. A year of furious writing and recording resulted in their second LP, "Try On The Marshmallow Overcoat." In 1989, they released the EP "Alive." Their success has been greater outside Tucson, though, as Timothy suggested during the release party for their second LP at **Club Congress** in March last year.

"You see, even though the band lives in Tucson, we understand that many folks here don't know us," he told party guests." We've been focusing on the international and European market instead. We would like to raise local consciousness of the band." They don't have that problem now.

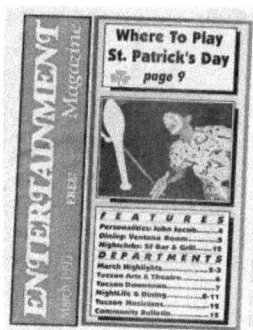

March 1993

Spring Fling cover

Tucson Bands Hold CD Release Parties

By Tina Alvarez
March 1993– Entertainment Magazine, page 12

The **Tucson Garden**'s Friday Nite Rock Party continues to rock on. On February 19th **Savant** began the evening with its style of thrash-rock sound. Because **Ysadora**'s lead singer was down and out with a sore throat, **Impact** filled in and they were as good as ever. The Los Angles based **Roxanne** was the headlining act and they were synchronized with their dance steps and "Motown meets Dance Fever" style of presentation. Again, despite less than ideal weather, the club had a good size crowd.

Slated to perform on March 5th are **Rozy Coyote**, **Stone Giant**, and **Tantrum**. Bands to appear at the Tucson Garden Saint Patrick's Day Blowout are **Dead Silence**, **Backlash**, **Prophecy**, **Way Station**, and **Stone Giant**. **Paul Thomas Productions**' **Jon Miller** is also putting out a newsletter that covers information regarding the various bands appearing at the venue. Way Stations' manager and promoter **Mike Buckels** was also at the rock party that night checking out the place since the group will be performing later in the month. Buckels described Way Station's music as "high energy rock."

The **Rembrandts**, whose second LP, "Untitled," is out on **Atco Records**, performs at the **Rock** March 10th. The main core of the band, consisting of **Danny Wilde** and **Phil Solem**, performed in Phoenix last month as part of their current tour.

Pulse will be holding a "fun dance party" at the **Downtown Performance Center** (DPC) on March 14th according to band member **Mike Olson**. The Sunday gig, which begins around 8:00 pm, will also feature **Mama Ritmo**, an all female Afro-Caribbean percussion band. Cover charge is $2. Olson said that those who want to see Pulse in the future can catch them at the DPC. "There are no commercial strings attached. I can sell what I want to sell there," he said, "instead of booze, dinners, etc. I took my marbles out of the game and now I'm playing my own game." Olson likes the creativity the DPC allows the play there.

Sand Rubies had their CD release party at **Club Congress** last month with **U & the Risk** opening. The self-titled CD is well worth the wait.

El Mariachi advertisement, February 1993, *Entertainment Magazine*, page 12.

Tucson Blues Legend, Sam Taylor Dies at 74

"I love what I'm doing. It's a gift and I'm thankful for it"
–Sam Taylor, 1994

January 11, 2009 – Entertainment Magazine On Line (EMOL.org)

Tucson, Arizona's former blues guitarist and singer-songwriter, **Sam Taylor**, passed away on Monday, January 5, 2009 at the age of 74, in his Islandia, New York home.

Among the performers he's played with are **Otis Redding**, **Sam and Dave**, **T-Bone Walker**, **Solomon Burke**, **Little Johnny Taylor** and **Big Joe Turner**, who called him the Crown Prince of the Blues. Taylor had spent a decade in Tucson, Arizona and was a staple on the local music scene. He left Tucson in 1996 to live with his family in New York.

Sam Taylor, who always wore his signature sailors' cap, was a frequent performer at the **Chicago Bar**, **Dirtbag's West**, **Hec & Wink's**, and **Jaime's** on 4th Avenue before he moved back to New York after the death of his son.

Bobby Taylor, Sam's son, died Monday, July 21, 1997 after a heart attack. Bobby, 39, was the leader of The **Real Deal**, a popular Tucson blues band.

Sam Taylor was inducted into the **Arizona Blues Hall of Fame** in 1997. He received the **Long Island Music Hall of Fame** recognition in 2006.

The **Sam Taylor's House of Swing** was a showcase for Sam Taylor, his band's talent, and guest appearances. Its brief incarnation was at the **Santa Rita Ballroom** in Downtown Tucson in December 1994. The club, sponsored by local music magazine *Roadhouse* [23] and **Chuck Gross's Thrillville**, featured artists like **Frankie Lee**, **King Ernest and the Wild Knights**, and the **Blue Monks**. Local musicians **Heather Hardy**, **Ed Delucia**, **Mike Nordberg** and **Paul Elia** joined Sam on stage.

Sam Taylor graphic by George Alford

---

[23] **Robert Zucker**, *Entertainment Magazine* publisher help produce the *Roadhouse* **Magazine**. The short-lived publication– only printed in December 1994– was published by **Robert Catz**.

Index: Volume 1

The following indexes are from each of the three volumes of ENTERTAINING TUCSON ACROSS THE DECADES. The first volume contains 310 pages and cover the years from the 1950s through 1985.

2

22nd Street, 16, 32, 48, 88, 172, 247

4

4 Cylinders, 176
4th Avenue, 56, 96, 120
4th Avenue Street Fair, 228

5

5th Avenue, 148

6

6th Street, 172

7

7-Eleven, 139

9

9th Street Checkers, 128, 217

A

A Tribute to Elvis Album, 66
Abelow, Jules, 26
Abril, Manuel, 47, 293
Ace, Frank, 47
Acedo, Jesus, 234, 258, 265
Aces High, 242
Addled Recording, 236
Affirmative, 226, 269, 276
Africa is at War by Uptones, 217
After The Gold Rush, 69
Aftermath, 180, 186, 187, 196, 199, 200, 209, 229, 242
Aguirre, Ernie, 99
Aikens, Rambler Kenton, 142
Aikens, Rick, 142, 143
Air Hockey, 88
Airtight, 84, 85
Al Bums, 154, 172, 206, 258, 266, 274
Al Perry and the Cattle, 194, 252
Al Smith's Pub, 271
Alameda Street, 26

Alamo, 62
Alday, Roxanna, 133, 134, 293
Aldridge, Rick, 165, 231
Aldus PageMaker, 288
Alev, Simon, 203, 293
Alexander, Ed, 77, 78, 82, 83, 94, 95, 104, 293, 294
Alford, George, 293
Ali, Azie, 228
All Bob Band, 270, 271
Allen, Gary, 59
Allen, Larry, 59, 66, 67, 273
Allen, Rex, 24
Allen, Rick, 116
Alvarez, Tina, 256, 293
Alvernon, 27
Ambush, 84
Amerikaans, 151
Amphitheatre High School, 118, 124, 142, 272
Amphitheatre Junior High School, 82
Anderson, Jim, 91
Anderson, Mark, 239
Andes, Linda, 169, 230, 246
Anglers, 147
Animation, 168
Anonymous Bluesmen, 190
Antariez Rayen, 110
Anti-Apartheid Benefit (1985), 266
Apache Drive-In, 31
Apocalypse Horns, 126
Aquillo, Cindy, 176, 293
Arem, Keith, 277
Aristocrats of the Range, 19
Arizona Cowboy, 20
Arizona Cowboy, Rex Allen, My Life Sunrise to Sunset, 24
Arizona Daily Star, 31, 101, 116, 138
Arizona Dance Hands, 44, 45
Arizona Historical Society, 260
Arizona Jobs for Graduates, 148
Arizona Kidney Foundation, 45
Arizona Opera Company., 251
Arizona Polo Association, 33
Arizona Summer Arts Festival, 249
Arizona Theatre Company, 240, 241, 251, 262
Arizona Women's Political Caucus, 162
Armagedeon, 217

Armstrong, Dean, 5, 17, 44, 45, 248
Armstrong, Greg, 129
Art Attack Records, 97, 222, 293
Arthur, Lamont, 253
Assassinators, 97
Assorted Images, 278
Asylum Records, 293
Atar, Mike, 59
Atari, 99
Atkinson, Brian, 293
Audience, 274
Audience Abuse, 117
Aztec Press, 13, 292

B

Babbitt, Bruce, 70
Backstage, 56, 97, 98, 121
Backstreet Boogie Band, 101, 233
Bad Brains, 121
Bad Element, 259
Bad Habit, 54
Bade, Richard, 127, 153
Bailer, Bryn, 77, 83, 293
Bailey, Connie, 265
Baker, Ace, 281
Baldwin, Andy, 186
Ball, Annie, 265
Ballyhoo Manny's, 48
Bambi Lounge, 53
Banshees, 16
Baron's Restaurant, 63
Barrrio Historico, 279
Barry Smith, 112
Base Six, 110
Bass, Hilary, 69, 293
Bassmen, 37
Battle of the Bands, 34, 37, 66
Beachcomber, 48
Beast de Resistance Street Pajama, 253
Beaudry, Bob, 241
Bednarek, Jim, 70, 77, 79, 104
Beetcher, Don, 78, 104
Beets, 266
Bego, Mark, 54
Believer, 209
Bellamy, Elizabeth, 119, 293
Beloved Ones, 39
Bendover Band, 57
Benedon, Bob, 154, 159, 165
Benny, Jack, 285

Berry, Jim, 48, 49
Big Roach Horns, 129
Bill Cashman, 57
Billy Templeton Band, 66
Biltmore Drive-In, 31
Bird, Kristi, 61
Birkenstock, 236
Bish, Bob, 98
Bissey, Thom, 211
Bitches Brew, 157
Black Angus, 246, 260
Black Flag, 181, 194, 204
Black Sun Ensemble, 234, 258, 265
Blackie Ranchette, 181, 194, 226
Blades, 186
Blake, Sam, 229
Blancato, Jacqueline, 151, 293
Blanche, Louis Virie, 217
Blankstrom, Alan, 180
Blanton, Carl, 213, 239
Blaze, 180
Bloodspasm, 237
Blue Lizard, 270
Blue Riddim Band, 217
Blue Wave, 252
Blues All Stars, 270, 277
Blues Company, 172
Bluewave, 269, 274
Bo St. Runners, 40
Bob and Bob, 251
Bob Cook's Bezerko Lounge, 98
Bob Meighan Band, 56, 97, 127
Boker, Steve, 81
Bomp Records, 156
Bono, Joe, 69
Boogie Man Blues Band, 269
Boomers, 170
Boon Docks, 270
Boot Hill, 66
Booth, Jeff, 247
Booth, John, 274
Booth/Baker Productions, 266
Borderline, 273
Borton, Vicki, 247, 274
Boss, Rick, 242
Bostrom, Derrick, 231
Bottom Line, 276
Boudreaux, Joseph, 215
Bourbon Street Five, 49
Bourbon Street Jazz Band, 48, 49
Boy Scout's Explorer's Post, 148
Boyd, Al, 49
Boyd, Bobby, 39
Bozec, Johnny, 65
Brady, Pat, 18
Brain Damage Orchestra, 218
Brain Dead/45 Grave, 181
Breakers, 38
Breathless, 266
Breeze, 126
Breeze, Connie, 215, 216, 238, 293
Brett, John, 234, 258
Broadway Blvd., 97, 110, 194, 244, 246, 260, 272, 273
Brock, Clifford, 213
Bromberg, Brian, 206, 265

Bromberg, David, 57
Brooklyn's, 218, 219, 223, 226, 228, 276, 277
Brooks, Brad, 239
Brown, Clay, 232, 233
Browning, Allen, 83
Browning, Jon, 128, 129
Bruce Babbitt, 70
Bryce, Rodney, 56
Buddy System, 206, 239, 274
Buel, Billy, 271
Bukunus, Dave, 215, 216, 279, 280
Bull Pen Lounge, 270
Burch, Shawn, 266, 276
Burkes, Billy, 45
Burkes, Sam, 57
Burning Bush, 217
Burroughs, Chris, 98, 133, 147, 223, 243
Bushwacker Steak House, 271
Bustamante, Sergio, 278
Butler, Ray, 272
Butterscotch, 41
Butz, Seymour, 221, 293
Buzzard, Clyde, 27
BZB Publishing, Inc., 2, 13, 311

C

Cabaret Attractions & Talent, 293
Cablewaves, 215
Cacavas, Chris, 131
Cacavas, Dorian, 226
Cactus Drive-In Theatre, 30
Café Olé, 219, 223, 269
Café Sweetwater, 56
Calhoon, Clayton, 194
Call, Paneen, 169
Camino Seco Blvd., 110
Campbell Avenue, 31, 172
Cannal, Dave, 266, 276
Cannon, John, 139, 154
Career Threads, 26
Carlos Murphy's, 260, 264
Carradine, Ted, 83
Carson, Johnny, 285
Carter, Jeff, 264, 293
Casey, 162, 215, 279, 293
Cashman, Bill, 97, 222
Casio, 150
Casler, Bob, 225, 259
Cason, Barbara, 194
Cass Preston and Ensemble, 63
Cassie-I, 161
Cat Blue, 119
Catalanotte, Peter "Splat", 230
Catalina High School, 110
Catback Mountain Band, 235, 248
Cattle, 170, 203, 207, 208, 226, 236
   Cattle release party, 226
Cattle Crossing, 236
Cavan, Jack, 48
Cavanaugh, Richie, 57
Central Air and the Air Brothers, 57
Chain Reaction, 142

Chameleons, 128
Chance Romance, 269
Chances Night Club, 98, 201, 202
Chandelle's Restaurant & Lounge,, 273
Channel 88, 96
Chaotic Allegiance, 168
Characters, 153, 157, 171, 177, 181, 184, 187, 194, 202, 240, 281
Charlie Pickett and the Eggs, 203
Chastain, Jean, 59
Chastain, John, 62
Cheers, 260, 267
Chicago Bar, 128, 269, 274
Chicken, 184
Chicken Coop, 177
Chicken House, 181
Cholla High School, 99
Choo Choo's, 56, 58
Chris Burroughs and the Nationals, 98, 121, 132, 133, 147, 157, 167, 168, 226
Christian, Van, 157, 202, 203, 207, 226
Chromatics, 97, 98, 120, 126, 247
Chuck E. Cheese's Pizza, 110
Chuck Wagon and the Wheels, 41, 57, 60, 61, 111, 157, 194, 226
Cinco de Mayo, 234, 255
Circle Jerks, 150
Circle K Stores, 222
Cirritto, Jamie, 228
City of Tucson Cable Office, 148
Civil Death, 120, 188
Class of '64, 233
Claussen, Susan, 249
Clayborne, Roy, 59, 62
Clean Dog, 98, 120, 126, 127, 144, 156
Click, Jim, 241
Club Europa, 97
Club La Jolla, 47
Cochran, Randy, 61
Comedia del Arte, 240
Comedy Boat, 281
Comedy Corner, 244
Comedy Zone, 240, 244, 260, 272, 282; newly reopened, 268; also see Karmel's, 267
Commonplace, Constance, 96, 135, 293
Community Food Bank, 69, 80
Community Media Services, 291
Compset 510, 288
Concourse, 202
Conflict, 98, 120, 121, 164, 168, 230, 247; demise of band, 169
Confused, 142, 143, 146
Congress Street, 26, 139, 181
Conklin, Steve, 176, 184
Connie and the Bandits, 265, 271
Contractions, 96
Cook, Bob, 98, 145
Cooke, Shep, 37, 40, 52, 53, 232, 233
Copper Star Café, 217

Copper State Recording Company, 47, 59
Cora's Café,, 50
Corona De Tucson Race Track, 59, 66
Corporate Whores, 120, 164, 230
Cory and Dave (his puppet), 267
Costin, Neil, 116, 172, 239, 247, 259, 274, 293
Country and Western Music Hall of Fame, 19
Country Club, 27, 244, 272
Country Club Lounge, 127, 152
Country Punks, 157
Country Sounds of Tucson, 59, 66
Country Swings Disco Sucks Chck Wagon & the Wheels, 60
County Club Lounge, 153
Cowboy Steakhouse, 127
Cowboy's, 98, 150, 167
Cowgirls, 98, 121
Cox Cable, 94, 105, 117, 181, 202, 212, 240
Cox Cable's Public Access Channel, 148
Cox, Danny, 152, 191, 195, 198, 226
Cox, Larry, 37, 52
Cox, Milton, 107
Craycroft Road, 273
Creative Entertainment, 221
Crews, Cheryl, 170
Cross, Fred, 112
Crosswind, 149
Crown Glass, 119
Cruising Speedway, 74
Cry Like A Rainstorm, Howl Like the Wind, 42
Culturecraft Int'l, 84
Cunneely, Kevin, 276
Curtis, Andrea, 144
Curtis, Ken, 18
Cushing Street Bar & Restaurant, 223

D

Daily, Pete, 48
Dairy Queen, 48
Dalen, Criss, 127
Dalen, Don, 127, 181, 227
Daley, Kevin, 209
Dalton Gang, 272
Dan Stuart, 131
Dan Woodberry, 270
Dance Attack, 202
Dance Attack (break dancing), 207
DanceTrax, 202
Dancing Dan, 152
Daniels, Jeff, 57, 84
Darnell, Pat, 239
Darwin, Danny, 89
Das Combo, 170
Dave, 244
David Bean Photography, 252, 293

David, Robert, 151
Davidson, Cathy, 225
Davis Monthan, 148
Davis Monthan Air Force Base, 61, 105
Davis Monthan Hispanic Day, 148
Davis, Mike, 107
Davis, Steven, 194
Davis-Monthan Air Force Base, 17
Dead End Records, 258
Dean Armstrong's Country Music Store, 17
Dean, David, 219
Dearly Beloved, 5, 37, 38, 39, 40, 52
Dearly's, 39
DeConcini, Dennis, 70
Deemer, Karl, 278
Defender, 99
DeForest, Calvert, 244
DeGrazia, Ted, 81
Déjà vu Photography, 238, 293
DeMers, Gerry, 128
Denman, John, 64, 65
Derald Fulton, 27
Desert City Six, 48
Desert Express Band, 273
Desert Fire, 266
Desert Riders, 271
Desert Show, 118
Desert Slim and the Fistful of Blues Band, 165
Desert Springs Rock Festival, 84, 85
Desert Tracks, 119
Desportes, John, 177
Dew, Tony, 194
Diamond's Box Office, 228
Dicambio, Mike, 213
Dickey, Debbie, 150
Die Kreuzen, 177
Die Like A Dog, 236
DiGiovanni, Michael, 88
Dirtadian, Armen, 260, 261, 262, 267, 272
Discount Records, 258
Disco-vision, 95
DiscRock, 87
Dissonance, 96
Distant, 274
Doc Zucker, 57
Dodge, Joe, 106, 147, 181
Dogs, 207
Dominguez, Leo, 59
Donath, Rob, 252
Donovan, Jack, 89
Dooley's, 97, 98, 127
Doss, Tommy, 18
Dotson, Rock, 239
Doubletree, 50, 249
Doubletree Inn, 260
Dow, Tom, 227
Dow, Tony, 181, 202, 227, 252
Doyle, Bill, 45, 293
Dozer, Bill, 164
Dr. Sax, 159

Dread Beat And Blood, 217
Dress Code, 247
Driftwood, 273
Dubwise, 219
Dubwise, Steve, 228
Dukowski, Chuck, 194, 204
Dunes, 48
Dunn, Ron, 35
Durrell, Kenny, 59
Dusty Chaps, 57, 61, 152, 157, 159
Dutiel, Curtis, 105, 293

E

E.S.S., 117, 120, 138, 150, 156
Eads, Rob, 119
Eagle, Bill, 49
Easter Seal Walk-a-Thon, 80
Eastman, Gary, 88
Easy But Not Cheap, 266
Eat to the Beat, 207
Eclipse, 119
Eddleblute, Caylah, 56, 152, 293
Edelbrock, Ed, 258
Edelbrock, Tony, 258
Edward, Michael, 239
eegee's, 85
Eek-a-mouse, 218
El Dorado Disco, 69
Eighty Go Ninety, 98, 111, 167, 269
El Casino Ballroom, 217, 218
El Con Mall, 49, 88, 228, 244, 272
El Pueblo Neighborhood Center, 82
El Rio Neighborhood Center, 82
Elem, Cornell, 148
Elk's Club, 219
Ellick, Chuck, 148
Embers, 180
EMC Entertainment, 293
Emery, Bill, 157
EMOL.org, 11, 13, 291, 292
Eneke, 223
Engle, John, 86, 293
English, Anne, 53
English, Steve, 236, 258
Enola Gay and the Tokyo Bombers, 207, 227, 231
Entertainment Magazine, 2, 11, 13, 117, 139, 222, 245, 247, 266, 270, 289, 291, 292, 293, 294
Entertainment Magazine On Line, 2, 13, 33, 291, 292
Entertainment Travel Business, 54
Epics, 84
Epps, Jimmy, 119
Erotics, 96
Espinel, Luisa (Ronstadt), 43
Espinosa, Fred, 220
Essig, Bonnie, 266, 276
Estell, Rex, 112, 164
Ethyl, 57
Etude, 211, 247
Europa Productions, 146, 166, 167
European Tan, 172
Evans, Paul, 271

Evening Star Productions, 97, 98
Every, David, 276
Executive Inn, 63
Exodus, 229

F

Faith, 267
Fan, Paula, 64
Fanatiks, 238, 239, 266
Farr, Hugh, 18
Farr, Karl, 18
Farzalo, David, 228
Father of all radio festivals, 292
Faucher, Charles, 149
Fay Anne's Memory Lane, 65
Feline, 184, 202
Ferguson, Jim, 281
Ferguson, Rob, 281
Ferrart, Steve, 127
Ferrone, Len, 49, 64
Fetish, 119
Feyline, 97
Fiction, 277
Fine, Pete, 126
Finney, Cliff, 199
Fintel, Dave, 162, 293
Fintel, Kay, 162, 293
Fire Fighters Hall, 265
Firehouse, 57
Fish Karma, 226, 236, 281
Fisher, Bill, 164, 169
Fisher, Mike, 277
Fisher, Shug, 18
Five More, 38
Five Of Us, 37
Flagstaff Lumberjack, 61
Flames, 266
Flash pinball game, 88
Flight, 151
Flipper Show, 202
Floating House Band, 41
Flowing Wells High School, 194
Fonda, 127, 169, 188, 204, 209,
   230, 235, 236, 245, 248, 293
Food Circus, 219, 237
Fool Around, 88
Foosball, 88
Forest Properties, Inc., 281
Forler, John, 244
Foundation for Creative
   Broadcasting, 139, 141
Fourth Avenue, 56
Fox Broadcasting Co, 285
Frank & Woody Show, 270
Frank Ace Combo, 47
Frank Ace Trio, 47
Frank and the Hurricanes, 270
Frank and Woody, 57, 59
Frank Kalil's Teen Town, 30
Freds, 98, 127, 153, 181, 184, 194
Free, Kevin, 276
Freiser, Manny, 40
Friendly Warning, 206, 269, 278
Ft. Lowell Depot, 272

Fuller, Tim, 225, 293
Fuller-Rey, Diana, 124
Furlow, Dick, 56

G

Galaxy 500, 218
Gallagher Theatre, 249
Gamble, Oscar, 89
Gamera, 57
Garber, Scott, 135, 136, 181, 182,
   183, 208, 226
Garcia, Ben, 67
Garrish, Madeline, 241
Gary Hood, 260
Gaslight Theatre, 50, 241, 260,
   262, 267, 272, 281
Gasper, Jim, 252
Gassen, Timothy, 112, 117, 150,
   293
Gate's Pass, 216
Gates Pass Inn, 62
Gates, Dan, 38, 40
Gavilan, Jorge, 157
Gazebo Restaurant and Nightclub,
   69, 71, 72
Geezers, 121
Gelb, Howe, 135, 136, 157, 181,
   183, 208
General Delivery, 53, 232, 233
Generations, 233
Genesis, 267
Gentle Ben's, 219, 259, 265, 269,
   270
Gentlemen After Dark, 98, 112,
   164, 169, 183, 206
George Hawke & the Cary Grants,,
   273
George, Stephan, 219
Giant Sand, 208, 226
Giant Sandworms, 5, 96, 97, 101,
   110, 121, 132, 133, 135, 136,
   137, 143, 156, 167, 181, 182,
   183, 184, 194, 208
Giant Sandwurms, 194, 208
Gilbert, Tim, 267
Gillie, Jim, 80, 81
Glassman, Terry, 159, 202, 246,
   268
Glenn, Johnny, 150
Glick, Roberta, 139
Glicksman, Elliott, 251
Glidewell, Michael, 234, 258
Global Village, 276, 277, 278
Glover, Fritz, 48
Goddard, Scott, 227, 237
Gold Mine, 88
Golder, David, 194
Golf 'n Things, 88, 214
Golf Links Rd., 17
Gomez, Richard, 232, 233
Gonnan, Mike, 237
Gonzales, Tomas, 211, 247
Gooch, Ron, 89
Goodwin, Darrell, 67

GoR, 131
Gorecki, Hope, 207, 227
Gowan, Gail, 271
Grabe's Record Center, 16
Graham and O'Leary Comedy
   Show, 240, 241, 251
Graham, Adam, 240, 241, 251, 267
Graham, Cheryl, 156
Graham, Chuck, 56, 110, 115, 116,
   256
Grams, Steve, 152
Granfalloon Saloon, 181, 233
Grant Road, 172
Gray, Gary, 89
Greased Pig Contest, 272
Greatbatch, Ron, 167
Greco, Mickey, 50
Green Acres Golfland, 88
Green on Red, 97, 130, 132, 144,
   150, 171, 196
Green, Jack, 111
Greenberg, Robert, 85
Greener, Bill, 72, 293
Greenspoon, Jimmy, 54
Gregory, Stewart, 267
Griffin, Anne, 89, 293
Griffin, Matt, 169, 195, 207, 230,
   246
Grodes, 37, 40
Gunther, Dan, 267
Gus & Andy's Steakhouse, 49, 64,
   65, 223
Guy, Carl, 51

H

Haas, Chuck, 35
Hall, Darwin, 215
Halper, Bruce, 176, 184, 227, 237
Hamilton, Michael, 16, 25, 30, 31,
   34, 35, 293
Hardy's Hamburger Restaurant, 72
Harmon, Charlee, 254
Harmon, Merle, 253, 254, 294
Harmonica Mike, 170, 191
Harmonica Mike's Traditional Blues
   Show, 191
Harp and Shamrock, 269
Harper, I.W., 77
Harper, Terry, 149
Harpo's, 254
Harris, Phil, 49
Harrison, John, 49
Harry, Neil, 61, 157
Hart, Mike, 89
Hartis, Randy, 215
Harvey's Boys, 110
Hatala, Steve, 242
Hauser, Marc, 216, 293
Hawk, John, 62
Hawke, George, 152, 157, 198,
   203, 273
Heath, Mike, 89
Heavy Axe, 108, 110
Hecklers, 120, 127, 147, 156, 157

Hegwer, Heidi, 203
Hellfire, 177, 181, 184
Henderson, Chrissie, 148
Herbert, David, 150
Heydt, Maggie, 154
Hi Top Stink's, 203
High Risk Venture Productions, 213
High School Hotline, 110, 115
High Sierra Jazz Band, 49
High Society Five, 49
Highbeam, 170
HIHO Club, 30
Hill, Danny, 203, 252
Hilton Hotel, 50, 63, 66
HMS, 210, 247, 266, 269, 274
Hockings, Jim, 48, 49
Hodges, Sharon, 244
Hole in Her Handbag, 198
Holiday Intermediate School, 262
Holle, Gary, 89
Holliman, Chris, 138, 226
Hollis, Jack, 49
Holloway, Mike, 222
Hood, Gary, 244, 251, 260, 267,
    268, 282
Hopkins, Andrea, 245
Hopkins, Richard, 245
Hornback, Lori, 116, 293
Horner, Lisa, 215
Hot Lucy, 177
Hot Rize, 271
Houseknect, Mark, 142, 143
How to Stuff A Wild Bikini, 147
Howard, George, 154, 159, 165,
    191, 219
Howard, Richard, 56
Howell, Tim, 168
Humphrys, A.V., 32
Husky Baby, 57

I

I Need to Know – Roc Lochner, 229
I'd Rather Smoke Butts Than Kiss
    Them, 254
Icon, 168, 169
Iconoclast International, 98, 117,
    120, 121, 138, 145, 150, 156
If, 203, 206, 207, 239, 252
iMac (2011), 289
Ingleman, Jim, 235
Intruders, 36, 37
Invisible Theatre, 249
Ipso Facto, 164, 181, 203
Irving, Edmund, 85
Isaiah, 207, 252
Itals, 217
Itule, Steve, 57
Itule, Tom, 57
Izia, 110

J

J.D. Rock, 177
J7, 97

Jack Cavan's Riverboat Six, 48
Jack Hollis, 49
Jacks (the band), 273
Jack's Pub, 98, 181, 183, 184, 186,
    201, 207, 219, 223, 226, 231, 237
Jacket Weather, 98, 117, 127, 138,
    150
Jack-in-the-Box, 75
Jackson, Russ, 16
Jacomes, 26
Jah Works, 161
Jah's Children, 217
Jamaican SunSplash, 217
Jane, Mary, 49
Jarman, Joseph, 219
Jasinowski, Bennie, 100, 107, 293
Jasinowski, Bob, 110, 111, 269
Jay, Mike, 186
Jaye, Joie, 100
Jazz Wars, 157
JD Rock, 186
Jeckle & Hyde's, 56
Jeff Haskell, 64
Jeff's Pub, 259
Jenson, John, 270
Jerome, Jane, 128, 144
Jerry Lewis Telethon, 80
Jerry's Lee Ho Market, 279
Jester's Court, 49, 50
Jewels, 121
JoBozec, Johnny, 65
John Denman Quintet, 64, 65
Johnies, 208, 226, 246
Johnnie's Drive-In, 16, 30, 35
Johnny Mann & the Country Kings,
    273
Johnoff, Nick, 164
Johnson, Robin, 112
Johnson, Scotty, 268
Johnston, Buddy, 119
Jon Sorrow, 41
Jonathan L, 2, 12, 59, 98, 121, 292,
    293
Jones, George, 271
Jonny Sevin, 5, 97, 98, 106, 110,
    111, 117, 120, 121, 138, 147,
    150, 156, 164, 171, 180, 196,
    207, 252
Jorge Gavilan and the Ovalteens,
    157
Joseph, Lee, 36, 96, 98, 106, 117,
    121, 127, 138, 156, 293
Juergens, Cliff, 68
Juneteenth Blues Festival, 191, 255
Just Us, 169, 177, 181

K

Kalat, Fred, 89
Kalil Bottling Co., 82
Kalil, Frank, 16, 30, 47
Karmel's Comedy Zone, 244, 267,
    281
Kaufman, Lance, 127, 138, 147,
    156

Kayci, 167
KBLE-FM, 212
Keaton's, 223, 266, 270
Keenan, Brooks, 154, 158
Keenan, Jeff, 144, 156, 181, 194,
    203, 207, 226, 236, 246
Keenen, Brooks, 165
Kelly, Joe, 88
Kennedy, Steve, 126
Kennedy, Susan, 126
Kepharp, Richard, 215
KEYX-FM, 292
KFIF, 30
KGVY, 44
KHOS, 25
KHYT, 86, 101, 104, 110, 111, 115,
    141, 215
KHYT's "Tucson Music Show", 150
KHYT's "High School Hotline.", 110
Kid Squid, 170, 191
KIKX, 118
Kimmel, Bob, 43
Kimsey, Jerome, 253
Kinder, John, 27
King, Dave, 273
King, Mike, 253, 254
King, Roger, 57, 254, 266
Kirkpatrick, Rick, 223, 243
Kirkwood, Chris, 231
KJOY-FM, 139
KLPX-FM, 12, 98, 101, 104, 114,
    116, 119, 125, 140, 141, 146,
    177, 186, 229, 255, 266, 292
Klymaxx, 216, 220
KMCR, 191
KMOP, 25
KOLD-TV, 44, 127
KOMA, 32
Koplin, Kelly, 59
KOPO-TV, 17
Kountry Tucson, 154
Kramer Frederick Leighton, 33
Krauss, Ilaina, 71, 90, 293
Krawzak, Phil, 126
Kritzer, Eric, 274
KRQ; see KRQQ
KRQQ-FM, 71, 80, 87, 101, 104,
    268
Kruiser Experience, 267, 281, 282
Krzyzanowski, Stephen, 281
KTKT-AM, 16, 17, 25, 30, 34, 38,
    47, 71, 77, 82, 94, 101, 104, 105
    format change, 104
KTKT-AM van, 77
KTKT-FM (96 Rock), 77, 83
    new station, 83
KUAT, 191, 249
KUAT-AM, 170, 234
KUAT-FM, 162
KUKQ-FM, 292
KUPD-FM, 12, 47
KVOA-TV, 222, 277
KVOI-AM, 249
KWFM-FM, 61, 98, 101, 116, 141,
    177, 191, 234

KXCI-FM, 139, 140, 141, 154, 157, 164, 168, 169, 170, 177, 191, 218, 234, 255, 259, 266, 268
KXEW, 141
KZAZ-TV, 101

L

L Mondo Combo, 153, 184
La Fiesta de los Vaqueros, 33
LaBeau, Gail, 32
Lain, Eddie, 49
Lambert, Bob, 156
Lamm, Ronnie, 99
Lance Kaufmann and the Soul Rebels, 194
Landers, Tracy, 88, 293
Landon, Michael, 222
Lanham, Roy, 18
Lariat Lounge, 271
Larkins, Tom, 127, 147, 183, 194, 226
Larkspur, 57
Larry Allen & Charley Yates, 273
Larry Allen Trio, 66
Larson, Galvin, 261, 293
Las Margaritas Restaurant Lounge, 118
Last Territory, 271
Latawiec, Jeff, 164, 165, 166, 168, 169, 171, 173, 177, 178, 180, 186, 196, 199, 209, 229, 242, 293
Laundryman, Robert, 184
LaViola, Nancy, 267
Lawson, Wes, 128
Leanne McCabe Band, 271
Lee Furr's Studio, 56
Lee, Gary, 272
Lee, Terry, 37, 40
Leibowitz, Dennis H., 213
Leinbach, Connie, 91, 293
Lemmol, Tom, 49
Lennon, John, 97
Leo Domingus & the Brakemen, 272
Leon, Roger, 221
Leonard, Johnny, 59
Leroy, JoAnna, 59
Les Seldoms, 97, 98
Lesher, Jan, 162, 280
Letty Shop, 26
Levinson, Marc, 244, 267, 268
Levitz, Lee, 241
Levy's, 26
Lewallen Brothers, 37, 46, 59
Lewallen, Cal, 46
Lewallen, Keith, 46
Lewallen, Tim, 46
LFB & the Apocalypse Horns, 119, 126, 247
Lil Abner's Steak House, 44, 248
Lil' John's Café, 25
Limbs, 120
Lincoln Street Bullies, 259
Lindskold, Graydon, 226

Lipson, Jeb, 168, 171
Livin' at the Deja View, 254
LJ's, 117
Lochner, Charlie, 178
Lochner, Robby, 169, 178, 242
Loder, Kurt, 156
Loeb, Marx B. III, 57, 152, 198, 203, 223, 243
Loeb, Marx, B. III, 57
Logga, 161
Long Island Sound, 206
Longhorn Saloon, 157
Lopez, Elaine, 148
Lopez, Lenny, 41
Lopez, Randy, 152, 198
Lopsided World of L, 12, 292
Los Hamsters, 169, 177, 195, 201, 202, 207, 226, 230, 231, 246
Los Lasers, 5, 57, 98, 127, 153, 157, 178, 191, 195, 197, 198, 203, 223, 226, 243
Losers Club, 223, 237, 243
Loudness One, 97, 98, 101, 121
Lounge Lizard, 227
Love Tractor, 181
Lowe's Ventana Canyon, 63
Lucky Wishbone, 27
Lumia, Angie, 253, 258, 266, 269, 276, 293
Lupo, Don, 154
Lux, Violet, 48
Lynde, Gordon, 222

M

M.I.A., 208
M.J., 83
M.P.S. Chunks, 164
Mac Nicol, Alex, 131
Mac Peters, Cactus, 21
MacBride, John, 139
Macintosh SE, 288
Mack, Ronnie, 265, 270, 272
MacWilliams, Skip, 232, 233
Mad Daddy's, 172
Madam X, 186
Magazine, 2, 11, 13, 117, 125, 139, 200, 222, 291
Magee, Sharon, 42, 293
Magi Productions, 264, 267
Magic Carpet Golf., 88
Mainstream Blues Society, 170, 293
Majors, Bob, 80, 81
Malibu Grand Prix, 88
Mamma and Pappa K., 273
Man Dingo Groit Society,, 269
Manandt, Frank, 270
Manhattan, 153
Manifest Destiny, 207
Mann, John E., 235
Mann, Johnny E., 248
Manny's, 66
Mansfeld Jr. High School, 164
Mapes, Kata, 161, 293

Marana High School, 49
Marauders, 150
March of Dimes, 78, 83
Marchek, Paul, 64
Marco, Joe, 48
Marie, Jan, 226
Marksberry, Jack, 235
Marley, Bob, 217
Marriott Hotel, 157, 159
Marschinke, Mark, 242
Marshall Building, 72
Martin, Tim, 60, 293
Martinez, Jack, 156, 157, 168, 171, 208, 226
Mary Jane, 49
Massacre Guys, 169
Master Promotions, 249
Materson, Jeff, 253
Maultsby, Chuck "Wagon", 61
Maultsby, Sharon, 61
Maverick, 248, 271, 273
Maximum Rock 'n Roll, 138, 150
Mayers, Darrel, 203
McAndrew, Pat, 154, 158, 159, 165, 191
McBride, Dyan, 265
McBride, Ronald, 265
McCabe, Freda, 118
McCabe, Leanne, 118, 124, 125, 294
McCabe, Leora, 118, 124, 293
McCall, Cash, 57
McCallion, Nancy, 224
McCallion, Neil, 259
McCanon, Rupe, 49
McCauley, Lainey, 63
McCauley, Pat, 63
McClure, Byron, 76, 293
McCoy, Dan, 81
McDonald, Bob, 49
McKale Center, 228
McKasson, Molly, 249
McKinley, Bob, 237
McMahon, David, 276
McReynolds, Randy, 147
Meat Puppets, 181, 184, 231
Meditations, 217
Medran, Rick, 111, 156
Meighan, Bob, 56, 57, 127, 232
Mellenger, Rick, 40, 41
Mellinger, Mark, 142, 143, 247, 274
Mellow, Lenny, 188
Memory Product, 96, 97, 150
Ménage a Trois, 96, 144
Merlin's, 56
Merrifield, Jane, 267
Mersky, Steve, 238
Mesa, JoAnn, 80, 293
Meshel, Andy, 276
Michael Landon Tennis Tournament, 222
Mickey Greco Quartet, 50
Microsoft Word, 288, 289
Midnight Express, 98, 143
Midnight Star, 216, 220
Midway Drive-In, 31

Mighty Flyers, 265
Mighty Sphincter, 177
Milan, Frank, 139
Miles, Larry, 114
Miller, Bryan, 83
Miller, Jim, 127, 203, 235, 269
Miller, Jon, 56
Miller, Milt, 56
Miller, Reggie, 35
Miller, Zebo, 128
Minter, Greg, 239
Minutemen, 194, 204
Miracle, 31
Miracle Mile, 56, 172
Miracle, Keith, 176, 269
Mirand, Wanda Jean, 265
Miss Tucson Trailer Court Contest,
    1960s, 17
Mobile Cubes, 184, 206, 239, 252
Moda Modeling Studio, 98
Moha, 218
Molly's, 294
Mols and Suzs, 249
Monahan, Jim, 274
Monke, Mike, 245
Montreal, 258
Moon Men, 119
Moor Rockers, 217
Morgan, Donna, 106, 293
Morgan, Howard, 260, 264, 267
Morris, Don, 27
Mosh, Tommy, 195
Moskowitz, David, 110, 114, 213,
    220, 239, 245, 247, 266, 276,
    293, 294
Mountain Newsreal, 12, 59, 291
Moxie, 38
MPS Chunks, 168, 169, 230
Mr. Bojangles, 58
Mr. FM, 191
Mr. Lucky's, 118
Mueller, Julia, 230, 236
Munguia, Larry, 211
Munoz, Andrea, 126
Murph, 167
Murphy, Pat, 184, 195, 198, 203,
    223, 243
Murray, Bill, 270
Murry, Bill, 77, 104
Muscular Dystrophy Dance-a-Thon,
    239
Museum of Art, 251
Musgrove, Verlon, 47
Music Box Lounge, 63, 66
Music Magazine, 168
Musiker, Av, 126

N

Nadine & the MoPhonics, 5, 224,
    225, 239, 258, 259, 266, 274
Nahan, Dave, 238
Naked Prey, 98, 157, 168, 203,
    209, 226, 229
Nass, Matt, 169

Nationals, 127, 147, 243
Neal, Wally, 48
Neck Romance, 266
Ned Sutton and the Rabbits, 98,
    144, 153
Neighbors, 177
Nelson, Dave, 17
Neon Prophet, 217, 218, 219, 228
Neville, Aaron, 42
New Deal, 96
New Outlaw, 248, 273
New Union Ramblers, 43
new wave, 164
New Wave concert, 101
Newland, Mark, 107, 110, 293
Newman, Donny, 70
Newman, Mark, 196
Newsreal, 2, 101, 167, 266, 289,
    291, 292, 293, 294;
    Newsreal 11th anniversary, 237
Nice 'n Easy, 63
Nicholas, Nick, 21, 293
Nick (Civil Death), 150
Night Rider, 119
Night Train, 56, 96, 98, 112, 153
Nino's, 98, 127, 143, 154, 156, 157,
    164, 166, 169, 171, 181, 184,
    203, 219, 226, 228, 237, 238,
    239, 246, 252, 267, 268, 270,
    277, 278, 282
Nitro, 110
Nolan, Bob, 18
Noyce, John, 99, 293
Nue Venue, 270, 276
Numbskulls, 194
Nutt, Joe, 199, 209
Nuttall, Rick, 222

O

O Bar O Cowboys, 21
O Team DJ's, 202
O'Brian, Sharon, 207
O'Conner, Tim, 273
O'Hayre, Sean, 69
O'Leary, Peter, 240, 251
Oasis Television, 107, 108, 215,
    269
Occasionals, 37
Odyssey, 99
Offret, Denis, 170, 191
OK Corral, 48
Olan Mills Studios, 179, 293
Old Buckskin Bar, 270
Old City Jail, 124
Old Pueblo Billiards, 88
Old Pueblo Jazz Band, 48
Old Time Fiddler's Contest, 45
Old Tucson, 178, 222
Old Tucson Gunfighters, 66
Olivas, Chris, 194
Olsen, Glenn, 50, 63, 65
One Free New World
    Uptones, 217
Only Oldies, 172

Only's, 156, 168, 169, 171, 180,
    186, 206, 208, 226, 237
OP, 138
Open Door Night Club, 44
Open End Halfway House, 260
Opera House, 33
Oracle Road, 31, 134, 157
Orange, Randy, 110
Original Jacks, 59
Ortho 28, 246
Osta, Emilo, 260
Otis Records, 172
Our Neighbor's S*CK, 177
Outcrowd, 206, 239
Outlaw, 196; move to Speedway,
    204
Outlaw Nightclub, 222
Ovalteens, 157
Oxbow, 57, 127

P

P.S. Bingo, 246
Pacific Coast League, 89
Pac-Man, 99
Palo Verde High School, 34, 283
Panama Pete's, 66
Pandemonium, 208
Paneen, 177
Papago O'Odham Reggae
    Rockers, 217
Park Avenue, 150, 194
Park Mall, 228
Parks, Jim, 121, 138, 144, 156
Parmenter, Doug, 61
Paulis, Rob, 238
Pawnbroker, 56, 97
PDQ Records, 172
Peace Corpse, 169
Pearl's Hurricane Bar, 96, 131, 144
Peart, Neil, 258
Pedestrians, 96, 168
Peep, Peep, Pop, Pop, 39
Pegram, Rick, 126
Pendleton, Pen, 150
Pennington Street, 26
Penny, J.C., 26
Pepin, Art, 48
Perillo, Joe, 194
Perry, Al, 146, 147, 156, 203, 207,
    236, 294
Perry, David, 126
Perry, Jim, 40
Perryman, Lloyd, 18
Person, Linda, 144
Persuasion, 118, 124
Pete Swan, 63
Peters, Dan, 38, 40
Peters, P. Joseph, 226
Phantom Hombres, 157
Phantom Limbs, 97, 101, 117, 121,
    144, 146, 156, 157, 181, 194,
    195, 203, 207, 226, 246, 252
PhD, Richardson, 17
Phenis, 138

Pills, 5, 96, 98, 101, 110, 112, 113, 121, 136, 150, 164, 207, 252, 294
Pima Air Museum, 168
Pima College Jazz Band, 49
Pima Community College, 13, 159, 213, 222, 224, 282, 292
Pima County Collaboration on Children and Youth, 82
Pima County Fair, 111, 124, 222
Pima County Fairgrounds, 84, 85
Pima County Golf Amateur Championship, 261
Pima County Public Libraries, 222
Pima Street, 172
Pinball, 88
Pink Dancing Elephant, 98
Pinky's Drive-In, 32
Pioneer Trio, 18
Pitts, Bill, 191
Pizza Pub, 247
Plan B, 277
Planned Parenthood, 110
Playbox Theatre, 262
Plimsouls, 146
Plush, 56
Plush Horse Pub, 272
Poco Loco Bar & Grill, 223
Polar Bar, 27
Porter, Fred, 41, 57
Post Time Pub,, 273
Pre Fix, 150
Pre-Fix, 150
Press, 266, 276
Preston, Cass, 63
Preston, John, 235
Pridy Stryange, 117
Prince Drive-In, 31
Privett, Tom, 252
Professional Internship Program, 148
Professor Paul, 170, 191
Progerian Youth, 177, 181, 195
Psychology Today, 145
Ptacek, Rainer, 98, 136, 156, 170, 206, 237; see also Rainer
Public Access Channel, 240
Pust, Joel, 278
Pyknotic Records, 234, 258

Q

Quick Draws, 48
Quine, Mike, 100
Quinstrels, 38
Quintanilla, Phil, 266
Quiros, Jay, 61

R

Rabbits, 144
Rabinowitz, Steve, 133, 147, 154, 243, 293
Radio 99
    see KTKT, 17
Radio Flyer, 265

Raffles Nightclub, 87
Ragged Bags Show, 184
Rain Parade's, 150
Rainer, 98, 136, 156, 170, 206, 237
Rainer & Das Combo, 206
Ramada Inn Hotel, 34
Ramada Tucson Resort, 69
Rampage, 84, 110
Ramsey, Mike, 59
Rancehausen, Joel, 247
Randy Orange Band, 119
Ras Dan, 161
Ras John, 217
Raw Power, 164, 177
Ray and Red's, 56
Ray, Johnny, 168, 171, 237
Razzmatazz, 184, 195
Record Room, 101
Red Knuckles, 271
Red Oak Review, 67
Redwood Gay 90s, 50
Reed, Tim, 242
Registers, 266
Reid Park Bandshell, 97, 234
Reid Park Zoo, 110
Reinhart, Mike, 227
Resistors, 146, 166, 181, 204, 231
Rex Allen Arizona Cowboy Museum and Rex Allen Days, 20
Rey, Aaron, 293
Rey, Aaron and Diana, 118
Rey, Diana, 265, 293
Reynolds, Nancy, 79
Rialto Theatre, 26, 33
Rich Brother Robbins, 86
Richards, Troy, 178
Rigberg, Jodi, 54, 293
Right in Our Own Backyard, 154
Rigole, Ernie, 57
Rillito Race Track, 271, 272
Rincon High School, 52, 82, 148
Rincon Optimist Blue Grass Festival, 271
Ripley, Rom, 41
Rising Star Productions, 217
Ritchie's, 16
Ritter, Rob, 83
River Roses, 202, 207, 226
Rivera, Michelle, 110
Rivera, Ricky, 110
Rivera, Veronica, 69, 293
Riverboat Six, 48
Riverfront Inn, 127
Riverfront Saloon, 154
Rivers, Bobby, 81, 104
Rivers, Mickey, 89
Rivers, Steve, 71, 80, 81, 87
Road Furniture, 160, 194, 202, 227, 231, 237, 246, 252
Road to Ruin, 157
Roadrunner Restaurant & Lounge, 235, 248
Roads to Moscow, 169, 172, 180
Roads, Dave, 236
Robbins, Rich Brother, 86
Robey, Dave, 156

Robinson, Laurie, 74, 293
Robinson, Tanya, 145
Roc Lochner, 169, 173, 177, 178, 180, 186, 196, 209, 229
Rock Doktor, 57
Rock West, 270
Rock, J.D., 180
Rockefeller's, 153, 168, 169, 177, 179, 180, 185, 186, 187, 196, 200, 237, 242
Rodriguez, Lupe, 100
Rogers, Roy, 18, 19
Rolling Stone, 156
Romantics, 106
Romeo and the New Deal, 96
Ron Devous Revue, 129
Ronstadt, Gilbert, 42
Ronstadt, Linda, 40, 42, 52, 59, 294
Ronstadt, Pete, 42
Ronstadt, Ruthmary, 42
Ronstadt, Suzi, 42
Rooty Kazootie, 57
Rose, Peggy, 50, 51, 63, 64, 65, 67, 68, 293
Rosen, Joan, 59
Rosen, Jon, 12, 167, 291, 292
Ross, Ed, 49
Round Up, 271
Roxy Nightclub, 196, 202, 205, 209, 229
Roy Clayborne & The Alamo, 62
Roy, David, 181, 194
Royce, 104
Rudrug, Jeff, 57
Ruiz, Rueben, 184, 252
Russell, Kirk, 77, 104
Rust, Gary, 272
Ryan, Chris, 234
Ryan, Joe, 267

S

S B&S Warehouse, 218
S.O.S., 121
S.S.K., 120, 121
Sabra, 272
Sabu, 110
Saddle and Sirloin, 50
Saddle City Band, 206, 222, 248, 273
Sahuaro High School, 82, 110
Salmon Brothers, 181
Salmon, Howard, 117, 120, 121, 144, 150, 207, 293
SALOC, 262
Salpointe High School, 49, 211
Salt River Ramblers, 271
Sambo's Restaurant, 59
Samoy, S. Castillo, 211, 224, 234, 258, 265, 268, 293
Samoy, Stephanie, 211, 293
Sample, Curt, 231
Sandworms, 136, 183
Sanford and Son, 283
Santa Rita High School, 82, 149

Santa Rita Hotel, 33
Sather, Red, 48, 49
Saunders, Al, 48
Saunders, Tim, 226
Savage Circle, 164
Savery, Peri, 176, 293
Sayer's Linen Shop, 26
Scappa, Stephan, 126
Schenkenberg, Joel, 117, 293
Schieffelin Hall, 48
Schockett, Bruce, 126, 128, 293
School of Journalism, UA, 292
Schotland, Robert, 210, 281, 293
Schottlaender, Brian, 138, 188, 293
Schrager, Chris, 184
Schultz, Jim, 48
Schuyler, Pete, 37, 40, 41
Schwartz, Mark, 77, 82
Scott, Phyner, 151
Sears, 26
Sed, Billy, 136, 183
Seed's, 177
Seekers, 41
Seger, Dave, 136, 183
Seldom, Chris, 138, 202
Seldoms, 117, 120, 121, 138, 156, 226
SeMi-Round Records, 133
Serfers, 96, 97, 101, 130, 131, 132, 144, 145, 196
Sevan, Pete, 63
Sevits, Wally, 241
Sferra, John, 128, 129
Shaar, Paul E., 27
Shag, 56
Shagnatty, 161, 217
Shaka, Richard, 200
Shake, 232
Shalamar, 216, 220
Shanty, 56
Sheehan, DeeAnn, 116
Shensul, Jill, 116
Sheraton El Conquistador, 269, 271
Sheraton Hotel Resort, 66
Sheraton Rio Rico, 266, 270
Shoemaker, Gerard, 247
Showtime, 274
Showtime Lounge, 274
Sidewinders, 239, 245, 247, 266, 294
Sievert, Nick, 251
Silent XChange, 151
Silver Room, 271
Silver Rose, 273
Silver Sage, 271
Simms, Stacey, 206
Simon Peter, 262
Simon, Mary, 149, 154, 157, 293
Simply Samples, 26, 105
Sin of Detachment, 117, 120, 121, 138, 156
Siqueros, Shawn, 200
Sisters Warehouse, 217
Skate Country, 86
Skinner, Gary, 59
Skinner, Rick, 59

Skyline, 168
Slick, Gracie, 174
Slit, 144, 150
Slitboy, 117, 120, 121, 150, 293
Slug, 188
Slutes, David, 160, 181, 245
Sluts, 121
Smith, Barry, 98, 113, 164
Smith, Brian, 112, 113
Smith, Ed, 45
Smith, Jeff W., 173, 293
Smith, Kaline, 254
Smith, Moses, 128, 217
Smith, Ross, 149
Smith, Stewart, 164
Smokey Covington, 218
Smokey's Nightclub, 161, 217
Smythe, Mark, 106, 164, 180, 196, 202, 207, 252
Sneaky Pete's Steak House, 273
Snowblind, 112, 187
Snyder, Eric, 237
Social Distortion, 121
Solomon, Larry, 214
Some Place Else, 91
Somerman, Steve, 69
Somerset, 100
Sommers, Kacie, 77, 79, 104
Sonic Drive-in, 16
Sons of Captivity, 218, 228
Sons of the Pioneers, 18, 294
Sorenson, Dan, 224, 259
Sorrenti, Frank, 213
Sorrow, Jon, 41
Sot Weed Factor, 37
Soul Rebels, 156, 170, 183, 223
Sound Factory Recording Studio, 169, 173, 194, 198, 234, 259, 266
South Forty, 67
Southern Arizona Entertainment Association, 265, 270
Southern Arizona Fiddler's Association, 265
Southern Arizona Light Opera Company, 262
Southern Arizona Youth Athletic Association, 82
Southwest Alternatives Institute, Inc., 2, 13, 117, 139, 222, 291
Southwest Comedy Jam, 267, 268
Space Invaders, 88, 99
Spam, 127
Spanish Trail Motel, 270
Spanna, 203
Spaulding, Neil, 49
Spectre, 168
Speed Sport, 17
Speedway Blvd., 27, 30, 32, 74, 75, 76, 87, 88, 91, 100, 150, 159, 165, 170, 172, 180, 217, 273
Speedway Domino's, 180
Speedways, 202, 247, 274
Spencer, Jimmy, 100
Spencer, Tim, 18
Splinter Brothers Warehouse, 194, 196, 217, 252, 269

Split Decision, 206
Splitsound, 40
Spontaneous Cheesemakers, 160, 181, 194
Sportsman, 271
Spring Fling, 206, 222
Springate, Bob, 48, 49
Sprouse, Daniel, 244
Squid, 167
SST Records, 231
St. Joseph's Hospital, 260
St. Paul, Michael, 151
St. Pierrex, Walt, 64
Stab in the Dark, 181, 194, 223, 227, 231, 237, 243
Stagg, Chris, 195
Stainless Steel Kimono, 98, 127
Stan Washmon, 272
Starr, Dan, 46, 62, 65, 293
Stars, 217
Stars & Bars, 273
State Theatre, 26
Statesboro Blues Band, 5, 154, 157, 158, 159, 165, 167, 170, 184, 190, 191, 219, 231, 234, 294
Steel Pulse, 128, 217
Steelink, Lawra, 127, 144
Steenken, Dan, 260
Steinfeld's, 26
Stern, Howard, 267, 268
Sterner, Mike, 144, 244
Stevens, John, 80, 81
Stevens, Phil, 269
Stewart, Rod, 174
Stewert, Bryan, 126
Stiebrs, Rudy, 48, 49
Stinky Felix, 57
Stitt, Duncan, 222, 273
Stockman, 119
Stone Avenue, 97, 217
Stone Poneys, 40, 52
Storm Warning, 186
Stowe, Brian, 107
Stowe, Dee, 67
Stowe, Jeff, 107
Stowgram, Jerry, 17
Straight Shot, 101
Strawn, Fla, 89
Stray Cat, 98, 127
Stray Theatre, 240
Stream of Consciousness, 41
Street Pajama, 111, 167, 181, 184, 206, 231, 253, 254, 266, 281, 294
Streetman, Cecilee, 126
Stumble Inn, 60, 152
Suarez, Mike, 249, 268
Subterranean, 97
Subterranean Blues Band, 101, 154, 159, 165, 190
Subterranean Blues Review,, 170
Sullivan, Mike, 62, 222
Summer Reggae Festival, 217
Summer Teen Discos, 1979, 82
Summerdog, 57, 84, 85
Sun Downers, 271
Sundance West, 125, 134, 157

Sundin, Michelle, 21, 24, 293
Sunnyside High School, 82
Sunset Rollerama, 30
Supercade, 99
Superwalk, 83
Surge, 100
Suspects, 96, 117
Suspicious, 156
Sutton, Ned, 98, 137, 144, 153
Suzan and the Erotics, 117, 156
Suzie Caruze, 97
Svendsen, Clarence, 49
SWA, 194, 204
Swamis, 127
Swan, Pete, 49, 63
Swing Inn Lounge, 271, 273
Swingin' Seven, 25

T

T.S.O.L., 177, 208
Tama, Vicki, 142
Tanque Verde Road, 88, 201, 241, 273
Tanque Verde Road,, 267
Tape Techronics, 168
Taylor, Sam, 294
TCC, 174, 186, 228
    see also Tucson Convention
        Center and Tucson Community
        Center, 244
TCCC, 279, 280
Teardrop Explodes, 121
Teen On-Line, 291
Tempest, 99
Temple of Music and Art, 190, 191, 218, 223, 239, 246
Templeton, Billy, 59, 66, 67, 269
Tender Trap, 50, 63, 262
Tepper, Carol, 104, 293
Tequila Mockingbird, 149, 186, 207, 208, 219, 223, 226, 240, 242, 244, 249, 252, 260, 266, 267, 268, 272, 274, 277, 281, 282
Terry & Zeke's, 157, 158, 159, 164, 165, 167, 170, 184, 187, 190, 191, 202, 204, 219, 223, 237, 246, 265, 268, 270, 272, 282
Terry O, 170, 191
THC, 169
The Air Show, 252
The Best and Worst of Chuck Wagon and the Wheels, 61
The Brewery, Bisbee, 239
The Bystanders, 150
The Good, The Bad and The Ugly, 157
The *Magazine*, 196, 293
The Rock, 169, 186, 196
The Tonight Show, 284
The Working Musician's Guide, 47
Thomas, Kevin, 62
Thompson, John, 52, 232, 293
Three American's, 117
Three Dog Night, 54

Thuringer, Franz, 126
Tin Ear Cocktail Lounge, 48
Tin Roof, 217
Tiny's Saloon, 61
Titan Valley Warheads, 271
Tofel, Joe, 125, 134
Tombstone, AZ, 48
Tommy O, 237
Tompkins, Richard, 232, 233
Tony Baloney and the Spontaneous Cheesemakers, 160
Tornado Foosball, 88
Tosh, Peter, 217
Tost, Bruce, 154, 159, 167, 231
Tovar, Jesse, 50
Tovi's Hoof & Horn, 270, 271
Toxic Shock, 229
Toys for Tots, 80
Trailblazers, 271
Traveling Show, 58
Travis, Rick, 169, 173, 177, 178, 242
Trax, 137
Treumann, Manny, 48
Triantulon, 169, 177
Triphon, Ken, 178
Triple C Chuckwagon, 18
Tropical Inn, 48
Troupe Deluxe, 119
Trout Unlimited, 97, 120
Tuccio, Jim, 271
Tucker, Kerry, 164
Tucker, Maureen, 164
Tucson Air Show, 211, 215
Tucson Baseball, LLC, 89
Tucson Blues Society, 223, 265
Tucson Blues Society's Blues Festival, 269
Tucson Cablevision, 94
Tucson Citizen, 67, 101, 110, 115, 116, 256
Tucson City Amateur Golf Champion, 261
Tucson City Council, 95
Tucson City Parks and Recreation, 82
Tucson Club Filharmonico, 43
Tucson Comics Association, 260, 268, 282
Tucson Community Air Show, 239
Tucson Community Cable Corporation, 162, 213, 214, 277, 279
Tucson Community Center, 66, 228, 26. TCC opening, 45; see also Tucson Convention Center
Tucson Community Center Music Hall, 101
Tucson Convention Center, 42, 174; see also Tucson Community Center
Tucson Film Commission, 249
Tucson Fire Department closes down Splinter Brothers, 276
Tucson Girls Ranch, 45
Tucson Hardcore Productions, 169

Tucson High School, 63, 162, 164
Tucson Home, 235
Tucson Jazz Society, 223
Tucson Job Corps, 148
Tucson Mall, 125, 228
Tucson map, 290
Tucson Mardi Gras, 47
Tucson Meet Yourself, 45, 255
Tucson Mountain Newsreal, 12, 291
Tucson Police Department, 76, 276
Tucson Public Libraries, 222
Tucson Rodeo Breakfast, 45
Tucson Rodeo Parade, 33
Tucson Strip, 17
Tucson Symphony Orchestra, 64, 159
Tucson Teen, 2, 11, 13, 69, 104, 117, 139, 222, 266, 289, 291, 292, 293
Tucson Toros, 89
Tucson Unified School District, 49, 148, 159, 165
Tucson Western International Telethon, 279, 280
Tucson Youth Sports, 110
Tucson YWCA, 13, 70, 82, 148, 270, 276, 277, 289, 291, 292
Tucson Zoological Society, 110
Tucson, Arizona's VirtualMall, 291
Tucson's Office of Cable Administration, 162
Tucson's Reggae Splash, 217
Tully, Tim, 267
Tumbles, 97
Tumbleweeds, 96, 97, 131
Turner, Craig, 67
Turner, Mike, 242
Twin Peaks, 202
Twinkle Brothers, 217
Twister, 266, 270
TWIT, 160, 181, 202, 215, 216, 279, 280
Two Bills, 157

U

U.P.S., 164, 168, 169, 177, 181, 184, 188, 195, 201, 202, 207, 231, 237; see also Useless Pieces of Shit
UA Cellar, 177, 181, 207, 226, 229, 244, 277; see also University of Arizona
UA Centennial Committee, 249
Ullestad, Neal, 217, 293
Unclaimed, 156
Uncle Henry's Original Kentucky Mountaineers, 18
Underground Newspaper Collection, 291
University Blvd., 70, 71, 172, 219, 277
University High School, 277
University Medical Center, 49

University of Arizona, 13, 70, 91, 151, 162, 167, 206, 209, 217, 222, 238, 262, 268, 282, 283
University of Arizona Ballroom, 209
University of Arizona Department of Journalism, 72, 292
University of Arizona Drama Department, 240
University of Arizona Library Special Collections, 289, 291
Up in the Sun, 231
Upsetters, 101, 128, 217
Uptones, 119, 128, 129, 217
Urban Guerillas, 98
Useless Pieces of Shit see U.P.S., 188

V

V-8's, 176, 184
  break up, 184
Valentino, Val, 41
Valley Fever, 117
Van, 131
Van Holzer, Katherine, 48, 293
Van Slyke, Peter, 260, 262, 267
Veg-a-matix, 207, 227
Vegas Kids, 246
Veins, 168, 171
Venet, John, 168, 247, 274
Vibrations, 30, 35
Vidal, Ray, 50
video games, 88, 99, 125
Videotex, 117
VideoWaves, 148
Vinnie-I, 228
Viper, 107, 108
Virgin Vinyl, 12, 98, 121, 140, 141, 142, 146, 160, 255, 257, 266, 292
Virgin Vinyl Christmas Concert, 202
Viscounts, 34
Visitor, 252
Voila, 240, 268
Volts, 107, 108
Von Glahn, Rich, 199
Voodoo Godhead, 121

W

Wade, Kinee, 219, 228
Waggoner, Chris, 231
Wagner, Chris, 181, 194
Wagner, Ed, 124, 125
Wagon Tracks Records, 61

Wah-Deh Connection, 218, 219, 226, 228
Waiting for Bardot – Los Lasers, 198
Walker, Balfour, 253, 254
Walker, Mike, 35
Walker, Tom, 37, 40, 41
Wall, Robin, 276
Walsh, Joe, 48
Walton, Johnny, 272
Wannabo, Dick, 273
Warner Cable, 94
Warren, Dale, 18
Washington, LaRue, 89
WASP, 186
Wasted Youth, 121
Waterson, Jack, 131
Watkins, Steve, 100
Watson, Winston, 112
Waxler, Dan, 168
Wayne Darnell and His Slick Band, 271
We're Here, 177, 186, 209, 242
Weasel, 57
Weather, Jacket, 121
Wedding Ring on the Bathroom Floor, 145
Wedekind, Susan, 267
Weeks, Tom, 84
Wellington White, 223
Wells, Robin, 83
Wells, Russell, 176, 184, 195
West, Rocky, 59
Westbound, 270, 271
Western Music Association, 19, 45
Westward Look, 47
Westwood Recording Studio, 41, 110, 127, 217, 254, 266, 276
Wetmore Road, 273
What Went Wrong, 201, 207
Wheatley, Chris, 226
Whistling Shrimp Records, 98, 121, 156
White Animals, 269, 276
White Lightning, 107, 108, 110
White Pages, 96, 117, 156
White Super Beings, 168
White, Greg, 57
Whitmer, Richard, 115, 293
Who's Who in the West, 45
Wild Thing, 195
Wildcat House, 132, 133, 146, 147, 167, 184
Will, Adrian, 181
Williams, Bill, 48

Williams, Guy, 25, 30
Williams, Ted, 88
Wilson, Doug, 252
Winstel Studios, 252
Wooden Nickel, 48
Workshop Music Store, 53, 105
Wren, Suzy, 144
WREX, 194, 201, 202, 203, 207, 209, 210, 229
Wrye, Margie, 294
Wylie, P.L., 240, 244, 249, 250, 260, 261, 264, 267, 268, 272, 281, 283, 293

Y

Yanks, 97, 126, 127
YAP; see also Youth Awareness Press, 87
Yard Trauma, 120, 138, 156
Yates, Charley, 67, 273, 293
Yates, Charlie, 59
Yberra, Xavier, 148
Young, Lydia, 135, 160, 180, 181, 182, 183, 184, 194, 197, 201, 202, 206, 207, 226, 230, 231, 243, 246, 252, 293
Young, Paul, 164, 169, 195, 237
Youngren, Liz, 202
Your Gain, 247
Youth Alternatives, 2, 11, 13, 69, 71, 81, 291, 292, 293
Youth Awareness Press, 2, 11, 13, 69, 80, 82, 84, 87, 101, 288, 291, 292, 293
Youth Cable Consortium, 148
YWCA Tucson, 148
  see also Tucson YWCA

Z

Zaestury, Ron, 245
Zavala, Cathy, 224, 259
Zelisko, Danny, 98
Zip's Record Traders, 101, 154
Z-Nine, 96
Zombie Burger, 27
Zucker, Bertram, 33, 293
Zucker, Letty, 105, 267
Zucker, Michael "Doc", 56
Zucker, Robert, 2, 13, 47, 58, 66, 69, 72, 75, 77, 82, 91, 117, 174, 222, 289, 290, 291, 292, 293, 294

Index: Volume 2

The second volume contains 223 pages and cover the years from the 1986 through 1989.

1

12th Avenue, 178, 206
1st Avenue, 39, 44, 60, 99, 107, 130, 202, 203, 204, 205, 206

2

2 DEFKREW, 152
22nd Street, 16, 57, 199, 202, 203, 205, 206, 207
26th Street, 203
29th Street, 100, 106, 203
2nd Avenue, 203
2nd Street, 206

4

4400 Club, 199, 202
4th Ave Street Fair, 134
4th Avenue, 19, 69, 122, 134, 172, 202, 203, 204, 205, 206
4th Avenue Merchants Association, 69
4th Avenue Street Fair, 134
4th Avenue Trolley, 134
4th Avenue Park, 149

5

5th Avenue, 29

6

6th Avenue, 16, 202, 203, 207
6th Street, 36, 100, 107, 149, 178, 182, 188, 202, 204
6th Street Pub & Grill, 152, 202

7

700 Club, 65

8

88-CRIME, 60
8th Street, 134

9

911, 112, 118
9th Street, 203

A

A Band Called Sam, 145, 156
A&M Records, 106
a.k.a. Theatre, 103
AB, 108
Abbey Records, 198
ABCO, 159
Abel and Allen, 130
Abel, Sonia, 130
Abeyta, Ted, 76
Abril, Manuel, 188, 191, 193
AC/DC, 35, 42
Acevedo, Jesus, 31, 37
Ackerley, Julian, 187
Adams, Ed, 22
Addled Records, 70, 130, 169
Aerosmith, 42
Affirmative, 19, 20, 21
Afram the Walrus, 182
Aftermath, 26, 88, 89
Aires Flamenco Dance Co., 102
Airport Inn, 202
Ajo Way, 203, 206
Akauldron, Viv, 84
Akhvan, Dan, 39
Al Bum's, 17, 19
Al Perry and the Cattle, 11, 102, 120, 169
Al Smith's Pub, 71, 202
Alday, Roxanna, 208
Alexander, Ed, 24, 25, 58
Alexandra's, 202
Alford, George, 63, 72
Alfson, Jon, 62
Alice in Wonderland, 127
All Stars, 114
All Stars and Feline, 162
All with Blood Spasm, 149
Allen Road, 86
Allen, Rex, 113, 153, 154, 208
Allen, Tony, 130
Allman Bros. Band, 65
Allman Brothers, 192

All-Stars, 131
Alperin, Misha, 199
Alpine Lodge, 22, 120, 172, 205
Alternative Press Syndicate, 209
Alvaro Road, 17
Alvernon Way, 17, 44, 100, 107, 202, 204, 205, 206
Amazon.com, 2
American Pie, 64
American Radio Theater, 191, 199
Americana Hotel/Quality Inn, 206
Amphitheater School District, 135
Anderson, Carole, 149
Anderson, Eric, 40
Anderson, Greg, 30
Anderson, Scott, 191
Andrew and the X-Rays, 42
Anklam Road, 203, 204
Apache Drive-In, 109
Apel, Robert, 108
Apollo Theater, 162
Apple computer, 40
Apple LaserWriter, 110
Apple Macintosh SE, 91, 110
Aquilino, Angelo, 39
Aradia Music, 173
Arandela, Kay, 56
Arem, Keith, 26, 34, 40, 46
Argan Wigs, 149
Arion, Thor, 122
Arizona Battle of the Bands of 1988, 111
Arizona Cardinals, 124
Arizona Civic Theatre, 50
Arizona Commission on the Arts, 81, 148, 154
Arizona Family Restaurant, 199, 203
Arizona Illustrated, 166
Arizona Inn, 202
Arizona Opera Company, 81, 82, 193
Arizona Theatre Company, 50, 111, 208
Armory Park, 22, 51
Armory Park Neighborhood, 19
Armstrong, Dean, 12, 22, 144, 208

Armstrong, Greg, 46, 77, 145, 155, 156
Armstrong, Steve, 124
Arnold, Carl, 52
Arnold, John, 188
Arram the Walrus, 149
Art Attack Records, 12, 22
Art in Arizona, 148
Arthur, Lamonte, 77, 101
Arthur/Brand Band, 101, 116
Arts in Education, 148
Asexuals, 31
Ash Alley, 33
Assorted Images, 28
Aston, Rollah, 100
Asylum, 48
At the Hop, 131, 202
ATC, 50
Atkins, Chet, 129
Atrophy, 91
Atwood, Frank Jarvis, 56
Auble, Marc, 65
Auburn Astros, 151
Audience, 20, 33
Audubon, 202
Austin City Limits, 124
Austin, Robin, 105
Autocatz, 77
Avatar of Visnu, 158
Aztec Inn, 202
Aztec Press, 210

B

B&B Café, 202
Babich, Greg, 49
Back Streets, 202
Backstreet Boogie Band, 65, 169
Bad Attitude, 124
Bad, A.J., 199
Baez, Joan, 93
Baja Arizona Music Cooperative, 102
Baja Arizona Pop Festival of 1988, 102
Baldwin, Adam, 130
Ball, Bill, 76
Ballash, Mike, 115
Ballet Arizona, 193
Ballet Folklorico Mexican Dancers, 22
Balloon Fiesta, 24
Band Called Sam, 173
Band X, 115

Banyon Tree, 202
Bar B-Q Ranch, 53
Bar M Cattle Co Steak House, 143
Bar M Cattle Co. Steak House, 53, 71, 152, 202
Barbara Bird and Da Fellas, 48
Baron's Restaurant, 120, 168, 195, 202
Barons, 186
Barrio El Hoyo, 193
Bascowitz, Danny, 185
Base, Rob, 152
Basek, Cindyrae, 76
Bashful Bandit, 192, 202
Batman, 170
Battle of the Bands of 1968, 165
Battle of the Bands of 1988, 135
Battle of the Bands of 1989, 158
Bayless, 107
Beach Boys, 24, 58, 63
Bear Canyon Merchants Association, 22
Bear Canyon Plaza, 22, 51
Bear Canyon Western Festival, 22, 51
Beastly, Melvin, 122
Beatles, 33, 122, 127, 132
Bedouin, 158
Beethoven, 73
Believer, 30
Bellybutton's Etc., 99
Bemis, Dave, 140
Bemis, Fran, 140
Benson Highway, 16, 203, 204, 205, 207
Benson, George, 71
Bentley's, 132, 172, 176, 177
Bentley's, 202
Berky's Bar, 57, 63, 116, 148, 184, 202
Berman, Sheryl, 68
Bernhardt, Robert, 129
Berry, Chuck, 165
Bessett, Rick J., 185
Best Kissers in the World, 102
Best of Tucson, 48
Best Western, 205, 206
Bevel, Mat, 149
Bickler, Kyle, 127, 176
Big "D", 22
Billy Ribs, 53
Billy Shears Band, 76, 85
Billy Templeton, 125
Biltmore Drive-In, 109
Bingaman, Lori, 21
Bird, Barbara, 48, 192
Birkett, Bernadette, 175

Bish, Scott, 100
Bissey, Thom, 61
Black Sabbath, 26, 159
Black Sun Ensemble, 31, 37, 120, 199
Blackwell, Melissa, 33
Blades, 44, 48, 57
Blanche, Louis, 21
Blask, Dave, 74
Blaster, 55
Blitz Creek, 102, 113, 123, 138, 143, 190
Blitzkrieg, 71
Block, Rory, 99
Blondie, 158
Blue J's, 124, 202
Blue Lizards, 57, 101, 161
Blue Note, 119
Blue Tigers, 48
Blue Wave, 33
Bluegrass Festival of 1988, 102
Bluegrass Festival, 1988, 102
Blues Co. Records, 18, 39, 145
Blues Festival at Reid Park, 1987, 84
Boardroom, 202
Bob and Jay, 108
Bob Dobb's, 100, 152, 202
Bob's Squeezy Snake Lounge, 206
Bobby and The All Stars, 161
Bobby Fuller Four, 165
Bobby McGee's, 57, 202
Bodden, Faith, 64
Bodine's, 202
Bojangles Saloon, 17, 202
Bolen, Harry, 167
Bolin, Harry, 127
Bondavi, 101
Bonds, Gary U.S., 114
Boney Brothers, 136
Boogie Animals, 49, 124
Boogie Man Blues Band, 19, 28, 34, 85
Bookman's, 182, 190, 202
Boomer's, 202
Boomer's Café Espresso, 177, 202
Boon Docks Lounge, 66, 97, 99, 120, 130, 202
Boone, Pat, 60, 61
Boosamra, Mareena, 76
Bopp Road, 52, 206
Borders, Keith, 116
Boswell, Darrin, 70
Bottom Line, 28
Bourbon Street Jazz Band, 162
Bowden, Charles, 67
Bowen & Bailey, 202

Bowes, John, 74
Bowkowski, Jeff, 45
Bowman, Dan, 65
Boyd, Kaye, 208
Bozec, Johnny, 179
Brady, Jim, 70
Brain Damage Orchestra, 21, 33, 48, 88
Brand, Scott, 101
Brett, Robert, 31, 37
Brewery (Bisbee), 63
Brewski's, 202
Broadway Blvd., 44, 72, 100, 122, 202, 204, 205, 206
Broken Horse, 102
Bromberg, Brian, 199
Bronwen, Tim, 20
Brook, Cedric, 130
Brooklyn's, 12, 18, 20, 21, 26, 27, 31
Brooks, Brad, 31, 38, 173
Brooks, Karen, 161, 162
Brotherhood, 162
Brown, Charles, 38, 40, 42, 45
Brown, Clarence, 83
Brown, Clay, 183
Brown, James, 176
Brown, Paul, 44
Brown, Roy, 167
Browne, John, 130
Broyles, Bill, 67
Buchanan, Dale, 40
Budnick, Aaron, 126
Buena High School, 156
Buggy Wheel, 16, 202
Bugs Bunny, 157
Bull Pen Lounge, 17, 52, 131, 202
Bullies, 28, 55
Bullpen Bar, 66
Bullring Band, 59
Bullring Bar, 59, 64, 202
Bum Steer, 202
Bunbuku Japanese Cuisine, 202
Bunnell, Deacon, 123
Burkes, Billy, 208
Burning Bush, 102
Burning Spear, 187
Bushwacker, 52, 53, 143, 152, 202
Butch Lord, 185
Butterfield Junction, 202
Butterfield, Paul, 126
Bynes, David, 162
BZB Publishing, 2, 210, 223

C

Cables, George, 73
Cactus Club, 202

Cactus Moon Café, 199, 202
Cadillacs, 166
Café Dorado, 202
Café Magritte, 104
Café Napoli, 32, 50, 202
Café Olé, 39, 40
Café Poco Cosa, 202
Café Quebec, 202
Café Sweetwater, 73, 115, 116, 133, 202
Caldwell, Tom, 44
Callahan, Steve, 158, 159
Camino Principal, 205
Camino Seco, 44, 99, 152, 204
Camp Family, 91
Campbell Avenue, 48, 53, 107, 109, 119, 199, 203, 204, 206
Campbell, Kevin, 35
Camper Van Beethoven, 158
Camper, Greg, 42
Canned Heat, 83, 99
Canyon del Oro High School, 156
Capitol Records, 162, 197
Cardinal Road, 17
Caribbean All Stars, 110
Carlin, George, 14, 51, 174
Carlos Murphy's, 116, 202
Carlson, Scott, 137
Carlton's Lariat Lounge, 204
Carmel's Restaurant, 32
Carolina Homestead, 202
Carranza, Carlos, 139
Carrere, Tia, 38
Carrillo Intermediate School, 193
Carroll, Scott, 62
Carroll, Zoe, 47
Carson, Johnny, 15, 175
Carter, Billy, 25
Carter, Scott, 50
Carvey, Dana, 185
Cary Grants, 48, 57
Cascade Lounge, 202
Case, Curtis, 123
Case, Peter, 35
Cashman, Bill, 12
Casler, Bob, 28, 55
Cason, Barbara, 175
Cass Preston and Ensemble, 168
Castaway Club, 202
Castillo, Samoy, 26
Catalina High School, 28, 105, 140
Catalina Highway, 22
Cate, Lou, 199
Catholic Boys, 158
Cattle, 11, 48, 70, 130, 169

Cavco Mobile Homes, 143
Cavern, 35, 37
Caywood, Gene, 69
CBS/Sony Records, 41
CBS-TV, 185, 198
Celebration, 57, 202
Central Park West, 100, 202
Chadbourne, Eugene, 158
Chambers, 106, 113, 153
Chambers, Becki, 153
Chambers, Tom, 113, 138, 143, 153, 154
Chambers, Tom and Becki, 148
Champaign Pyramid, 162
Chance Romance, 34, 125, 146, 155
Chances, 107
Chances Night Club, 11
Chandelle Restaurant, 202
Chapman, Tracy, 171
Charles, Ray, 139
Chastain, John, 197
Cheek, Molly, 175
Cheers, 107
Chelsea's, 202
Cherry Bay, 131
Cherry, Carl, 46
Chiara, Nick, 42
Chicago Bar, 15, 19, 33, 46, 47, 48, 55, 62, 63, 84, 144, 148, 202
Chicago Store, 104
Child Protective Services, 143
Children's Fund of TMC Foundation, 93
Chopin, 73
Chu, Randy, 78, 124, 199
Chuck and Bob, 108
Chuck Wagon and the Wheels, 66, 99
Church Avenue, 72, 119, 206
Churchill's Shelter, 203
CIGNA Healthplan, 60
Cigna Michael Landon Celebrity Tennis Classics, 60
Circle K, 69, 138
Circus Lounge, 195, 199, 203
City Art Walk, 173
City of Tucson, 36
Clarion Hotel, 205
Clark, Brian, 61
Clark, Dick, 25, 58, 135, 165
Clark, Gary, 110, 112, 114
Clark, Gary L., 106
Clark, Mike, 17
Clarke, Stanley, 121
Clash, 130

Clauson, Dewey, 22
Clayburn, Ray, 146
Clayburn, Roy, 197
Cliff Manor, 203
Cline, 122
Club Congress, 79, 148, 149, 176, 182, 203
Club Kaos, 203
Club La Jolla, 203
Clubhouse, 203
CoCo's, 108
Coffee, Etc., 124, 172, 203
Coke, Alex, 73, 74
Col. Sander's, 107
Cole, Nat King, 168
Cole, Richie, 73
Collette's West, 203
Collins, Albert, 3, 142, 156
Collins, Judi, 72
Columbus Blvd., 99
Comediennes Band, 59
Comedy Club, 203
Comedy Live!, 32
Comedy Sportz, 119
Comedy Store, 14, 108, 175
Comedy Zone, 12, 23, 32, 68, 108
Comelin, Jean Paul, 193
Community Media Services, 110
Community Outreach Program, 102
Como, Perry, 189
Comstock Children's Foundation, 60
Congress Street, 103, 104, 148, 202, 203, 205
Conklin, Steve, 57, 95
Connection, 74, 115, 116, 133, 166
Conqueroos, 176
Consequential Images, 34
Constant Creation, 84
Cooke Cable, 136
Coors Beer, 36, 39, 60
Coors Lite, 94
Coplin, Tom, 54, 152
Copper Moon, 131
Cora's Café, 178
Corcoran, Tim, 30, 75, 120, 128
Corea, Chick, 116, 121
Corkill, Brian, 76
Cormier, Beaux, 39
Coronado Theatre, 107
Corporation for Public Broadcasting, 150
Cossu, Scott, 18
Costello, Elvis, 61
Costin, Neil, 71
Coulter, Ron, 41, 90
Country Club Road, 100, 204

Country Kicker, 17
Cowboy's, 57, 107, 203
Cowell, Mitzi, 112, 161, 162
Cox Cable, 12
Cox, Kathy, 42
Cox, Milt, 118
Coy, Fred, 176
Coyote's, 199, 203
CPW, 100
Craft, Beverly, 133, 140, 144, 155, 160, 166, 192
Craft, John, 21
Craycroft Road, 32, 106, 107, 204
Crayon Club, 203
CreateSpace, 2
Cromm, Susan, 60
Cross, Ruth, 69
Crossroads, 203
Crosswind, 21
Crowley, Cheryl, 42
Crown, Joe, 108
Crypticier 5, 36
Crypticies, 36
Cryptics, 36, 37
Crystal Palace Playhouse, 203
Crystall, Joseph, 208
Culver, Donna, 167
Culver, Sammy, 167
Cummins, Chris, 117, 123
Curbtones, 112
Curtis, Andrea, 65
Curtis, Bobby, 186
Curtis, Mark, 158
Curtis-Olson, Andrea, 130
Cushing Street Bar, 171
Cushing Street Bar & Restaurant, 100, 203
Cypress Records, 106

D

D.A.V., 20, 187
D.N.A., 95
Da Fellas, 48
Daddy Jack's, 119, 124
Daddy Jack's Sports-A-Rama, 130, 135
Dahlstrand, John, 134
Daily, E.G., 20
Daisy Mae's Steakhouse, 203
Dan Del Santo World Beat, 124
Dan Washuk, 42
DanceTrax, 11
Daniel (Moore) and Friends, 136
Daniel Sprouse, 68
Danner, Gene, 186
Dark as Day, 131

Dave Pratt and the Sex Machine Band, 60, 94
Dave Sunderman, 102
Davis Monthan Air Force Base, 144
Davis, Bette, 64
Davis, Chris, 95
Davis, Doug, 77, 101, 116, 133
Davis, Miles, 121
Davis, Phil, 20, 101, 116, 133
Davis, Spencer, 114
Dead Air, 149
Dean Armstrong and the Arizona Dance Hands, 22
Dean Armstrong's Country Music Store, 144
Dean, David, 46
Dean, Kelley, 118
Decker, Jimmy, 167
Dee, Terry, 140, 141
Déjà Vu Nightclub, 32, 33, 45, 57, 203
Del Santo, Dan, 124
Del Shays, 131
Denman, John, 74, 164, 208
Dennis Mitchell and the Wilsons, 131
Dennoncourt, Bob, 71
Denver, John, 171
Department of Journalism, 210
DePavia, James, 97
Depoty, Dave, 196
Depoty, Hank, 137
Derby, Robbin, 36
Derunan, John, 164
Desert Express, 17, 52, 143
Desert Fire, 78
Desert Garden Lounge, 203
Desert Inn, 203
Desert Rose, 203
Desert Rose Canyon Band, 192
Desertfire, 30
Desktop Publishing, 91, 110
Devito, Karla, 36
Dewey Parker and the Shakedowns, 135
Diamondback, 111
Dickey, Debra, 178
Dickie Tucson and the Speedways, 59, 60
Diddley, Bo, 114
Diehl, Larry, 28, 183, 184
Dillard's Ticket Outlets, 190
Dillenger, 35, 44, 48, 110, 111, 158
Dion, 166

Dire Straits, 159
Dirtbag's West, 199, 203
Discount Records, 18, 21, 30, 31, 37
Discovery Inn, 203
Disneyland, 190
Distant, 31, 33, 38, 40
Dixieland Jazz Band, 156
Do Deo's, 203
Dodajk International, 149, 158, 203
Dodson, Roc, 38
Domino Theory, 39, 131
Don & Donna, 17
Don Chandler's Lounge, 203
Don Stevenson, 17
Donath, Rob, 21
Doors, 95
Dos Locos, 203
Dotson, Ron, 31
DoubleTree Hotel, 95, 100, 187, 203, 204, 206
DoubleTree Lounge, 31, 34, 203
Dougherty, Dan, 119
Dove, Tommy, 40
Dover Trench, 136
Downtown Performance Center, 203
Doyle, Chris, 30
Dr. Demento, 70
Dr. Lee, 84
Dr. Omega Trip, 149
Drachman Street, 203, 205
Drakides, Nick, 124
Drexel Road, 16, 202
Drifters, 114
Driftwood Lounge, 203
Drinking Gourd, 203
Drive-In' Movie Theaters, 109
Dry Heaves, 62
Dunn, Suzie, 182
Duran Duran, 70
Dusenberry, Bruce, 69
Dusty Chaps, 99
Dusty Roads, 22
Dycus, Bill, 180, 185
Dykinga, Jack W., 67
Dylan, Bob, 177

E

Earle, Shay, 53
Eastwood, Clint, 108
Easy Street Lounge, 195, 199, 203
Eat to the Beat, 182
Eddie & the Tide, 60
Eddie's Cocktails, 203
Edelbrock, Tom, 126
Edge, Travis, 158
Edmonson, Earl, 190

Edmonson, Travis, 22
Edmundston, Errol, 167
Edwards, Mike, 31, 38
Eerie Vox, 157
El Jabala, 100
El Casino Ballroom, 77, 124, 203
El Centro Bar & Grill, 203
El Con Mall, 12, 23, 30, 44, 57, 91, 206
El Jabala, 107
El Kabong, 57
El Mariachi, 80, 203
El Mesquital, 203
El Parador, 203
El Presidio Park, 72
Elbow Room, 203
Elia, Paul, 45, 125
Ella, Paul, 125, 155
Elm Street, 202
Elmer's Pub, 203
Embassy Suites, 203
EMOL.org, 2
Empathy, 131
Emrie, Bill, 196
Enchiladas, 107
Energy, 155
Entertainment Magazine, 2, 3, 11, 13, 31, 36, 40, 44, 58, 60, 76, 91, 92, 94, 97, 106, 110, 112, 114, 115, 121, 124, 128, 132, 150, 157, 160, 174, 176, 188, 191, 208, 209, 210
Entertainment Magazine On Line, 2
Ervin, Tom, 74
Escallier, Steve, 77
Essex, Doug, 34
Estefan, Gloria, 86
Euclid Avenue, 97, 204, 206
Evarro, Rick, 135
Evenson, Dean, 160
Evenson, Dean and Dudley, 199
Evenson, Dudley, 160
Everly Brothers, 135, 167
Executive Inn, 168, 203
Exodus, 91
Expressions, 56
EZ ROCK, DJ, 152

F

Faded Images, 131
Faith, 185
Falinski, Paul, 21
Fall From Grace, 157, 158
Famous Sam's, 100, 106, 203
Famous Sam's III, 152, 176
Fan, Paula, 164
Fanatiks, 18, 30, 121

Fast Break, 131, 152
Fastbreak, 54
Faulk, Sabra, Frank, 123
Fawcett, Farrah, 39
Faye Anne, 107
Faye Anne's Memory Lane, 100, 107, 111, 179, 186, 203
Fed Marts, 107
Feline, 133
Felix, Joey, 40
Ferganchick, Julia, 177
Ferrone, Len, 164, 208
Festival in the Sun, 187
Fiction, 26, 34, 40, 46
Fiesta, 203
Fiesta de los Vaqueros, 51, 93
Fiesta Melons, 182
Figueroa, Miley, 59
Fine, Pete, 21
Fine, Sam, 208
Fineline, 203
Finnegan's, 203
Finney, Cliff, 26, 88
Fintel, Dave and Kay, 60
Firehouse, 203
Firestone, Roy, 15
First Strike Studios, 18, 21
Fish Karma, 120, 130, 169
Fisher, Mike, 26, 34, 40, 46
Flaming Lips, 84
Fleetwood Mac, 90
Fleetwood, Mick, 90
Fletcher, Liz, 115, 116, 133, 166
Flower Hour, 36
Flowing Wells Road, 52, 53, 202
Flying V, 203
Fock Rock Duo, 166
Fogelberg, Dan, 171
Folklorico Mexican Dancers, 51
Food Giant, 107
Foothills Center, 204
Foothills Jazz Quintet, 74
Forbes, Dave, 37
Ford, Lita, 128
Foreman, George, 180
Fortner, Dave, 146
Fossdal, Chris, 39, 189
Foundation for Creative Broadcasting, 19, 36, 150
Fourth Avenue Merchants Association, 70
Fourth Avenue Social Club, 203
Fox Broadcasting Co., 175
Foxy's Café & Lounge, 181, 203
Frankie and the Hurricanes, 131

Frankie Goes to Hollywood, 38
Franklin, Jimmy, 17, 22
Frazier, Ralph, 130
Freeway Road, 102
French Quarter, 112, 116, 148, 203
French, Victor, 12
Fridkin, Dennis, 21
Friendly Warning, 19
Friendship Club, 39
Frighetti, Vince, 112, 114
Frog Mountain Blues, 67
Front, 131, 199
Ft. Lowell Depot, 124, 203
Ft. Lowell Road, 99, 203
Fuller, Tim, 48
Futons, etc., 134
Fuzzy's, 203

G

Gallagher, Tim, 55
Gallahad, 125, 155
Gallegos, Alex, 77
Galleria, 119
Ganz, Bill, 148, 153
Garber, Scott, 65, 79
Gargoyle's, 204
Gargus, Rory, 41, 90
Gariss, R.C., 125
Garris, R.C., 155
Gary Clark and the Original Blues All Stars, 114
Gary Rust Band, 22
Gaslight Theatre, 50, 71, 72, 73
Gasper, 21
Gassen, Scott, 178
Gassen, Timothy, 37, 178
Gates Pass Inn, 197
Gates Pass Steakhouse, 204
Gee, Nancy, 84
Gelb, Howe, 11
Gelb, Ricky, 182
Gemco's, 107
General Electric, 70, 134
Generations, 152, 204
Genesis, 64, 68, 176, 185
Gentle Ben's, 18, 43, 46, 48, 55, 57, 63, 73, 97, 98, 99, 106, 199, 204
George Hawke and the Cary Grants, 48, 57
George, Erik, 21
George, Stefan, 21, 208
Germain, Marv, 173
Geronimoz, 204
Get Hip Records, 177
Gettinger, Lee, 127, 176
Ghost Riders In the Sky, 195
Giacomazza, Carl, 198, 208

Giant Sand, 11
Giant Sandworms, 3, 11, 65, 79
Giant Sandwurms, 11
Gibson, Hoot, 53
Gibson, Wendy, 53
Giffney, Steve, 146
Gila Bend, 131
Gilbert's Plush Horse Pub, 204
Gilmour, David, 128
Girls, 158
Gissleman, Gary, 111
Glassman, Terry, 12, 32, 44, 97, 110, 112
Global Village Nightclub, 19, 205
Glombecki, Gerry, 102, 208
Godfrey, Arthur, 198
Godunov, Boris, 82
Goeringer, Conrad, 134
Goldberg, Susan, 111
Golden Ass, 91
Goldthwait, Bobcat, 110
Golf Links Road, 202, 204, 205
Gonzales, 204
Gonzales, Tom, 61
Goodberry, Dan, 196
Goodbooks, 134
Goodman, Greg, 75, 128
Goodridge, Mary **Anne**, 86
Goodridge, Mrs., 87
Gould, Hal, 88
Gowing, Gail, 123, 138, 143, 190
Graffiti's, 130, 204
Graham Central Station, 35
Graham, Adam, 64, 68, 185
Gramm, Lou, 90
Granada Avenue, 203
Grand Master Flash, 162
Grand Prix Motors, 60
Granfalloon Saloon, 92, 99, 106, 112, 181, 204
Grant Road, 100, 182, 202, 203, 204, 205, 206
Grant Road Pub, 204
Grant, Amy, 112
Grateful Dead, 149, 150, 182, 199
Gravity Recording Studios, 77, 78
Gray, Jerry, 16
Great Peace March, 20
Greco, Mickey, 74, 84, 178
Green Dolphin, 99, 204
Grey, Joel, 138
Griffin, Matthew, 36
Griffin, Michael, 36
Griffith, Daniel, 50
Griffith, Gail, 48
Griffith, Jim, 81

Griffith, Joshua, 48
Groove Garden, 132
Ground Zero, 131
Grubsteak, 204
Guess Who, 132
Guitar Player, 140
Guitar, Johnny, 136
Guitars, Etc., 102
Gulotta, James, 92
Gus & Andy's, 164, 204
Guy, Carl, 198, 199
Gwyn, Kenny, 126

H

Hacienda del Sol Guest Ranch, 112, 138, 143, 152, 153, 204
Hacienda del Sol Road, 204
Hackensack, 74, 120
Hadden, Sean, 101
Hager, Michael, 208
Haggerty, Mike, 134
Hall, Arsenio, 182
Hall, David, 21
Hall, Doug, 62
Halloween's Haunted Ruins, 86
Halper, Bruce, 28, 115
Hamilton, Michael, 109, 118, 135, 144
Hamilton, Rita, 190
Hamilton, Scott, 118
Hamlisch, Eduard, 129
Hammond, John, 99
Hampton Inn, 204
Handi-Dogs, 131
Handi-Dogs of Tucson, 131
Hans Naughty, 157
Hanson, Pete, 176
Hard Rain, 131
Harmonica Mike, 19, 28
Harp and Shamrock, 204
Harper, Terry, 21
Harris, Craig, 43, 97
Harrison, Wesley, 151, 174
Harry, Neil, 22, 100
Haskell, Jeff, 74
Hastings, Fox, 52
Hastings, Mike, 52
Hatch, Mike, 136
Hatchett, Molly, 128
Hawk, John, 197
Hawke, George, 48, 57
Haynes, Allyn, 53
Haynes, Billy, 53
HBO, 185
Head East and Head West, 11
Hearns, Thomas, 180
Heartsongs, 124
Hec & Wink's, 204
Hecklers, 169
Hedges, Michael, 132

Heiderman, Kevin, 117, 123
Heithaus, Eric, 30, 78
Helderman, Kevin, 139
Helgison, Odin, 122
Helper, Bruce, 139
Hemwell, Drew, 189
Hendrix, Jimi, 115, 191
Henning, Doug, 40
Herberger Theatre Center, 111
Herd, Don, 199
Hermenitt, Lisa, 192
Herzog, B, 42
Heston, Charlton, 59
Hewlet, Jay, 185
Hi Corbett Field, 176
Hidden Valley Inn, 52, 204
Hideout, 126, 204
High Beam Blues Band, 48
High Noon Saloon, 204
High Rise, 78
Highbeam, 62
Highbeam Blues Band, 83, 84
Hilton East Hotel, 204
Hilton Hotel, 168
Hilton Inn, 207
Hilton, Eric, 34
His Boy Elroy, 131
HMS, 19
Hodges, Sharon, 64
Hoeft, Jenny, 166
Hoff, Jack M., 107
Hoff, Stacey, 66
Holiday Inn, 95
Holiday Inn Downtown, 200
Holiday Inn Holidome, 57, 204
Holiday Inn Palo Verde, 185
Holiday, Bob, 25, 58
Holidome Resort, 22
Holloway, Mike, 12, 100
Holloway, Red, 73
Hollywood Records, 107
Holmes, Peter, 173
Holt, Dave, 102
Home Den, 204
Hood, Gary, 120, 185
Hooker, John Lee, 83
Hopkins, Rich, 65, 130
Horrible Fetters, 158
Horse 'n Round, 204
Hoskinson, Vicki Lynn, 56
Host, 102, 122, 136, 157
Hot Property, 120, 125, 154
Hot Pursuit, 120, 125, 154, 155
Hot Shot, 34
Hotel Congress, 104
Houghton Road, 16, 205, 206

Houlihan's, 126, 204
House of Large Sizes, 149
Howard Johnson's, 207
Howard, George, 183, 184
Howard, Mike "the Duck", 84
Huayucaltia, 204
Humane Society, 190
Humphries, Mike, 88
Hungry Ear, 149, 182
Hunter, 111
Huntley, Ron, 30, 78
Hurricanes, 131
Hutch's, 100, 204

I

I-10, 100
Iafelice, Butch, 31, 36
IF, 18, 20
Illusions, 204
Improv, 64
In CaHoots, 46, 48, 53, 57, 89, 107, 204
In Your Face Horns, 136, 145, 155, 156
Ina Road, 64, 204, 205, 207
Inasense, 85
Inner Fear, 199
Insane Jane, 116, 133, 166
Insect Mystery Zoo, 173
Intima, 106
Intima Records, 199
Ireland's Post Time Pub, 100, 104, 110, 124, 204
Iron Maiden, 26
Irvington Road, 178
Isla Tiburon, 204
Isley Brothers, 63
Itchy Foot Moe's, 173
Ivans, Jack, 130

J

J.C. Vigilantes, 51
J.J. Nickels, 204
J.R. Garner & 3-Wheel Drive, 124
Jack's Pub, 12
Jack-in-the-Box, 108
Jackson, Earl, 196
Jackson, Kevin, 176
Jaime's Bar & Grill, 204
Jamaica Bay, 204
James, Brion, 42
January, Johnny, 88
Japanese Kitchen, 204
Jarret, Keith, 121
Javelina Cantina, 96, 100, 204
Jazz Festival, 112
Jazz Showcase, 73
Jazz Terrorists, 48, 57
Jazzberry Jam, 74

Jed Paradies and the Jazz Terrorists, 48, 57
Jeff's Classical Records, 21, 39
Jeff's Pub, 21, 33, 41, 44, 47, 49, 50, 75, 85, 99, 112, 204
Jeff's Pub, Camino Seco, 118, 120, 152, 165
Jeff's Pub, Tanque Verde, 99
Jeffers, Scott, 30, 75, 128
Jefferson Airplane, 106, 116, 127
Jeffrey, Dave, 136
Jeffries, Dave, 196
Jennings, Waylon, 138
Jerry Gray and the Country Diamonds, 16
Jerry Lewis Telethons, 26
Jerry's Ming House, 107
Jesse's Music World, 178
Jin's Lounge, 199
Joachin, Pete, 49
Joe & Vicky's Place, 120, 135, 143, 204
Joey Suicide, 157
John Booth, 19
John Bowes Quartet, 74
John Denman Group, 74
John Denman Quartet, 74
John Denman Quintet, 164
John Walton, 155
John, Elton, 114, 128, 132, 188
Johnny H., 28
Johnny Law, 102, 136, 157, 182
Johnson, Ben, 151
Johnson, Don, 71, 113, 148, 153
Johnson, Jay, 108
Johnson, Sally, 191
Johnson, Susan, 117, 123, 131, 137, 139, 146, 154
Jonathan L, 95
Jones, Jesse, 127, 176
Jones, Mark, 33
Jones, Plato, 46
Jones, Rick "Shadow", 70
Jordan, Stanley, 132
Journey, 90
Joy, Jessie, 64
Judas Priest, 41, 78, 158
Juergens, Cliff, 195, 196
Junior Chamber of Commerce, 110

K

K Mart, 107
K.C. and the Sunshine Band, 114
KAIR-AM, 25, 58

Kaiserman's, 107
Kamikaze, Larry, 62
Kappy's, 204
Kardomah Café, 93
Karl Records, 18, 30
Karma's, 120
Karmel's, 12
Karotsky, Bob Kay, 137
Katz & Jammer, 17
Katzel, Bill, 130
Katzel, Celia, 130
Kaur, Singh, 199
Kazan, Lainie, 69
KBLE-FM, 12
KCEE-AM, 24, 58
KCUB-AM, 22
KDTU-TV, 39, 60
Keating, Bridget, 79
Keaton's, 18, 204
Keck, Darryl, 88, 91
Keel, Matt, 64
Keenan, Brooks, 183, 184
Keenan, Jeff, 11
Kelly T., 33
Kelly, Gene, 69
Kelly, Tim, 35, 92
Kennedy, Leon, 106
Kennedy, Robert, 59
Kent, Dean, 145, 155, 156
Kerang, 92
Key Club, 34
KGUN-TV, 39
KHYT-AM, 25, 31, 40, 46, 58
Kimes, James, 44
King Diamond, 89
King, B.G., 31, 36
King, David, 17
King, Martin Luther Jr., 71
King, Roger, 18, 30
Kinney Road, 167, 206
Kiss, 24, 58
Kitt Peak, 68
KJMM-FM, 128
KLPX-FM, 12, 21, 62, 182
Knudson, David, 42
Kodaka, Gary, 28
Kolb Road, 44, 99, 207
KOMA-AM, 109
Kon Tiki, 204
Kool & The Gang, 71
Kool-MoeDee, 162
KOPO-TV, 144
Korp, Annemarie, 37
Kountry Kicker, 52, 53
KPOL-TV, 92
Kramer, Leighton, 51
Krause, Stuart, 62
KRQQ/ KNST, 60
KRQQ-FM, 40
Kruiser, 64
Kruizer, 68
Krystal, 40
KTKT-AM, 25, 58, 144

KUAT-AM, 166
KUAT-TV, 166
Kuitart, Gary, 113
Kuitert, Gary, 71
KUPD-FM, 39, 60, 94, 95, 97, 176
Kupeers, Stu, 21
Kurures, 74
Kuryakin, 160
KVOA-TV, 26
KWFM-FM, 25, 58
KXCI-FM, 12, 19, 21, 27, 34, 36, 39, 71, 80, 102, 124, 149, 150, 182
KZAZ-TV, 39

L

L Mondo Combo, 20
L.S.D.– Lower Sonoran Desert, 169
La Cañada Drive, 204
La Cholla Blvd., 204
La Fuente, 204
La Placita Café, 204
La Placita Village, 204
La Vista Lounge, 204
Laff's Comedy Night Club, 100, 108, 185, 204
Lalo's, 204
Lamb, Kim, 166
Landon, Michael, 9, 11, 12, 24, 60, 208
Lang, Mark, 62
Lange, Kathy, 189
Lariat Lounge, 152, 204
Larkins, Tommy, 196
Larroquette, John, 81
Larry and the Vibrations, 135
Larry Redhouse Quartet, 121
Larson, Boon, 196
Las Cruces, 79
Las Posadas, 193
Last Flite, 33
Last Round Up Band, 17, 52, 136, 196
Last Territory, 204
Lavin, Linda, 31
Law,, 157
Law, Johnny, 102, 136, 182
Lazy V, 204
Lazy-V, 17
Leanne McCabe Band, 66, 100
LeBirec, Paul, 152
LeBrec, Paul, 54
LeClerc, Jean, 39
Led Zeppelin, 35, 191
Lee, Fred, 196
Lee, Gina, 117, 123
Lee's Catering, 190
Legends, 107

Legler, George Phar, 86
LeKawa, Dave, 166
Lennon, John, 124
Leonard, Johnny, 22
Leonard, Sugar Ray, 180
Leprechaun, 204
Lesher, Jan, 20
Lester Street, 203, 205, 206
Levelle, Craig, 105, 124
Levinson, Marc, 12, 23
Lewallen Brothers, 152, 165
Lewallen, Cal, 165
Lewallen, Keith, 165
Lewallen, Tim, 165
Lewallen, Timothy, 208
Lewis, Diann, 76
Li'l Abner's Steak House, 22, 204
LifeForce, 147, 179, 200
Liggens, George, 21
Lil Abner's Steak House, 12
Lil' Anthony's, 166
Lillie, Dave Jr., 131
Lillie, Dave Sr., 131
Linders, Tommy James, 131
Linsey, J.P., 146
Lintecum, Russell, 132
Lipson, Jim, 21, 34
Little Anthony's, 204
Little Britches, 204
Little Feat, 114
Loco Records, 18, 21, 30, 61
Loeb, Marx, 79
Loew's Ventaña Canyon, 168, 203
Loews Ventaña Canyon, 95, 202
Lofton, Ken, 151
Lohr, Buffington, 20
Loll, Ron, 21
Lomax, 131
Lonely Trojans, 182
Long Wong's, 204
Long, Shelly, 149
Longbranch Saloon, 16, 17, 204
Look, 21
Lookout Lounge, 84, 112, 204
Loose Change, 134
Loring, Gloria, 60
Los Lasers, 3
Los Mayas, 204
Lou Ross Agency, 198
Loutzenheizer, Mark, 34
Love, Bob, 39, 208
Love, Gary, 74
Love, Randy, 178
Lovin' Spoonful, 165
Low Max, 182

Lowery, Randy, 140
Lowry, Randy, 69
LRQ, 121
Lucky Dollar, 204
Lugo, George, 34
Lumia, Angie, 18, 20, 27
Luminarias, 193
Lupo, Jeff, 45, 117, 123
LXIX, 131
Lykins, Chris, 92
Lynch, Dan, 162

M

Mac Williams, Skip, 65
Mac, Jimmy, 97
Mac's Place, 85, 205
Mack, Billy, 17, 22
Mack, Ronnie, 16, 22
Mackey, Eric, 34
Mad Dog Mandanici, 64, 68
Madachy, Mike, 49
Maddog, 149, 182
Madonna, 159
Madrugal, Rich, 158, 159
Magazine, 3, 210
Magee, Dan, 178
Magic Healing Springs Cave, 86
Magnum, 75, 125, 155
Mahan, Patrician, 102
Main Street, 206
Malicious, 131
Mammoth Records, 130
Mandanici, Virgil, 68
Manilow, Barry, 189
Mann, Johnny E., 12
Manor, Carl, 186
Manowar, 88
Mantnegro, Julio, 180
Marcarchick, John, 182
Marchant, Jeff, 145, 155, 156
Marchek, Paul, 164
Marie, Jan, 20
Marl, Marley, 162
Marquez, Xavier, 77, 115, 133, 145
Marriott Hotel, 95
Mars Hall Records, 21, 120, 135
Marshal KGUN, 39, 208
Marshall, Heather, 91
Marshmallow Overcoat, 102, 148, 169, 177, 178
Marsound, 21
Martin, Chris R., 158
Martin, Doug, 77, 139
Martin, Wade, 123
Martinez, Billy, 121
Martinez, Jack, 27
Maslak, Kesbaven, 199

Mat Bevel and the Little Dinks, 149
Matlock, Don, 81
Matrix, 48
Matthews, Dave, 90
Matthews, Matt, 31
Mattingly, John, 71, 138, 143, 190
Maultsby, Chuck, 100
Maverick, 12, 196
Maverick King of Clubs, 196, 205
MCA Records, 198
McAndrew, Pat, 183, 184
McAndrew, Patrick, 208
McCabe, Leanne, 66, 99
McCallion, Lisa, 55
McCallion, Nancy, 29
McCallion, Neil, 55
McCartin, Jim, 43
McCartney, Paul, 24, 157
McCauley, Lainey, 168
McCauley, Pat, 168
McCaw Cablevision, 43, 46
McCleese, Raynard, 68
McCormic, Angela, 40
McCracken, Janet, 149, 157, 169, 173, 176, 182
McCreary, Denise, 116, 133
McCrum, Lillemor, 80
McFadden, Aladin, 70, 125
McGee, Suzanne, 59
McGhie, Jack, 21
McGinnis, P., 70
McGovern, Maureen, 129, 144
McGraw's Cantina, 205
McGregor, Chuck, 180, 181
McGuire's Saloon, 205
McKinney, Will, 120
McLaren, Caribou, 123
McLaughlin, Peter, 113, 190
McPhearson, Charles, 73
Mean Babies, 131
Meat Puppets, 149
MediaTek, 36
Medina, Joey, 180, 181
Medina, Raul, 118
Meditations, 130
Megaw, Peter, 73
Meighan, Bob, 190
Melon, Eric, 100
Mendoza, Earl, 61
Mendoza, Ernie, 18
Merril, Pat, 16
Merrill, Erick, 173
Merski, Steve, 18
Metal Forces, 92
Metallica, 26, 88, 187
Metzger, Michael, 150
Meyer Street, 203

Miami Sound Machine, 189
Micha's, 205
Michael Landon Tennis Tournament, 24
Mickey Greco Quartet, 178
Middle Finger Show, 149, 182
Midvale Park, 93
Midway Drive-In, 109
Mike Porter Quintet, 74
Milan, Frank, 150
Miller, Jim, 20
Miller, Jimmy, 79
Miller, Jon, 97, 99, 140
Mills Brothers, 80
Mills, Leticia, 122
Miner, Franne, 44, 47, 48, 49, 52, 54, 55, 57
Minter, Greg, 31, 38
Miracle, 109
Miracle Mile Strip, 204, 205
Mirage, 205
Misalidas, John, 45
Miss Tucson Trailer Court, 144
Missailidis, Jon, 45
Mission Road, 203
Mobile Cubes, 21
Molina, Gabe, 152
Monrow, Jeff, 20
Monroy, Miguel, 18, 176
Monte V, 205
Monteleone, Gary, 34
Montgomery, Wes, 115
Moonstruck, 205
Moore, Daniel Patrick, 136
Moore, Joel, 158, 159
Moore, Lhia, 42
Moore, Melba, 58
Mophonics, 48, 57, 60
Moquin, Rick, 45
More Than Pizza, 96
Moreno, Ted, 177
Morgan, Debra, 46
Morgan, Howard, 29, 32
Morgan, Tom, 62
Mormon, Dwane, 122
Moses, Agnes, 69, 71, 72, 80, 81, 87, 102, 103, 108, 128, 129, 134, 153, 170, 193
Moskowitz, David, 65, 77, 79
Moss, David, 31
Motherless Child, 116
Mothers of Invention, 34
Motley Crue, 35
Mountain Men, 22
Mourning Glories, 102
Mouseketeers, 114
Mozart, Wolfgang, 82, 129
Mr. Catfish, 205

Mr. Lee and the Soul Patrol, 106, 110, 192
Mr. T, 185
Mt. Lemmon, 102, 120, 172, 190
Mt. Lemmon Alpine Lodge, 22, 205
Mt. Lemmon Community Center, 67
Mt. Lemmon Ski Valley, 102
Mt. Lemmon's Octoberfest of 1988, 120
MTV, 148
Mudbuggs, 11, 84, 85, 91, 99, 115, 149, 182, 190, 199, 205
MudSharks, 199
Mueller, Julia, 70, 130, 169
Mulatto, 149
Multiple Sclerosis Society, 39
Mungia, Larry, 59
Muñiz, Dan, 162
Muñiz, David, 161
Munson, Arvid, 145
Munzer, Annette, 193
Murphy, Ben, 60
Murphy, Eddie, 185
Murphy, Pat, 20
Murphy, Wendy, 192
Music Box, 168
Music Box Lounge, 205
Music Instructor's Collective, 179, 200
Musicland, 73
Myers, Joe, 132

N

Nadine and the Mophonics, 27, 29, 35, 48, 57
Naggs, Pete, 42
Nahan, Dave, 18
Naked Prey, 65, 102
Nallin, Mike, 42
Nam Jam, 199
National Western Music Association, 113
Naturals, 106, 137
Navy Leapfrog Parachute Team, 93
Nazareth, 70
NBC-TV, 12
Necromancer, 30, 75, 78, 120, 128
Nelson, Dave, 144
Nelson, Lance, 62
Nelson, Willie, 167
Nemes, Scott, 175
Nemesis, 44, 47, 55
Neon Moon, 205
Neon Prophet, 46, 101
Nethermist, 157

Nevada Smith's Saloon, 205
New Blues Tigers, 44
New Circus Lounge, 205
New Highbeam Blues Band, 44
New Loft Theatre, 53, 91, 188
New Orleans Lounge, 205
New Orleans West, 205
New Potatoes, 102
New Ronnie Mack Sundowners with Billy Mack, 22
Newman, Mark, 11, 208
Nickerson, Ross, 71, 95, 113, 138, 143, 190
Nicklin, Glenda, 34
Niec, Ed, 90
Niece, Ed, 41
Night Ranger, 90
Night Shift Tavern, 205
Night Train, 107, 205
NightLites, 185, 205
Nino's, 20, 21, 26, 34, 37, 42, 44, 79, 107, 205
No Bull, 149, 182
Nogales Highway, 17, 202, 206
Nolan, Bob, 52, 113
Nolan, Margaret, 103
Northern Arizona University, 73
Northstar, 21
Nostros Teamwork Program, 97
Notables, 131
NRG, 125
NueVenue, 18, 19, 26, 27, 28, 29, 30, 31, 205
Nugent, Ted, 158
Nun, Joe, 26
Nuñiz, David, 112
Nutt, Joe, 88
Nuttall, Rick, 12

O

O Sole Mio, 107
O'Conner, Mark, 30
O'Conor, Hugo, 72
O'Donnell, Brian, 95, 176
O'Hare, Tom, 114, 115, 116, 121, 127, 132
O'Malley's, 205
O'Shaughnessy's, 80, 100, 205
Oasis, 27, 205
Oasis TV, 44
Obsessions Night Club, 163, 205
Obsidian, 111
Off The Rock, 192
Oiling, Sam, 86

Oktoberfest International, 39
Old Father Inn, 205
Old Pueblo Trolley, 69, 134
Old Spanish Trail, 204
Old Tucson, 22, 71, 73, 91, 103, 106, 108, 138, 143, 144, 154
Olsen, Glenn, 133, 168, 178, 179
Olson, Craig, 74
Olson, Lute, 152
One-Eyed Jack's, 205
Onion John, 131
Only Oldies, 18, 107
Only's, 27
Oracle Road, 11, 100, 119, 164, 202, 204, 205, 206, 207
Orange Empire R.R. Museum, 69
Orange Grove Road, 203
Orbison, Roy, 135
Orders, Keith, 133
Oriental Garden, 205
Original Blues All Stars, 110, 112
Osmond, Donny, 15
Ostberg, Neal, 30
Outback, 205
Outfield, 41
Outlaw, 11, 107, 205
Oved, Dan, 21

P

P, 125
Pacific Beach Club, 205
Pack, Tim, 64
Padilla, Diane, 130
Pain Bank, 149, 182
Palm Rock, 205
Palmer, Robert, 33
Palmer, Vicky, 143
Palo Verde High School, 13, 174
Palo Verde Road, 22, 203, 204, 206
Palomino Restaurant, 205
Pancho's, 205
Pandy, Ron, 136, 138
Panico, Mike, 178
Pantano Road, 100, 179, 203, 204, 206
Paradies, Jed, 48, 57
Paradox, 74
Paris, Charles, 170
Park Avenue, 149, 182, 204, 205, 206
Park Inn, 202, 207
Park Mall, 51, 100, 202
Park Theater, 87
Parker, Dewey, 135

Parque Viente de Agosto, 72
Passion, 189
Pastorius, Jaco, 126
Pat & Laing Duo, 100
Patrick & Associates, 60
Patty Sage and the Sahuaros, 16
Paul Revere & The Raiders, 165
Paul, Stanley, 136
Paulo's Restaurant, 80, 205
Paulus, Rob, 18, 121
PDQ Records, 39
Peace by the Soundings Ensemble, 199
Peggy Rose & Company, 179
Pelicans, 131, 199
Pendleton, Dayle, 102
Pennington Street, 207
Pennington, Thomas, 142, 144
Pennyland, 86
People's Yellow Pages, 36
Pepper's Lounge, 112
Pepsi Cola, 39, 60, 94
Perrodin, Mark, 130
Perry, Al, 11, 70, 120, 130, 158, 169
Pete and Fred, 176
Pete Fine Dan Oved Group, 21
Peter, Paul and Mary, 71
Peters, Dan, 118
Peters, Randy, 57
Peyton Place, 53
Phantom Limbs, 11, 65, 102, 169
Phil Stevens, 19
Philadelphia Pub, 205
Phillips, Bruce, 192
Phillips, Leigh Ann, 186
Phillips, Todd, 47
Pierce, Martha, 134
Pierce, Rick, 191
Pierre, 161
Pima Community College, 13, 21, 71, 73, 188
Pima Community College Journalism Department, 210
Pima County Board of Supervisors, 67
Pima County Courthouse, 72
Pima County Fairgrounds, 135
Pima County Superior Court, 188
Pima Road, 203
Piney Hollow, 134
Pink Cadillac Café, 122, 157, 205

Pink Floyd, 128, 132, 191
Pink'es, 205
Pione, Gary, 34
Pknotic Records, 37
Plain Jayne, 111
Plan B, 20
Plaza at Williams Center, 130
Plaza Bar, 205
Plaza Hotel, 73, 205
Plimsoul, 35
Plotner, Craig, 105
Plumer Avenue, 206
Poco Loco, 44, 55, 144, 205
Pointer, Anita, 91
Police, 61, 159
Pollo Elastico, 131, 173, 176, 182
Pollock, Terry, 136, 138
Poor Boys, 17
Pops Concerts, 129
Porter House Singers, 97
Porter, Barbara, 186
Porter, Mike, 74
Porter, Rick, 100, 186
Porter's House, 93, 186, 205
Post Time Pub, 22, 84, 100, 104, 110, 123, 124, 204, 205
Pratt, Dave, 39, 60, 94, 97, 128
Presley, Elvis, 35
Preston, Cass, 168
Preston, Johnny, 17
Pretenders, 55
Primavera Foundation for the Homeless, 100
Prince, 41
Prince Drive-In, 109
Prince Road, 100, 135, 203, 205
Privett, Tom, 21
Psychedelic Furs, 71
Psychedelicatessen, 149
Ptacek, Rainer, 79, 208
PTL Club, 64
Pueblo Inn, 202, 205, 206
Puhl, Geoff, 31, 36
Puku Puku Lounge and Taco Bar, 63, 99, 108, 119, 205
Putney's Street Pub, 100, 205

Q

Queensryche, 88, 91, 128
Quiet Lyze, 42, 44
Quincy's, 205
Quinn, Ron, 223

R

Radio Free America, 57, 62
Radio Ground Zero, 182
Radio Radio, 114
Radisson Suites, 74, 202
Rainer, 79, 102, 136, 138
Ramada Airport, 204
Ramada Inn, 203
Ramada Inn Downtown, 135
Ramones, 130
Ramsey, Dan, 40
Ramsey, Jon, 34
Randolph Tennis Center, 60
Rare Illusion, 85
Rawls. Lou, 168
RCA Records, 130, 158, 196
Reagan, Nancy, 64
Real Deal, 160, 162
Rebel, Kat, 173
Rechel, Joe, 65
Record Bar, 28, 30, 107
Red Dog Café, 71
Red Oak Review, 199
Red Squared, 102
Redbone, Leon, 80
Redhouse Band, 121
Redhouse, Larry, 121
Redhouse, Lenny, 121
Reel, 122, 205
Reid Park, 62
Reid Park Bandshell, 104
Reinsmen, 113
Renegades, 192
Reno Calice and Jazz, 74
Replacements, 127
Resort Drive, 202, 203
Restless, 120, 126
Restless Records, 199
Revenant, 131
Revivers, 131
Rex Allen and the Sons of the Pioneers, 153
Rhoades, Spyder, 122, 149, 182
Rialto's, 130, 199, 205
Rich, Buddy, 121
Richards, Billy Joe, 114
Richards, Keith, 136
Richardson, Leon, 115
Richardson, Phil, 144
Richie, Lionel, 24, 58
Rick Evarro and the Castaways, 135
Rick Porter's House, 100, 107, 186, 205
Rick's Oasis Club, 205
Ride, 131
Riders in the Sky, 113, 154, 195

Riders of the Purple Sage, 154
Riff Raff, 44, 47, 95
Rillito Downs, 39, 60, 94, 95, 97
Rillito River Revue, 112
Rincon High School, 25, 58
Riordon, Eileen, 40
River Road, 48, 53, 60
River Roses, 102
Rivers, Joan, 15
Rizzardi, Mark, 113, 138, 143, 190
Roadies, 95, 112, 124
Roadrunner Restaurant and Lounge, 109, 124, 167, 205
Roads, Dave, 70, 130, 169
Roberts, Bert, 59
Roberts, Eric, 33
Robinson, Lee, 52
Roc Lochner, 44, 55
Rock, 206
Rock 'n Roll on Cable TV, 136
Rock Island Café, 205
Rock Palace, 176
Rockefeller, 11, 41, 85, 90, 97, 99, 107
Rockefeller's, 205
Rockers for Recall Benefits, 1987, 84
Rocket 88s, 99
Rocking E Saloon, 205
Rode Way Inn, 34, 205, 206
Rodriguez, Gilbert, 145
Rodriguez, Lou, 139
Rodriguez, Paul, 39
Roger Road, 17, 131, 204
Rogers, Roy, 52, 154
Rogers, Susan, 112
Rolling Stones, 63, 127
Romancer, 78
Romero Road, 17, 131, 202, 207
Ronstadt, Linda, 118
Roo Huntley Revue, 120
Rose, Peggy, 147, 164, 167, 168, 177, 178, 179, 186, 195, 196, 198, 199, 200
Rosenthal, Sandy, 50, 208
Ross, Glynn, 81, 82, 194, 195
Rough, Susie, 80
Round Up Saloon, 16, 52, 110, 136, 143, 196, 205
Rowdies, 124, 131, 136
Roxy, 55, 77
Roxy Nightclub, 11
Roy Clayburn & The Alamo, 197
Royal Sun, 205

Rozy Coyote, 158, 199
RROC-TV, 136
Ruiz, Rubin, 21
Rundle, Lynne, 24
Runes Café, 205
Rush, 159
Rusty Geer German Band, 120
Rusty Lantern, 205
Ruthrauff Road, 100, 203, 205, 206
Ryan, Ronnie, 158, 159
Rybke, Blaine, 21

S

Sabino Canyon Road, 204
Saddle City Band, 12, 22, 52, 66, 136, 196
Sage, Patty, 16
Sage, Robin, 16
Sahlin, Chris, 35
Sahuaros, 16
Sainz, Paul, 182
SALOC, 32
Salvage, Joe, 33
Sam Burkes, Ted, 76
Sam's Tavern, 106
Samaniego House, 119, 206
Sammy C., 167
San Agustin del Tucson, 72
San Agustine Cathedral, 72
San Francisco Bar and Grill, 206
San Jacinto Records, 130
Sanchez Restaurant, 107
Sanders, Tim, 20
Santa Catalina Mountains, 67
Santa Fe Bar and Grill, 206
Santa Rita Avenue, 36
Santa Rita High School, 56
Santana, 121
Sasnatt, Tom, 64
Savant, 111
Saw Mill Café, 206
Sawmill Café, 124
Schlossberg, Steve, 50
Schwartz, Zoom, 62
Scofield, John, 121
Scorpions, 42
Scots Pipers, 81
Scott Avenue, 204, 206
Screen Actors Guild, 108
Sea, 102
Seattle Opera, 193
Sedlmayr, Billy, 79
Seemes, Doris, 186
Segovia, Andre, 132
Selby, Jackie, 95
Sellers, Tommy, 152
Señor Wences, 15
Señora Sands, 206

Serito, Jamie, 46
Serpa, Louise, 93
Serres, Mick, 166
Sertich, Ginny, 30
Sex Machine Band, 39, 60, 94, 97
Sex Pistols, 122
Sex Snacks, 131
Seymour, Daryl, 35
Sgt. Pepper's, 206
Shakespeare, 194
Shakespeare in the Park, 193
Shakespeare, William, 62, 82, 87
Shakey's Pizza Parlor, 107
Sham, Fred, 64
Shandling, Garry, 13, 14, 15, 174, 175
Shark's, 120, 206
Sharp Rain, 111
Shaw, Bobby, 73
Shayka, Richard, 26, 88
Shear DeLights, 76
Shears, Billy, 76
Shed, 191, 206
Sheehan, Doug, 94
Shenanigan's, 206
Sheraton El Conquistador, 33, 95, 203, 204, 206
Sheraton Pueblo Inn, 102, 206
Sheraton Rio Rico, 57
Shirley's, 206
Shnanigan's, 43, 68, 111
Shooters, 206
Short Circuit, 62
Short Stories, 18, 34, 44, 61
Shriner, Wil, 24, 60, 69
Sidewinders, 65, 79, 102, 130, 131
Silent Rage, 41
Silver Knight Photography, 26
Silver Room, 34, 111, 112, 206
Silver Screen Lounge, 206
Silver, Steve, 46
Silverbell Road, 204
Silverman, Robert, 44, 47
Simon and Garfunkel, 176
Simon, Chris, 152
Sin, Mike, 157
Sing, Glenn, 30
Sipes, Jeff, 84, 115, 145
Sirkis, John, 18
Sitting Duck Studios, 70
Ski Valley, 120
Ski Valley Lodge, 206
Skin Yard, 149
Skowron, Rick, 92
Skyclad Records, 148, 177
Skyclad Records/Get Hip Records, 177

Skynyrd, Lynyrd, 65
Slayer, 91
Sloth, 102
Slutes, David, 65, 70, 130
Slye, Leonard, 52
Small Paul, 162
Small Paul and the Drivin'
  Wheel, 95
Smiley, Sam, 87
Smith, Moses, 62
Smith, Ross, 21
Smith, Taylor, 61
Smith's, 107
Smithereens, 127
Smokey's, 206
Smokin' Joe, 48
Smothers Brothers, 99, 108
Smuggler's Inn, 204
Sneak Joint Lounge, 57, 77,
  199, 206
Sneak Joint West, 100, 206
Sneaky Pete's, 206
Snider, Eric, 36
Soap, 108
Soft Cell, 46
Solarium, 206
Somers, Suzanne, 66, 77
Somerset Club, 34, 40, 57,
  139, 206
Songdog Café, 206
Sons of the Pioneers, 52,
  113, 153, 154
Sons of the Western Plains,
  148
Soto, Bobby, 196
Soul Patrol, 192
Sound Factory, 18, 21, 26,
  27, 28, 31, 61, 71, 79,
  184, 190
Sound Factory Recording
  Studio, 11
Soundings of the Planet,
  160, 199
Sounds of Tucson, 124
Soundscapes, 119
South Forty, 143, 199, 206
Southbound, 196
Southern Arizona Light
  Opera Company, 32
Southern Arizona Old Time
  Fiddlers Association,
  128
Southwest Alternatives
  Institute, 2, 36, 150,
  188, 209
Spalding, Milton, 196
Spandex, 158
Sparky, 185
Speake, Mark, 21
Spector, Phil, 157
Speedway Blvd., 11, 12,
  44, 53, 59, 99, 107, 119,
  199, 202, 203, 204, 205,
  206, 207

Speedway Saloon, 176,
  199, 206
Speedways, 59, 60
Spellbound, 110, 111
Spencer, Tim, 113
Spinnaker, 173, 199, 206
Splinter Bros. & Sisters
  Warehouse, 206
Splinter Brothers
  Warehouse, 12
Spock, Benjamin, 13
Sports Page Lounge, 206
Sports-A-Rama, 119, 130,
  206
Sportspark, 39
Spotlight Attractions, 198
Spring Fling, 30, 46
Springfield, Rick, 114
Springsteen, Bruce, 159
Sprouse, Daniel, 61, 62, 64,
  65, 70, 75, 76, 78, 83,
  84, 86, 106, 124, 126,
  128
Spud Boy, 33
Squares, 131, 182
St. Bonaventure Hall, 196
St. Claire, Audrey, 56
St. Clair-Tarbill, Audrey,
  95
St. Elizabeth of Hungary
  Clinic, 60
St. Pierrex, Walt, 164
Stab in the Dark, 57
Stacey, Cynthia, 171
Stafford, John, 189
Stallone, Sylvester, 106
Starks, Burney, 208
Starr, Bonnie, 147, 200
Starr, Dan, 200
Starr, Dan, 136, 138, 147,
  159, 165, 171, 179, 183,
  189, 191, 197, 200
Starr, Steve, 208
Statesboro Blues Band, 3,
  18, 48, 60, 63, 183
Statman, Arthur, 74
Steely Dan, 114
Steenken, Daniel, 72
Steiniunes, John, 50
Steppenwolf, 110
Stern, Howard, 12
Stetson Nightclub, 206
Stevens, Phil, 61
Stingrays, 206
Stitt, Duncan, 136, 138,
  196
Stogsdill, Jim, 128
Stomer, Mike, 131
Stone Avenue, 202, 203,
  205, 207
Stormy Weather, 124
Stowgram, Jerry, 144
Strange Daze, 94
Stray Cat, 107, 206

Streed, Sarah, 67
Street Gypsy, 199
Street Legal, 40
Street Pajama, 3, 12, 48,
  77, 101, 112
Striker, Eric, 176
Stringi, Joe, 40
Strom, Kelly, 193
Stuart Anderson's Black
  Angus, 95
Studebaker's, 119, 206
Stumble Inn, 140, 206
Styx Stomper, 63
Submarine, 107
Subterranean Blues Band,
  169
Sudbury, Beth, 208
Sullivan, Mike, 12, 197
Summerhaven, 120, 205
Summerset Suite, 73
Summit Studios, 31, 78, 94,
  123, 124, 199
Sumter Drive, 202
Sundance East, 206
Sundance East and West,
  107
Sundance West, 206
Sunday Blues Jam, 144
Sunderman, Dave, 112, 120
Sundowner, 206
Sundowners, 17, 22
Sunrise, 56, 125, 155
Sunrise Drive, 202
Surge, 40, 139
Surgical Steel, 30
Sussman, Kenny, 54, 152
Sutton, Ned, 48, 57
Swan Road, 44, 100, 204,
  205, 206
Swan, Pete, 168
Swanson, John, 42
Sweat, Keith, 185
Sweet Baby, 149
Swing Inn Lounge, 17, 206
Swinging Sensations, 100

T

T. J. Canyon Band, 124,
  167
T.U.S.D. Centralized
  Media, 46
Tailgators, 44
Tailor Made, 42, 43, 97, 98
Tailor, Susan, 45
Taj Mahal, 124
Talking Heads, 21
Tanque Verde Road, 11,
  22, 44, 99, 202, 203,
  204, 205, 206, 207
Tap, Donny, 17
Tarantelli, Rick, 130
Tarbill, David, 95
Tavern On The Green, 198

Taylor, Beatrice, 161
Taylor, Bobby, 3, 160, 161,
  163, 208
Taylor, Jacques, 161, 162
Taylor, James, 177
Taylor, Pamela, 59, 64
Taylor, Sam, 3, 63, 77, 101,
  115, 138, 142, 144, 145,
  156, 160, 173, 208
Taylor, Sandra, 161
Taylor, Suzanna, 45
T-Bones Sneak Joint, 112,
  146
TCC, 108, 138, 143, 176,
  187
TCC Exhibition Hall, 20,
  98
TCC Music Hall, 129, 187
Tchaikovsky, 129
Teen on-line, 209
Teeters, Howard, 65
Telluride Bluegrass
  Festival, 113, 138, 143,
  190
Temple of Music and Art,
  100, 111, 206
Temple of the Arts, 81
Templeton, Billy, 34, 199
Temptations, 185
Tender Trap, 66, 100, 107,
  168, 178, 206
Tenth Street Dance works,
  149
Tequila Mockingbird, 12,
  20, 21, 23, 26, 32, 33,
  38, 42, 43, 44, 47, 48,
  50, 55, 57, 64, 68, 89,
  106, 108, 110, 112, 116,
  118, 120, 163, 185, 189,
  190, 206
Terry & Zeke's, 12, 18, 23,
  32, 44, 48, 83, 84, 97,
  99, 176, 183, 184, 206
Terry & Zeke's Again, 97,
  99, 104, 107, 110, 112,
  176, 199, 206
Texas Rangers, 154
The Comedy Zone, 50
The In Your Face Horns,
  138
The Jack's, 22
The Santa Fe, 17
The Tonight Show, 14
The WAVE, 128
Theloneus Monster, 149
Theobold, Dennis, 197
Thomas, Kevin, 197
Thomas, Sonia, 161
Thomasson, Jim, 147
Thompson, Ed, 134
Thornydale Road, 204
Three On A Match, 21
Tia Elena, 106, 206
Timbuk 3, 70

Tin Ear Cocktail Lounge, 206
Tiny's Saloon, 206
Titan Valley Warheads, 71, 102, 113, 138, 143, 153
To Be Announced, 49
Tohono O'odham, 81
Tommy Tucker Blues Band, 48
Tone Loc, 152
Toole Avenue, 203
Top Dogs, 192
Torrez, Luis, 77
Touch of Country, 16
Touchstones, 62
Tovar, Jesse, 74, 178, 183, 184
Tovi's Hoof & Horn, 143, 206
Toxic Ranch Records, 182
Toys for Tots, 110, 131
TPRCT, 193
Tragic, 149
Transatlantic Management, 102
Travis, Jim, 119
Travis, Randy, 197
Trend, 136, 176, 182
Triple C Chuckwagon Lounge, 52, 120, 206
Triple C Ranch, 142
Triple Shot, 65
Trolley's, 206
Troop, 152
Trouble, 155
Tu Madre Records, 31
Tucci, Michael, 175
Tucker, Ed, 30, 75
Tucker, Marshall, 110
Tucker, Tommy, 48
Tucson Action Core, 149
Tucson and Pima County Libraries, 13
Tucson and Pima County Recreation Centers, 13
Tucson Auto Mall, 119
Tucson Balloon Fiesta, 93
Tucson birthday of 1987, 72
Tucson Bluegrass Festival, 39
Tucson Blvd., 100, 203, 204, 206
Tucson Chronicles, 209
Tucson City Council, 43, 130, 188
Tucson Classics, 11, 60
Tucson Community Cable, 136
Tucson Community Cable Oasis Award, 26
Tucson Community Center, 108

Tucson Convention Center, 103
Tucson Electric Power, 70
Tucson Entertainment Magazine, 69, 81, 209
Tucson Entertainment Music Awards of 1988, 94
Tucson Festival Society, 193
Tucson Fire Department, 12
Tucson Friends of Traditional Music, 36
Tucson Fumbles, 206
Tucson Garden, 97, 99, 107, 110, 111, 120, 121, 138, 140, 141, 142, 143, 145, 158, 176, 199, 206
Tucson Gilbert & Sullivan Repertory Co., 73
Tucson Greyhound Park, 106
Tucson High School, 122
Tucson J.C. Vigilantes, 93
Tucson Jazz Society, 80, 84
Tucson Legends, 85
Tucson Mall, 51
Tucson Mardi Gras, 176
Tucson Mardi Gras of 1987, 59, 60, 95
Tucson Mardi Gras of 1988, 94, 95, 96, 97
Tucson McGraw's, 206
Tucson Meet Yourself, 128
Tucson Mountainmen, 51
Tucson Mountains, 16
Tucson Musician's Showcase, 150
Tucson Open University, 91, 188
Tucson Optimist Club, 39
Tucson Parks & Recreation Department, 104
Tucson Parks and Recreation Community Theatre, 193
Tucson Parks and Recreation Department, 102
Tucson Pima Arts Council's, 43
Tucson Police Department, 12
Tucson Public Access Cable, 26
Tucson Residence Foundation for the Mentally Retarded, 60
Tucson Rock Festival, 98
Tucson Rodeo, 22, 51, 91, 93
Tucson Rodeo Beard Contest, 22

Tucson Rodeo Dance, 22, 93
Tucson Rodeo history, 51
Tucson Rodeo Parade, 24, 51, 93, 150
Tucson Symphony Orchestra, 74, 101, 129, 133, 164
Tucson Teen, 3, 36, 58, 60, 69, 94, 105, 110, 122, 150, 176, 209, 210
Tucson Toros, 176
Tucson trolley, 69, 134
Tucson Unified School District, 188
Tucson Vigilantes, 22
Tucson Warehouse and Transfer, 158, 173, 206
Tucson Y.W.C.A., 19, 29, 31, 36, 110, 188, 209
Tucson, Arizona Boys Chorus, 187
Tucson, Meet Yourself of 1987, 81
Tucson/Pima Arts Council, 81
Tucson/Pima County Historical Commission, 72
Tumors, 31, 35, 36
Tunes of Tucson, 31
Tunnel Music, 114
Turner, Bret, 41, 90
Turner, Mike, 118
Turner, Ted, 70
Turtles, 165
Tutt, Terie, 125, 154
TW&T (see Tucson Warehouse & Transfer), 173
Twin Peaks, 26, 40, 42, 50, 53, 65, 112, 118, 126, 173, 206
Twister, 33, 45, 56, 57, 85, 117, 123, 125, 139, 155
TWIT, 34, 42
Two Cities, 110, 111
Tyler, Dave, 55
Tyndall Avenue, 57, 97, 203, 204, 206

U

U & the Risk, 38
U2, 38, 71
Uncle Bob Show, 39
Uncle Milty, 95
Unicorn, 206
Union Grove Bluegrass Festival, 71
United Way, 36
Units, 78
University Area Plan, 1989, 188

University Blvd., 19, 26, 29, 97, 202, 204, 205, 206
University Commons, 97, 99, 106
University High School, 46
University of Arizona, 13, 14, 19, 25, 58, 72, 73, 99, 126, 151, 156, 166, 174, 188, 209, 210
University of Arizona Cellar, 30, 46, 97, 98, 182, 206
University of Arizona Centennial, 69
University of Arizona Centennial Founders Day Parade, 69
University of Arizona Crowder Hall, 103
University of Arizona Drama Department, 87
University of Arizona Gallagher Theatre, 176
University of Arizona Library Special Collections, 209
University of Arizona Radio/TV, 30
University of Arizona School of Music, 116
University of Arizona Student Union, 87, 97, 182
University of Arizona Student Union Cellar, 176
University of Arizona's Master of Fine Arts, 87
University of Arizona's Southwest Folklore Center, 81
University Square, 188
Unwinder, 206
Up With People, 68
Uribe, Tony, 84

V

Vagabundo, 206
Valencia Road, 17, 202, 204, 207
Valens, Ritchie, 165
Valenzuela, Patti, 146
Valley of the Moon, 84, 86, 87
Van Dusen, Charlie, 21
Van Gogh's Italian Restaurant, 124, 206
Van Slyke, Peter, 50, 72
Vandross, Luther, 71
Vanyon Tree, 207
Vega, Susan, 171
Veltman, Alan, 145

Ventures, 118, 135
Venus, 116, 133, 166
Venuti, Joe, 81
VFW, 196
Victoria, Willie, 130
Victoria's, 207
Vidal, Ray, 178
Viet Nam Blues, 132
Village on Broadway, 100
Virden, Chris, 55
Virgin Vinyl, 12, 21, 95
Viscount Suites, 207
Vision, 111
Vision Quest, 22
Visitor, 40, 41
Vista's, 207
Volgey, Tom, 108
Von Glahn, Rick, 88
von Holtzer, Katherine, 97
Vonglahn, Rick, 26
Voxx Records, 35, 37

W

W.C. in the Fields, 207
Wachter, Dick, 69
Wade 'N Highwater, 110, 123, 124, 131
Wagon Wheel, 207
Wahl, Doug, 131
Wahoolic Cajun Band, 102
Wailers, 130
Waldron, Chris, 195
Wales, Josey, 108
Walker, Tom, 28
Waller, Julianna, 128
Walsh, Mike, 84
Walton, John, 125
Walton, Karl, 125, 154
Wanebo, Dick, 143
Warner, Kathy, 47
Washington, Oliver, 139

Wayne Darnell and his Slick Band, 16
We're Here, 110, 111
Webb, Dave, 17, 196
Webb, Dorris, 17
Weber, Chris, 128
Webner, Paul, 192
Weinglass, Steve, 126
Weird Harold's, 16, 207
Weisberg, Tim, 106
Welding, Rob, 49
Wesley, Careron, 65
West Wind, 52
Western music, 113
Western Music Association, 138, 143, 148, 154
Western Music Festival, 113
Western Way Circle, 205
Westin La Paloma, 74, 95, 116, 202, 203
Westin La Paloma's Cactus Club, 85
Westward Look, 63, 73, 84, 112, 204, 207
Westward Look Lookout Lounge, 124
Westwood Studios, 18, 30, 34, 123
Wetmore Road, 206
Wetzel, Harold, 16
Whalen, Rocky, 34
Whataburger, 107
Wheatley, Chris, 20
Whiskey's, 207
White Rabbit, 106, 112, 127, 176
White, Charles, 191
White, Lavinia, 21, 208
White, Michael, 191
White, Pat, 140
Whitney's, 207

Wilber's, 207
Wilbur Smith Associates, 70
Wild, Wild West, 207
Wildcat, 151
Wildcat House, 207
Wildcat's Rock Café, 131, 207
Wilde, Kim, 118
Will, Edith, 84
William Morris Agency, 185
Williams Center, 130
Williams, Hank, 197
Williams, Jack, 72
Williams, Joe, 168
Wilmot Road, 57, 168, 199, 202, 204, 205, 206
Wilson, Brian, 120
Wilson, Dan, 21
Wilson, Paul, 175
Windham Hill, 18
Windows, 106
Windy Cities Bar and Grill, 207
Winwood, Stevie, 155, 156
Wisehart, 97
Wisehart, Troy, 43, 97
Wolftung, 40
Wong, Nancy, 150
Wong's, 207
Wood, Jack, 74
Woods, Doug, 158, 173
Woods, Ruby, 81
Woolco's, 107
Wooten, Howard, 74
Works, 34
Workshop Music & Sound, 149
Wrath, 48
WREX, 12
WREX Records, 122, 149, 182

WTBS, 148
Wylie, P.L., 13, 23, 174
Wymen on Wheels, 36
Wyte Hott, 111

X

XL, 158, 159
X-Rays, 42

Y

Yaqui, 81
Yardbirds, 165
Yes, 159, 176
Yeung, Tony, 131
Young, Irene, 171
Young, Neil, 21
Young, Paul, 208
Youth Alternatives, 110, 176, 209, 210
Youth Awareness Press, 110, 176, 209, 210
Youth Services Bureau, 209
Yox, David, 54

Z

Z Club, 207
Zappa, Frank, 34
Zimmerman, Brian, 92
Zip's Records, 18, 30, 38, 61
Zip's Video, 107
Zucker, Robert, 2, 31, 36, 94, 110, 188, 208, 209, 210
Zwiebel, Alan, 175
ZZ Top, 65

Index: Volume 3

The third volume contains 228 pages and cover the 1990s.

"

"A" Mountain, 24, 157

1

100 Iced Animals, 168
1-2-1, 115
12th Avenue, 66, 210
1st Avenue, 44, 57, 66, 83, 166, 206, 207, 208, 209, 210

2

22nd Street, 67, 96, 166, 206, 207, 208, 209, 210, 211
26th Street, 207
29th Street, 207
2nd Avenue, 207
2nd Street, 105, 126, 210

3

3rd Avenue, 105

4

4400 Club, 206
45-Grave, 98
4H, 118
4th Avenue, 88, 90, 105, 153, 204, 206, 207, 208, 209, 210
4th Avenue Merchants Association, 105
4th Avenue Social Club, 151
4th Avenue Street Fair, 105, 153, 165

5

5th Avenue, 105
5th Street, 105

6

6th Avenue, 56, 166, 206, 207, 210
6th Street, 105, 206, 208
6th Street Merchants, 160
6th Street Pub & Grill, 206

7

7N7 Recording Studio, 90, 92
7N7 Sound Studio, 99
7th Street, 105

8

8th Street, 105

9

9th Street, 14, 105, 207

A

a.k.a. Theatre, 57
Abbey, Edward, 198, 199
ABC-TV, 27
Abeyta, Ted, 74
Able, Dave, 102
About Face, 78
Abril, Manuel, 10, 13, 15, 18
Access Unlimited, 53, 59
Ace, 169
Ace, Frank, 24, 25
Actors' Equity Association, 49
Addled Records, 195
After Midnight Band, 139
Aguirre, Jaimie, 30
Airport Inn, 206
Ajo Way, 40, 56, 66, 207, 210
Al Perry and the Cattle, 152, 165, 168, 179, 185
Al Smith's Pub, 206
Alabama, 106
Alameda Street, 82
Alan, Marshall Jack, 132
Alchemy Rhythm Band, 108
Alday, Roxanna, 212
Alexander, Bill, 50
Alexandra's, 206
Alford, George, 204
All Night Perchesi Club, 168
Allande, Pedro, 156
Allen, Gary, 38
Allen, Larry, 38
Allen, Marty, 21
Allen, Rex, 42, 82, 86, 101, 133, 212

Allen, Rex, Jr., 86
Almighty Honeywagon, 195
Alpaugh, Robert, 49
Alpine Lodge, 208
ALS Association, 62, 65
Alternative Press Syndicate, 213
Alvarez, Tina, 97, 103, 114, 119, 129, 133, 136, 138, 140, 143, 144, 146, 151, 157, 161, 164, 165, 166, 167, 168, 171, 173, 175, 176, 179, 182, 185, 186, 189, 191, 192, 193, 194, 195, 196, 202
Alvernon Way, 206, 208, 209
Amato, John, 50
Amazon.com, 2
American Automobile Association, 149
American Radio Theater, 173, 175
Americana Hotel/Quality Inn, 210
Anderson, Betty, 88
Anderson, Chaton, 69
Anderson, Jamie, 175
Anderson, Joanne, 156
Anderson, Kerry, 101
Anderson, Pete, 88
Anderson, Scott, 110
Anklam Road, 207
Ansley, Willie, 170
Anthony, Eric, 154
Anti M, 50
Antigone Bookstore, 109
Apollo Theater, 120, 147
Appice, Vinny, 179
Arc Angel, 146
Argent, John, 89
Ariana Records, 146
Aristocrats of the Range, 52
Arizona Anthem Poetry Contest, 198
Arizona Blues Hall of Fame, 1997, 204
Arizona Charlie's Casino, 148
Arizona Civic Theatre, 48
Arizona County, 146
Arizona Daily Star, 145, 175, 186, 203
Arizona Daily Star-Tucson Citizen, 166

Arizona Dance Hands, 54, 55, 101
Arizona Family Restaurant, 21, 27, 207
Arizona Historical Society, 68, 126, 156
Arizona Historical Society Fiesta Committee, 126
Arizona Historical Society Museum, 126
Arizona Inn, 206
Arizona Kidney Foundation, 55
Arizona Music and Conference Showcase of 1991, 97
Arizona Opera Company, 12
Arizona Rainforest Alliance, 37
Arizona Rock Wars of 1993, 162, 167, 171, 192
Arizona State University, 137, 177
Arizona Theatre Company, 18, 39, 48, 49, 57, 172, 212
Arizona's Best Kept Secrets, 179
Arizona's Best Kept Secrets Showcase, 197
Arki, 98
Arm & Hammer, 114
Armstrong, Dean, 54, 55, 101, 132, 175, 212
Armstrong, Gene, 145, 175
Arnold, Dennis, 159
Art Attack, 39
Arthur, Lamonte, 187
Asleep at the Wheel, 43
ASUA Concerts, 39
Asylum Records, 34
At The Hop, 206
Atar, Mike, 38
ATC, 18, 39, 48, 49, 57
Atco Records, 140
Atkins, Chet, 25
Atlas/Polygram Records, 143
Atrophy, 185
Audubon, 206
Auel, Jean, 60
Augustine, Nick, 144
Austin, Ada Redd, 26
Austin, Robyn, 60
Avalon, 27

Ave Fenix, 132
Avid Diva, 144
Avra Valley, 42
Ayame, 12
Aylward, Daniel, 27
Aztec Inn, 206
Aztec Press, 214

B

B&B Café, 206
Bachelier, Lisa, 145
Bachman Turner
    Overdrive, 166
Back Streets, 206
Back to Basix, 162
Backlash, 136, 138, 140
Backstreet Boogie Band,
    73
Bad Habit, 50, 78
Bad Love, 41
Baez, Joan, 34
Bajarius, Rudy, 162
Baker, Mary, 165, 175
Baldry, John, 136
Ball, Bill, 74
Bambi Lounge, 81
Banta, Victor, 71
Banyon Tree, 206
Bar M Cattle Co. Steak
    House, 32, 112, 206
Barajas, Ismael, 136
Barajas, Rudy, 63
Barkulis, Greg, 175, 186,
    191
Baron, Kenny, 13
Baron's Restaurant, 21, 27,
    206
Base, Rob, 178
Bashful Bandit, 206
Bassel, Aaron, 192
Battle of the Bands of
    1988, 63
Battle of the Bands of
    1991, 64, 75, 84, 114
Battle of the Bands of
    1992, 130
Battle of the Bands of
    1993, 161, 171, 192,
    193
Battle of the Bands of
    1994, 192, 193
Battle of the Bands of
    1995, 192
Bauer, Holly, 90
Baum & Adamson's Tire
    Co., 166
Beach Boys, 74
Beachcomber, 67
Bear Down Nut Brown,
    158, 159
Beastie Boys, 194
Beat Farmers, 136
Beatles, 14, 41, 74, 111,
    112, 151, 183, 190, 194

Beaver's Concert Band, 67
Beck, Jeff, 190
Bego, 78
Bejarano, Rafael, 188
Bell, Eric, 170
Bell, Steve, 64
Ben's Summer Wheat, 159
Benson Highway, 54, 83,
    166, 207, 208, 209, 210
Bentley's, 44, 79
Bentley's, 206
Benton, Brooke, 58
Berggoetz, Brian, 50, 76,
    87, 88
Berky's Bar, 74, 103, 206
Bernhardt, Robert, 19, 57
Berry, Chuck, 89, 178
Berry, Jim, 67
Best Western, 209, 210
Betty and the Bebops, 88
Betty Stress, 84, 85, 114,
    130, 174, 176
Beyond Records, 167
Big Bang Rodeo, 175
Big Brothers of Tucson, 62,
    65
Big Bug, 50, 76, 90
Big Country, 133
Big Deal, 157
Big Joe Turner, 204
Big Sisters of Tucson, 62,
    65
Bighead Todd, 183
Billboard, 168
Billy Shears Band, 74
Billy Templeton, 38
Bird, Kristi, 44
Bituates, Rob, 97, 98
Black Crowes, 183
Black Moon Graffiti, 175,
    185
Black Mountain, 156, 157
Black Sabbath, 17
Black Uhuru, 188
Blackburn, Sean, 101, 132
Blakeman, Robert, 33, 34
Bleckov, Andrew, 84
Blind Blake, 194
Blood Spasm, 195
Blu, Rose, 48
Blue J's, 206
Blue Light Blues Band,
    172, 176
Blue Lizards, 103, 136,
    152, 185
Blue Monks, 185, 204
Blue, Jimmy, 22
Blue, Victor, 60
Blues Brothers, 103, 104
Blues Crusher, 162, 176
Blues Light Blues Band,
    186, 187
Blues Traveler, 183
Boardroom, 206
Bob Dobb's, 206

Bob Meighan and the
    Shake, 72
Bob's Squeezy Snake
    Lounge, 22, 210
Bobby McGee's, 206
Bobby Taylor and the Real
    Deal, 125, 173, 202
Bobby Taylor and the Real
    Deal featuring Karen
    Brooks, 45, 179
Bodine's, 171, 206
Bojangles Saloon, 15, 206
Bolen, Mark, 30, 31
Bolin, Harry, 116, 123
Bombers, 75
Bond, Kirby, 83
Bone Mama, 145
Bone, Dyan, 61
Bonko, Richard, 185
Bono, Chastity, 129
Boogie Man Blues Band,
    26, 185
Boogie Night, 37
Bookman's, 206
Boomer's, 162, 206
Boomer's Café Espresso,
    206
Boon Docks Lounge, 39,
    83, 206
Boone County, 112
Boone, Pat, 65
Boone, Rob, 152
Boozehounds, 175
Bopp Road, 210
Borders, Keith, 179
Boston's, 179, 186
Boswell, Darrin, 120
bottleneck slides, 199, 201
Bourbon Street Five, 67
Bourbon Street Jazz Band,
    66, 67
Bow'ry Boyz, 136, 138
Bowen & Bailey, 114, 185,
    206
Bowman, Kevin, 90, 165
Box of Cherries, 136, 138
Boxes, 136
Boyd, Al, 67
Boyd, Kaye, 212
Brady Court, 39
Brady, Jim, 179
Brady, Pat, 51
Brain Damage Orchestra,
    20, 37, 93, 103, 119,
    130
Brain Pudding, 171
Braun, Muzzy, 101
Brayman, Matthew, 127
Breadwinners, 93, 130
Breeze Band, 191
Brennion, Rick, 199
Brett, Robert, 173
Brewski's, 206
Brickel, Edie, 109
Bridges, Beau, 118

Brigadier Jerry, 122
Briggs, David, 143
Brilliant Fools, 186
Broadway Blvd., 27, 101,
    124, 141, 142, 206, 208,
    209, 210
Brobeck, Eric, 161, 193
Broken Romeo, 14, 64, 91,
    114, 144, 174
Brokenhorse, 114
Bromberg, Brian, 13
Brooks, Brad, 24
Brooks, Karen, 45, 120,
    125, 147, 173, 179
Brothers Figaro, 62
Brown, Charlie, 18
Brown, Clay, 72
Brown, James, 25, 115,
    125, 169
Brown, Kim, 99, 133
Brown, Maxine, 58, 184
Brown, Paul, 104
Browne, Jann, 62
Brykas Records, 146
Buckels, Mike, 140, 151
Budweiser, 24, 183
Buena Vista Theater, 168,
    193
Buggy Wheel, 206
Bulk Records, 48
Bull Pen Lounge, 94, 206
Bullring Bar, 74, 88, 206
Bum Steer, 117, 171, 206
Bunbuku Japanese Cuisine,
    113, 126, 206
Burd, Ken, 186
Burke, Solomon, 184, 204
Burkes, Billy, 55, 212
Burkes, Sam, 74
Burkhalter, David, 163
Burnquist, Kris, 99
Burroughs, Chris, 145
Bush, George, 105
Bushwacker, 136, 139, 206
Butch Diggs, 26
Butterfield Junction, 36,
    206
Bynes, David, 45
Byrds, 34, 79
BZB Publishing, 2, 214,
    228

C

Cactus Brothers, 186
Cactus Club, 206
Cactus Moon Café, 83, 206
Cadillacs, 178
Café Dorado, 206
Café Napoli, 206
Café Poco Cosa, 206
Café Quebec, 206
Café Sweetwater, 58, 128,
    176, 206
Camacho, Rene, 152

Camino Principal, 209
Camino Seco, 102, 208
Campbell Avenue, 62, 207, 208, 210
Campbell, Glenn, 39
Campbell, Mike, 143
Campbell, Vincent, 113
Canadian Broadcasting Network, 36
Candlebox, 179
Canyon del Oro High School, 90
Canyon Ranch, 142
Capitol Records, 11, 43, 80, 147, 167
Caramba, 176
Carlone, Chris, 24
Carlos Murphy's, 148, 206
Carlton's Lariat Lounge, 208
Carolina Homestead, 206
Carson, Johnny, 81
Carter, Benny, 13
Carter, Linda, 124
Cascade Lounge, 206
Cash, Johnny, 107, 198, 200
Cashman, Bill, 162
Cass Preston Quartet, 21, 27
Castaway Club, 84, 85, 206
Catalanotte, Peter, 81
Catalina High School, 18, 19
Catalonotte, Peter, 195
Cats, 163
Cattle, 92, 114, 146, 152, 157, 165, 168, 179, 185
Catz, Robert, 204
Cavan, Jack, 66
Cavern, 162
CBGB's, 103
CBS-TV, 62
Cedeno, Andujar, 154
Celebration, 89, 206
Celebrity Tennis Classics, 62, 65, 118
Central Park West, 206
Centurions, 74
Chain Gang, 188
Chamberlain, Gordon, 139
Chambers, 101, 106, 132
Chambers, Becki, 77, 107
Chambers, Tom, 42, 77, 107
Chandelle Restaurant, 206
Char's, 128
Charisma Records, 120
Charles, Grey, 41
Charles, Ray, 190
Chastain, 112
Chastain Gang, 112
Chastain, Jean, 38, 199
Chastain, John, 111
Chelsea's, 206

Chemoux, Joe, 29, 39
Chenier, C.J., 130
Cherry Poppin' Daddies, 175
Cherry, Carl, 63, 120, 188
Chevelles, 112
Chicago Bar, 20, 24, 46, 63, 120, 148, 162, 172, 187, 204, 206
Chicago White Sox, 154, 170
Chip, Amo, 122, 187
Chitlin Circuit, 59
Chrysalis Records, 69, 75, 194
Chuck Gross' Thrillville, 204
Chuck Wagon and the Wheels, 42, 43, 44, 89
Church, 133
Church Avenue, 209
Churchill's Shelter, 206
CIGNA Healthplan, 62
CIGNA Michael Landon Celebrity Tennis Classics, 65
Circus Lounge, 207
Cirrito, Jaime, 63
Cirrito, Jamie, 188
City of Tucson, 163
Civil Death, 152
Clampetts, 171
Clapton, Eric, 183
Clarion Hotel, 209
Clark, Dale, 96
Clark, Darren, 15
Clark, Toni, 55
Class of 64, 73
Classix, 39
Clayburn, Roy, 38
Clayton, Mr., 68
Cliff Manor, 207
Climenhagg, Joel, 200
Clinton, Bill, 159
Clipman, Will, 119, 130
Club Congress, 15, 29, 31, 37, 64, 75, 92, 136, 140, 144, 146, 157, 162, 171, 179, 185, 186, 192, 195, 207
Club Filharmonico, 35
Club Kaos, 207
Club La Jolla, 25, 169, 207
Club X, 64
Clubhouse, 207
Coasters, 178
Cobb, Allison, 56
Cobras, 75
Cochran, Randy, 43
Cochren, Sallie, 115, 119, 124, 126, 132
Coe, David Allen, 200
Coffee, Etc., 207
Cohen, 177
Coke, Alex, 13

Cole, Gary, 60
Cole, Richie, 13
Colin, Bob, 17
Collette's West, 71, 207
Collins, Albert, 128
Coltrane, John, 13
Comedy Club, 207
Comedy Corner, 46
Comstock Records, 77
Congress Street, 44, 57, 75, 141, 206, 207, 209
Conklin, Steve, 24
Connection, 22
Convertino, John, 40
Conway, Jill, 178
Cook, Cathy, 19
Cooke Cable, 63
Cooke, Sam, 58, 190
Cooke, Shep, 72, 73, 80, 81
Copeland, Kelly, 106
Copland, Aaron, 57
Copper Bowl, 60
Copper State Recording Company, 25, 38
Copperhead Pale Ale, 159
Cordes, Mark, 136
Corkill, Brian, 74
Corliss, Stan, 132
Cormier, Beaux, 139
Corona De Tucson Race Track, 38
Cortez, Harry, 16
Cosmic Boogie Tribe, 50, 76, 168
Cosmic Jackhammer, 50
Costin, Neil, 37
Cotton Eyed Joe, 39
Counterproposal, 130
Country and Western Music Hall of Fame, 52
Country Club Road, 66, 71, 208
Country Kings, 112
Country Knights, 83
Cowboy Fiddlers Hall of Fame, 55
Cowboy Gospel Jamboree, 42
Cowboy's, 207
Cowell, Mitzi, 119
Cowhey, Harriet, 19
Cox, Larry, 80
Coyote's, 41, 136, 138, 207
CPW. See also Central Park West
Cracker Jack, 123
Crash Landing Productions, 90, 123
Cray, Robert, 128, 190
Craycroft Road, 208
Crayon Club, 207
Crazy Heart Band, 83
CreateSpace, 2
Creedence Clearwater Revival, 74

Crist, Joey, 167, 168
Crosby, Stills and Nash, 106
Cross, David, 136
Crossroads, 207
Crowbar, 164
Crystal Palace Playhouse, 66, 207
Crystall, Joe, 23
Crystall, Joseph, 212
Crystall, Martha, 23
Cullen, Ed, 200
Cullen-Kasdan Productions, 198, 200
Cultural Exchange Council, 92
Cultural Exchange Council of Tucson, Inc., 163
Cummins, Chris, 24, 100
Cure, 14
Curtis, Ken, 51
Cushing Street Bar, 93, 95, 109, 130
Cushing Street Bar & Grill, 73
Cushing Street Bar & Restaurant, 121, 207

D

Dabney, Amo Chip, 110
Daily, Pete, 66
Dairy Queen, 66
Daisy Mae's Steakhouse, 207
Dalton, Lacy, 39
Daly, Jan, 130
Damned, 40, 79, 116
Dan Stuart Quartet, 157
Daniel, Jeff, 37
Danson, Ted, 169
Dave Clark Five, 190
Davi, Bob, 26
David, Derick, 10, 186
Davis Monthan Air Force Base, 43
Davis, Chris, 24
Davis, Doug, 13
Davis, Lavernne, 55
Davis, Phil, 128, 172, 176, 187
DB Studios, 29
Dead Line Screamers, 75
Dead Silence, 140
Deadly Amez, 145
Dean Armstrong and the Arizona Dance Hands, 101
Dean, Brian, 183, 185, 202
Dean, Bryan, 190
Dean, Dave, 63
Dean, David, 188
Dearly Beloved, 80, 81
Dee, Joey, 183
DeeJaye, 20

Deep Purple, 22
Déjà Vu Nightclub, 207
Dekara, 75
DeLear, Gillian, 76
DeLeary, David, 50
DeLucia, Ed, 81, 204
DeMarr, James, 32
Demon Records, 40
Denfeld, Mic, 181
Denman, John, 21, 26, 27, 212
Dennis Mitchell and the Wilsons, 50, 99
Department of Journalism, 214
Derringer, Rick, 84
Desert Canyon Rose Band, 21
Desert City Six, 66
Desert Garden Lounge, 207
Desert Inn, 207
Desert Reign, 88, 90, 91, 96
Desert Reign, the tape, 76, 99
Desert Rose, 207
Desert Sons, 101, 132
Devo, 15
Dezo, Mark, 179
Diamond, Lou, 53
Diamond, Neil, 63
Diaz, Rick, 101
Dickey, Debra, 29, 78, 79, 116
Diddley, Bo, 127, 146, 183, 190, 191
Died Pretty, 40
Dietrich, Margo, 169
Dillard's, 56
DiMaggio's, 102
Dion, 88
Dionysus Records, 29, 53, 75, 116
Dirtadian, Armen, 18, 19
Dirtbag's West, 58, 59, 204, 207
Discovery Inn, 207
Disney channel, 58
Disneyland, 28
Do Deo's, 207
Dodajk, 75
Dodajk International, 15, 207
Dog and Pony Show, 186
Doggybag Records, 157
Dolen, Mickey, 178
Doll House, 146
Domineaux Device, 139
Dominguez, Leo, 38
Don Chandler's Lounge, 207
Doobie Brothers, 22
Doors, 40, 79, 81, 89, 116, 146
Dormer, Chris, 171, 192

Dos Locos, 207
Doss, Tommy, 51
Doubletree Hotel, 118, 207, 208, 209
DoubleTree Lounge, 207
Dover Trench, 50, 76, 103
Dow, Tommy, 152
Downtown Performance Center, 75, 97, 103, 138, 140, 145, 164, 180, 195, 207
Downtown Saturday Night, 37, 75, 90
Dr. Crayola and the Sophomores, 89
Dr. Demento, 42
Drachman Street, 207, 209
Drakes, 168, 185
Dread Zeppelin, 175
Drexel Road, 206
Driftwood Lounge, 207
Drinking Gourd, 88, 207
Droopy Gopher, 200
Drop Dead Records, 98
Dudas, Steve, 129
Duncan, Daniel, 177
Dunes, 67
Dunlop, Cathy, 129, 136, 139, 165, 175
Dunlop, Elizabeth, 165
Dunn, Andrew, 84, 85
Dunn, Ron, 46
Dunn, Suzie, 175
Dupont, Christopher, 83
Durrell, Kenny, 38
Dusty Chaps, 43
Dusty Roads, 83
Dylan, Bob, 72, 178

E

Eagle, Bill, 67, 68
Eagles, 151
Earl's Family, 75
Easterbrook, Jim, 101, 132
Eastwood, Clint, 58, 107
Easy Street Lounge, 21, 27, 207
Eat to the Beat, 64
Eberlein, Eb, 44
Economidis, Greg, 185
Eddie's Cocktails, 83, 84, 101, 207
Eden, Barbara, 58
Edmonson, Earl, 95, 199
Edmonson, Travis, 198, 200
Edmonton Trappers, 155
Edward, Bob, 146
Edwards, Don, 101
Edwards, Mike, 138, 146, 185
Eisenhower, Dwight D., 67
El Casino Ballroom, 207

El Centro Bar & Grill, 152, 207
El Con Mall, 57, 62, 67, 118, 210
El Mariachi, 140, 207
El Mesquital, 40, 207
El Parador, 141, 207
El Presidio, 82
El Presidio Historic District, 82
El Presidio Park, 44, 92, 163
Elbow Room, 207
Electric Ballroom, 193
Electric Light Orchestra, 166
Electric Prunes, 79
Elegance Car Club, 92
Elektra Entertainment, 33, 35
Elektra Records, 120
Elia, Paul, 146, 204
Elks Lodge, 21, 27
Ellington, Duke, 13
Elm Street, 206
Elmer's Pub, 207
Embassy Suites, 12, 207
Emery, Ralph, 36
EMI Records, 120
EMOL.org, 2, 181, 203
Energy Records, 164
Engle, David, 170
English Cathy, 136, 139, 165, 175
English, Anne, 81
English, Steve, 29
Enriquez, Demitri, 175, 191
Ensign Records, 69
Ensign/Chrysalis Records, 75
Entertainment Magazine, 2, 3, 13, 24, 26, 30, 39, 50, 53, 58, 59, 76, 88, 90, 99, 144, 181, 204, 212, 213, 214
Entertainment Magazine On Line, 2, 181, 203
Entertainment Travel Business, 77
Epiphany Records, 196
Ernie's, 150
Escalante, Claudio, 156
Espinel, Luisa (Ronstadt), 35
Estefan, Gloria, 97
Estrada, Erick, 65
Euclid Avenue, 208, 210
Everywhere West, 132
Ewers, Faye, 83
Executive Inn, 207
Exile, 53, 61
Eye Pennies, 157
Eye, Steve, 75, 180

F

FABCO Enterprises, 30, 31
Fabulous Fifties Fiesta, 165
Face Records, 116
Faded Images, 99
Fahey, John, 81, 89
Faires, Jay, 70
Fake McCoys, 145
Falinski, Paul, 11
Fall From Grace, 97, 98, 103, 114, 185
Faltin, Craig, 37
Famous Sam's, 58, 179, 207
Famous Sam's #3, 100, 113
Famous Sam's #6, 100
Fara, Frank, 77
Farr, Hugh, 51
Farr, Karl, 51
Favron, Gary, 16
Faye Anne's Memory Lane, 16, 21, 27, 207
Feast of St. Agustine, 156
Feder, Mike, 154
Fells, 75
Ferron, 109
Ferrone, Len, 21, 27, 67, 212
Ferrugia, Thomas, Jr., 193
Ferrugla, T.J., 161
Festival in the Sun, 57
FHP Health Care, 126
Fiden, Bob, 70
fiesta, 156, 207
Fiesta de los Sentidos, 15
Fiesta de los Vaqueros, 56
Fiesta del Presidio, 15
Fine Stream, 123, 175
Fine, Pete, 11
Fine, Sam, 212
Fineline, 180, 207
Finnegan's, 12, 207
Finstrom, Matt, 90
Fintel, Dave, 65, 119
Fire and Fury Records, 183
FireFox, 181
Firehouse, 99, 207
Fireworks Festival, 1990, 24
Fisher, Eldonna, 11
Fisher, Paul and Muriel, 165
Fisher, Shug, 51
Fisherman, 62
Fixx, 82
Flagstaff Lumberjack, 44
Flannery, Mike, 45, 120
Fleetwood, Mick, 74
Fleming, Alisa, 60, 71
Fleshworld, 175
Fligg, Keith, 10
Floating House Band, 81
Floating Opera, 89
Flock of Seagulls, 84, 90

Flow, 191
Flowing Wells Community Effort Council, 83
Flowing Wells Road, 206
Flying Cossacks, 56
Flying J Wranglers, 101
Flying V, 207
Flying W Wranglers, 42, 101
Flynn & Flynn Music, 188
Flys, 146
Fogelberg, Dan, 109
Fogerty, John, 74
Foley, Jim, 199
Folk Alliance, 129
Foot of Black Mountain, 156
foot of the Black Mountain, 157
Foothills Center, 208
Forans, Kevin, 99
Forbes Travel Guide, 137
Forbidden Pigs, 62
Ford, Mary, 22
Ford, Tennessee Ernie, 36
Fort Lowell Depot, 83, 105
Fortress Records, 99
Foundation for the Extension and Development of the American Professional Theatre, 49
Four Gents, 112
Four Leaf Clover Productions, 36
Four Pigs, 175, 191
Fourth Avenue, 153
Fourth Avenue Social Club, 119, 157, 162, 165, 207
Fourth Avenue Street Fair, 167
Fox, 89
Foxy's Café & Lounge, 207
Fraidy Cats, 157
Frank Ace Combo, 169
Frank Ace Trio, 25
Frank and Woody, 38
Frank Lloyd Vinyl, 179
Franklin, Aretha, 147
Franklin, Ben, 74
Frederick, 21, 27
French Quarter, 207
Fridkin, Dennis, 11
Friedman & Jobusch, 68
Frost, Robert, 10
Ft. Lowell Depot, 121, 207
Ft. Lowell Road, 83, 207
Ft. Lowell Shopping Center, 166
Fuentes, Ruben, 33
Fuller, Craig, 35
Funky Bonz, 157, 175, 176, 179, 186, 191

Furno, Joe, 50, 53, 76
Fuzzy's, 207
FX, 63

G

Gainey Ranch Hyatt, 177
Galaxy Brothers, 11
Gamelan, 175
Garces, Francisco, 156, 157
Garcia, Pete, 171, 192
Garcia. Johnny, 185
Gargoyle's, 166, 207
Garnelan, 123
Garrecht, Sarah, 129
Gary Pucket and The Union Gap, 178
Gary Rust and The Country Kings, 112
Gaslight Theatre, 18, 89
Gaspar, Jim, 146
Gassen, Scott, 29
Gassen, Timothy, 29, 53, 79, 116
Gates Pass, 42
Gates Pass Steakhouse, 207
Gavin Report, 144
Gelb, Howe, 40, 196
Gelb, Ricky, 48
General Delivery, 72, 81
Generations, 73, 74, 83, 91, 207
Genesis, 115
Gentle Ben's, 13, 67, 110, 138, 158, 159, 161, 179, 185, 192, 208
Gentlemen After Dark, 186
George Howard and the Roadhouse Hounds, 127, 185, 187, 190
George, Stefan, 93, 103, 130, 175, 185, 212
Georgie & the Starlighters, 58
Gerard, Kevin, 115
Geronimoz, 208
Gerroll, Daniel, 57
Get Hip Label, 116
Get Hip Records, 29, 53
Giacomazza, Carl, 212
Giannetta, Monique, 16
Giant Sand, 40, 48, 62, 196
Gila Bend, 37, 50, 62, 92, 116, 152, 157, 179
Gilbert's Plush Horse Pub, 208
Gilkison, Eliza, 109
Gillespie, Dizzy, 13, 198, 200
Gilmore, Ralph, 95, 199
Ginger, 186
Gladys Knight and the Pips, 183
Glassen, Jim, 39
Glitterhouse Records, 197

Global Village Nightclub, 209
Glombecki, Gerry, 195, 198, 199, 200, 201, 212
Glover, Fritz, 66
Gold Hill Inn, 135
Goldberg, David, 74
Goldberg, E.L., 188
Golf Links Road, 27, 84, 206, 208, 209
Gomez, Richard, 72, 185, 190
Gonzales, 208
Gonzales, Luis, 154
Gonzalez, Nicole, 57, 58
Gonzalez-Gonzalez, Pedro, 86
Good News Newspaper, 133
Goodberry, Dan, 21
Goodman, Benny, 11
Goodman, Steve, 199
Goodrich Tires, 183
Gordon, Dave, 105
Gordon, Robert, 185
Gordon, Stephan, 186
Gordon, Tony, 14
Gore, Tipper, 98
Gosdin, Vern, 101
Gothic Swank, 176, 179
Gould, Leslie, 112
Gouramie Records, 172, 176
Grace Chapel, 186
Graffiti's, 208
Graham, Sylvia, 120
Grain of Salt, 43
Grammy Hall of Fame, 52
Grams, Steve, 199
Granada Avenue, 207
Granfalloon Saloon, 208
Grant Road, 206, 208, 209, 210
Grant Road Pub, 114, 144, 146, 171, 192, 208
Grant, Rex, 45, 120
Grass Roots, 178
Grateful Dead, 78
Graves, Todd, 97
Gravity Man, 123
Gray, Simon, 57
Greco, Mickey, 21, 27
Green Dolphin, 63, 164, 167, 208
Green on Red, 136, 157
Greenspoon, Jimmy, 77, 78, 151
Grey, Troy, 139
Griffith, Jim, 92
Grimble Wedge, 123, 138, 157, 164, 174, 176
Gross, Chuck, 204
Grubsteak, 208
Guerrero, Lalo, 92
Guitar Player, 194, 195

Guitars, Etc., 152
Gulezian, Michael, 194
Gulotta, James, 185
Gunga Din, 138, 161, 164, 172, 174, 176
Gus & Andy's, 21, 27, 67, 208
Guthrie, Woody, 201

H

Haas, Chuck, 46
Hacienda del Sol Guest Ranch, 208
Hacienda del Sol Road, 208
Hackensack, 13
Hadley, Bob, 89
Hager, Michael, 212
Haggard, Marty, 39
Haggard, Merle, 111
Halitosis, 179
Halper, Bruce, 69, 186
Hamilton, Fonda, 152
Hamilton, Michael, 28, 46, 52
Hammes, Tom, 179, 196
Hammett, Rebecca, 48
Hampton Inn, 208
Hancock, Herbie, 146
Handlin, Gus, 39
Hankai Electric Tramway, 153
Hardy, Heather, 183, 199, 202, 204
Harold Ramsey & Associates, 32
Harp and Shamrock, 208
Harrigan, Dan, 103
Harris, 33
Harris, Emmylou, 35, 39, 82, 83, 116
Harris, Phil, 67
Harrison, Clint, 21, 27
Harrison, John, 67
Harrison, Lois, 27
Harry, Neil, 43, 195
Haskell, Jeff, 26
Hatch, Mike, 199
Havalinas, 62
Hawke, George, 95
Hawkins, Chris, 50, 76
Hayans, Michelle, 162
Hayduke, George, 198, 199
Hayes, Fred, 37
Haynes, Michelle, 168
Head, Jim, 179, 196
Heart of Steele Band, 83
Heat, 167
Hec & Wink's, 101, 102, 104, 120, 124, 125, 128, 179, 204, 208
Hegarty, Mike, 46
Helen Hammer, 37, 50, 76
Hendrix, Jimi, 87, 193, 195
Henry, Butch, 16

Herberger Theatre Center, 49
Herman's Hermits, 190
Hernandez, Bob, 125, 128
Herrera, Bobby, 31
Hi Busse and the Frontiersman, 101
Hi Corbett Field, 154
Hidden Valley Inn, 87, 208
Hideout, 208
High Fidelity, 195
High Noon, 101
High Noon Saloon, 102, 208
High Plains Drifters, 36
High Society Five, 67
Hillerman, Tony, 50, 53
Hilton East Hotel, 208
Hilton Inn, 210
Himmel Park, 44
Hirsh, Larry, 143
Hobbs, James, 180
Hockings, Jim, 66, 67, 68
Hohokam Indians, 157
Holiday Inn Holidome, 208
Holiday Inn Palo Verde, 132
Holliday, Billie, 128
Hollis, Duane, 157, 165
Hollis, Jack, 67
Holloway, Red, 13
Holly, Buddy, 56, 74, 116
Holman, Paul Gary Leonard, 63
Holmes, Peter, 24
Holzer Katherine, 66
Home Den, 208
Homestead Records, 40
Hoodoo Gurus, 40
Hoodoo Kings, 185
Hook, John, 177
Hooker, John Lee, 127, 191
Hope Thieves, 99
Hope, Bob, 39
Hopkins, Rich, 69, 143, 144, 168
Horse 'n Round, 208
Host, 15, 20
Hostetler, David, 17, 123
Hot Pursuit, 21, 162
Houghton Road, 208, 210
Houlihan's, 98, 113, 208
House of Blues, 198
House of Fabrics, 62, 118
Houston Astros, 154, 170
Houston Expos, 170
Howard Johnson's, 210
Howard, George, 127, 185, 187, 189, 190
Howling Wolf, 190
Howsare, Timothy, 103, 108
HTML, 181
Huayucaltia, 208
Hudson, Gary, 65

Hudson, Mark, 129
Hudson, Virginia, 133
Hulstedt, Eric, 161, 171, 193, 194
Humphrey, Paul, 55
Hunnewell, Pennie, 50, 76
Hunter, Peter, 147, 154
Hurricanes, 94
Hutch's, 208
Hyatt, Michael, 111
Hyde, Mike, 114
Hyderman, Kevin, 179
Hyper Text Mark Up Language, 181

I

IBM, 50
Ice Cream Headache, 168
Ice Nine, 76
Iglesias, Julio, 125
Igor's Cowboy Jazz Band, 101
Ike and the Aces, 183
Illusions, 208
Impact, 136, 138, 140
Impoppable, 175
In Cahoots, 208
In Your Face Horns, 53, 58
Ina Road, 166, 208, 209, 210, 211
International Death Stomp, 174
Invisible Records, 133
Invisible Theatre, 57
Ireland's Post Time Pub, 208
Irvington Road, 56
Isaaks, Chris, 62
Isla Tiberon, 166
Isla Tiburon, 162, 192, 208
Issachs, Bud, 101
Itchy Scratchy, 50, 76
Itsy Bitsy Spiders, 176

J

J.C. Skinner, 111, 112
J.J. Nickels, 208
Jack Cavan's Riverboat Six, 66
Jacks, 112
Jackson, Earl, 171
Jackson, Hal, 110
Jackson, Herb, 60
Jackson, Millie, 58
Jacob, Daniel, 142
Jacob, Dianne, 141
Jacob, Donald, 142
Jacob, John, 141, 142
Jacob, Loretta, 142
Jagger, 183
Jagiello, Greg, 17, 81, 90, 99, 123
Jaguar, 183

Jaime, Hector, 99
Jaime's Bar & Grill, 138, 144, 157, 162, 204, 208
Jaime's Revenge, 41
Jamaica Bay, 208
James, Etta, 128, 190
James, James and Frank, 36
James, Michael, 16
James, Steve, 201
Jane, Mary, 67
Jane's Addiction, 138
Jankowski, Bob, 118
Janos, 134, 135
Japanese Kitchen, 61, 165, 208
Jargo, Si, 162, 164, 171, 186
Jarvis, Francesca, 156
Javelina Cantina, 208
Jazz Logic, 37
Jazz Menagerie, 26
Jazz Night Downtown, 75
Jazz Terrorists, 26, 37
Jazzberry Jam, 152
Jed Paradies and the Jazz Terrorists, 37
Jeff's Pub, 101, 113, 208
Jeff's Pub, Camino Seco, 88, 102
Jefferson Airplane, 89, 107
Jeffrey, Dave, 152
Jeffries, Dave, 104
Jellyfish, 62
Jennings, Waylon, 198, 200
Jenott, Jerry, 60
Jerome's, 137
Jester's Court, 67
Jin's Sneak Joint, 16, 20
Joaquin Brothers', 163
Job Corps, 68
Joe & Vicky's Place, 208
Joe Rush & Right Now, 196
Joe Rush and Right Now, 175
Joey Dee and the Starliters, 203
John Denman Quartet, 26
John, Elton, 104
Johnnie's Drive-In, 47
Johnny Balls, 157
Johnny Garcia Band, 185
Johnson, Brian, 99, 133
Johnson, Kennard, 189
Johnson, Lyndon, 65
Johnson, Robert, 128, 190
Johnson, Robin, 186
Johnson, Sandra, 120, 125
Johnson, Scott, 114
Jones Brothers, 90, 123
Jones, George, 111
Jones, Plato, 63, 188
Joplin, Janis, 178
Jorgenson, Elaine, 64
Joseph, Lee, 29

Juden, Jeff, 154

K

K.A.L.R., 162
K.V. & Band, 114
Kaiser, 136
Kaiser, Fred, 153
Kakascik, Suzie, 146
Kalil, Frank, 25
Kappy's, 208
karaoke, 113
Karen, Garth, 179
Keane, Bill, 200
Keaton's, 208
KEDJ-FM, 171
Keel, Andy, 41
Keel, Tom, 41
Keeylocko, 50
Keith, Kevin, 114
Keleher, Jim, 96
Kelly, Shawn, 139
Kelly, Tim, 185
Kennedy Center For The Performing Arts, 105
Kennedy, John F., 73
Kennedy, Tom, 175, 191
Kenny Durell Band, 101
Kept in the Dark Records, 17, 123
Kerr, Darren, 171, 192
Kessler, Bob, 137, 138
Kessler, Esta, 137
Key to Arizona Local Rock, 162
KGUN-TV, 166
KGVY-AM, 23, 54
KHHR-TV, 130
Kidd Squidd, 107, 182
Kimmel, Bob, 34
Kimsey, Jerome, 187
Kinetic Vibes, 130
King, 183
King Crimson, 136
King Earnest, 185
King Ernest and the Wild Knights, 204
King, B.B., 58, 72, 190, 198
King, David, 87
Kinney Road, 21, 210
Kino, Eusebio Francisco, 119
Kinsey, Jerome, 172, 176, 183, 202
Kittrell, Leon, 178
KKLD-FM, 144
Kleespie, Thomas, 177
KLPX-FM, 24, 115, 175, 185, 192
KMSB-TV, 50
Knowles, Marlene, 17
Kolb Road, 166, 210
KOLD-TV, 54
Kon Tiki, 148, 208

Kool & the Gang, 166
KOOL-FM, 61, 74
Koplin, Kelly, 38
Kort, Brent, 175, 186, 191
Koshmideron, Rosemary, 55
Kottke, Leo, 195
Kotzambasis, Sandra, 177
Koz, John, 76
Krider, Dylan, 177, 178
Kristofferson, Kris, 198, 200
KTKT-AM, 25
KTKT-FM, 24
KTUC-AM, 71
KUAT-TV, 177, 178
Kuhn, Bill, 152
Kuhn, Mike, 104, 120, 152
KUPD-FM, 165, 192
KVOA-TV, 177
KVOI-AM, 133
KWFM-FM, 44
Kwiatkowski, Ladmo, 177
KXCI-FM, 15, 44, 60, 71, 99, 101, 107, 130, 142, 164, 182, 189, 199
KZRX-FM, 139

L

L Mondo Combo, 37
La Cañada Drive, 208
La Cholla Blvd., 208
La Fiesta de San Agustin, 126, 156
La Frontera Center, 62
La Fuente, 208
La Placita Café, 208
La Placita Village, 208
La Sota, Kim, 181
La Vista Lounge, 208
Lacey, Sean, 21
Laff's Comedy Night Club, 208
Lain, Eddie, 67
Lalo's, 208
Landon, Cindi, 118
Landon, Michael, 62, 65, 118, 212
Lanham, Roy, 51
Lariat Lounge, 40, 208
Larkins, Tommy, 157
Laser Karaoke, 113
Last Round Up Band, 83
Last Territory, 208
Latin Express, 175
Laughlin, Eddie, 167
Lawlor Events Center, 151
Lazy Bones, 176
Lazy V, 208
Leadbelly, 190, 194
Leavenworth, Brett, 89
Led Zeppelin, 193
Lee, 185
Lee, Frankie, 204

Lee, Gina, 24, 100
Lee, Katie, 101
Lee, Peggy, 72
Leech, Craig, 114
LeKawa, Dave, 178
Lennon, John, 74, 183
Leonard Hall Naval Academy Band, 73
Leonard, Johnny, 38
Leprechaun, 166, 208
Leroy, JoAnna, 38
Lester Street, 207, 209, 210
Leukemia Society of America, 118
Levin, Hal, 19
Levitz Furniture Co., 149
Lewallen Brothers, 38, 102
Lewallen, Timothy, 212
LFC, Inc. Foundation, 62
Li'l Abner's Steak House, 54, 208
Liberty Recording, 186
Licavoli, Peter, 64
Life Magazine, 65
Lightning & Prism Productions, 170
Like Minded Idiots, 162
Lipson, Jim, 103, 119, 130
Litteer, Scott, 167
Little Anthony's, 208
Little Britches, 208
Little Eva, 88
Little Sisters of the Poor, 186
Little, Vernon, 99
Lizarraga, Danny, 171, 192
Llorenz, Juan Bautista, 119
Lobo Rangers, 101, 132
Loco Records, 172
Loew's Ventaña Canyon, 21, 27, 60, 207
Loews Ventaña Canyon, 206
Loghry, Douglas, 172, 174
Lommel, Tom, 67
Long Island Music Hall of Fame, 204
Long John Baldry, 136
Long Wong's, 157, 161, 208
Longbranch Saloon, 208
Lookout Lounge, 20, 166, 208
Lopez, David, 26
Los Angeles Dodgers, 170
Los Chanquitos Feos, 15
Los Elegantes, 186
Los Familias, 62, 65
Los Lasers, 37, 95, 114
Los Lobos, 118, 143
Los Mayas, 208
Los Parachicos, 126
Lost Prophet, 76
Loumeau, Greg, 133
Love, Bob, 212

Love, Randy, 29
Low Max, 48
Lucky Dollar, 28, 31, 208
Luminurios, 168
Lupo, Jeff, 24, 100
Lux, Violet, 66
Lynch, Dan, 45, 120, 144
Lynd, Gordan, 39
Lynn, Jeff, 28
Lynn, Loretta, 32

M

Mac's Place, 61, 101, 166, 208
MacArchick, Johnny, 48
Machines of Loving Grace, 168
MacIntire, John, 65
MacWilliams, Skip, 72
Maddalozzo, Steve, 186
Madman Productions, 186
Magazine, 3, 214
Magee, Dan, 29
Magee, Sharon, 33
Mages, Mike, 133, 162
Mahon, Bobby, 36, 50, 76
Main Avenue, 15, 82, 134
Main Street, 210
Maine Course, 125
Major Lingo, 37, 119
Malaby, Tony, 13
Malone, Seamus, 130
Mama Ritmo, 140, 145
Mammoth Records, 70
Maniac Kill, 138, 146, 185
Maniac Records, 128
Mantis, 136, 138
Many Hands Courtyard, 44
Manzanita, 37
Mapes, Geri, 101
Maranatha School, 68
Marco, Joe, 66
Margolies, Lee, 177
Maria's, 185
Marley, Bob, 188
Marley, Rita, 122
Marley, Ziggy, 122
Marquees, 46
Marquez, Xavier, 26, 63
Marquez, Xavier, 188
Marsalis, Branford, 37
Marshal KGUN, 212
Marshall, Heather, 15, 20, 21
Marshmallow Overcoat, 20, 29, 40, 50, 53, 75, 79, 116
Martin, Doug, 125, 128
Martinez, Joe, 89
Marty Allen Band, 21
Maryott, Cantrell, 119
Mason Jar, 41
Mason, Dave, 84
Masterson, Jeff, 185, 190

Masterson, Liz, 101, 132
Maultsby, Chuck, 43
Maultsby, Sharon, 43
Maverick King of Clubs, 94, 96, 112, 131, 208
Maxi Priest, 188
McAndrew, Patrick, 212
McCabe, Leanne, 40
McCain, Buck, 86
McCallion, Nancy, 151
McCann, Mary, 145
McCanon, Rupe, 67
McCarthy, Declan, 31
McCartney, Paul, 74
McCauley, Pat, 20
McDonald, Bob, 67
McDonald, Mike, 172, 174
McDowell, Rody, 39
McGraw's Cantina, 208
McGuire's Saloon, 39, 208
McLaughlin Broadcast Services, 144
McLaughlin, Alan, 144
McMahan, Gary, 101
McMahon, Pat, 177
McMufflin, Ev, 120
McPherson, Charles, 13
McReynolds, Randy, 90, 172
McWilliams, Skip, 102
Megaw, Peter, 13
Meighan, Bob, 72, 95
Mello, Lenny, 152, 157
Mellon, Mark, 57
Men of the West, 86
Menagerie, 133
Mendoza, Ernie, 79
Menius, Art, 129
Mercy Seat, 75, 99
Merrill, Erick, 24
Metallica, 192
Meyer Street, 141, 207
Meyers, Wendi, 133
Micha's, 209
Michaels, Ardy, 114
Mickey Greco Quartet, 27
Mikulik, Joe, 170
Miller Brewing Co., 183
Miller, Jon, 136, 138, 140
Miller, Orlando, 170
Miller, Reggie, 47
Milsap, Ronnie, 111
Milwaukee Brewers, 170
Ministry, 64
Minus 1 Café, 124
Minus 9, 123
Miracle Mile Strip, 208, 209
Mirage, 209
Mirror Mirror, 50
Mission Road, 40, 207
Mississippi Delta players, 194
Mitchell, Dennis, 99

Mobil Travel Guide, 137, 149, 150
Mock, Earl, 55
Moe, Rick, 99
Mofford, Rose, 48, 49
Molly Who..., 81
Mollys, 81, 151, 152, 175, 199
Mollys & McGuire, 50
Momma Stud, 62
Mondo Guano, 21, 75
Mondragon, Mike, 145
Mongellis, 185
Monk, Theloneus, 13
Monkees, 178
Monroy, Miguel, 115
Monsoons, 193
Montana Blue & The Big Sky Cowboys, 132
Montana, Patsy, 42, 101
Monte V, 46, 192, 209
Montgomery Ward, 57
Monton, James, 170
Moonlight Ramblers, 111
Moonstruck, 209
Moreira, Airto, 73
Morganfield, Megha, 168
Morin, Tim, 42, 93
Moses, Agnes, 18, 19, 57
moshing, 186
Motorcycle Music Festival, 192
Mount Lemmon Blues Festival, 127
Mountain Pig, 50, 76
Mousey Award, 203
Mox, Dan, 113
Moxie Entertainment, 113
Mozilla, 181
Mr. Catfish, 209
Msatson, Mark, 194
Mt. Lemmon, 44, 200
Mt. Lemmon Alpine Lodge, 208
MTV, 44, 53
Mudbuggs, 14, 17, 20, 37, 41, 42, 64, 68, 75, 84, 209
Muddy Waters, 22, 128, 190
Muller Music, 152
Muñiz, David, 128, 172, 176, 186, 187
Munoz, Omar, 81
Munson, Arvid, 152
Murphy, John, 10, 99
Murphy, Michael Martin, 101, 105
Murphy, Pat, 104
Musgrove, Verlon, 25
Music Box Lounge, 113, 209
Music Maniac, 130
Music Voice Magazine, 139, 144, 186

Musicade, 16
Musician's Institute of L.A., 44
Musiker, Av, 171
Musselwhite, Charlie, 127, 191
Muzzy Braun and the Boys, 101

N

Naked Prey, 152
Nam Nam Records, 32
Namesake Series, 145
Napkins, 15
National Academy of Television Arts and Sciences, 177
National Organization for the Reform of Marijuana Laws, 164
National Tombstone Epitaph, 68
Naughty, Hans, 97
NBC-TV, 105
Neal, Kenny, 189
Neal, Wally, 66
Necropolis, 138
Needham, Sybil, 156
Nelson, Willie, 43, 83, 198, 200
Neon Moon, 166, 187, 209
Neon Prophet, 63, 90, 120, 123, 136, 152, 175, 188
Neptune, John John, 30, 31
Nevada Smith's Saloon, 122, 209
Neville, Aaron, 33, 35
Nevilles, 111
Nevin, Phil, 154, 170
New Artist Concert Series, 20
New Bohemians, 109
New Circus Lounge, 209
New Loft Theatre, 17
New Orleans Lounge, 157, 162, 164, 167, 168, 174, 175, 176, 192, 209
New Orleans West, 209
New Potatoes, 152
New Seekers, 81
New Union Ramblers, 34
Newman, Francesca, 39
Newman, Ilana, 46
Newman, Mark, 212
Newport, Rick, 120
Newsreal, 103
Nicholas, Nick, 51, 54, 101
Nicholson, Jack, 103
Nicholson, Rik, 17, 123
Nickel Creek, 132
Nigerian All Stars, 114
Night Crossings, 16
Night Shift Tavern, 209
Night Train, 119, 209

Night Watch, 124, 128
Nightlites, 209
Nilsen, Norm, 168
Nilsen, Norm Jr., 167
Nino's, 209
Niyah, Zebbhi, 122
Nogales Highway, 206, 209, 210
Nogueira, Manuel, 114
Nolan Spencer Foundation, 42
Nolan, Bob, 51
Nolaz Bar, 128
Nordberg, Mike, 183, 202, 204
Nordine, Jean, 105
NORML/Rock for Pot Tour '93, 164
Norteño Music Festival, 94
North American Folk Music and Dance Alliance, 129
North China, 117
Nossem, Ed, 167
Novak, Ralph, 34
November Criminals, 144, 162
November Guest, 10
Nowhere Dreamer, 138
NueVenue, 209
Nugent, Ted, 43
Nuttall, Joel, 164

O

O.J. Ekemode and the Nigerian All Stars, 114
O.K. Chorale, 101, 132
O.K. Corral, 66
O'Connor, Sinead, 69
O'Connor, Tim, 93, 94, 114
O'Conor, Hugo, 82, 156, 157
O'Gorman, Chris, 10, 99, 133
O'Gorman, Scott, 99, 133
O'Haire, Bob, 55
O'Hern, Jeffrey, 133
O'Malley's, 176, 193, 209
O'Shaughnessy's, 16, 209
Oakland A's, 154
Oakridge Boys, 106
Oasis, 209
Obsessions Night Club, 209
Ockham's Razor, 162, 171, 174, 192
Oden, Josie, 180
Offret, Dennis, 199
Old Father Inn, 209
Old Main, 69
Old Pueblo Jazz Band, 66
Old Pueblo Trolley, 153
Old Spanish Trail, 208

Old Time Fiddler's Contest, 55
Old Town Artisans, 82
Old Town School of Music, 198
Old Tucson, 27, 42, 77, 101, 179
Oliver, David, 179
Olson, Hans, 145
Olson, Michael and Wendy, 179, 185
Olson, Mike, 93, 140
One Blood, 109, 114, 179
One to One (1-2-1), 115
One Way Productions, 168
One-Eyed Jack's, 174, 175, 176, 192, 209
Open Inn, Inc., 62, 65
Open Season, 76
OPJB, 66
Oracle Road, 27, 57, 206, 208, 209, 210, 211
Orange Grove Road, 207
Orbison, Roy, 89
Organ Donors, 76
Oriental Garden, 113, 209
Origin, 90
Original Delta Slider Blues Bottleneck, 195, 198
Original Jacks, 38
Ortez, Frank, 180
Osbourne, Ira, 110
OSH II Productions, 76
Out of Nowhere, 26
Outback, 166, 175, 177, 209
Outlaw, 209
Overcoat, 53, 75, 76, 78, 79, 90, 116, 123, 129
Owens, Buck, 195

P

P.D.Q. Records, 17
Pacific Beach Club, 20, 209
Pacific Coast League, 154, 170
Pagliaro, Nicole, 22
Pakulis, Kevin, 93, 94, 114
Paladians, 62
Palm Rock, 114, 209
Palo Verde Road, 132, 207, 208, 210
Palomino Restaurant, 209
Pananler, Dave, 24
Pancho's, 209
Panico, Mark, 29
Panico, Mike, 78, 79, 116, 123
Pantano Road, 27, 102, 124, 207, 208, 210
Pantano Stables, 172
Pants Palace, 56
Papion's II, 185

Papp, Joseph, 33
Paradies, Jed, 26, 37
Park Avenue, 14, 56, 208, 209, 210
Park Inn, 206, 210
Park Mall, 195, 206
Parker, Patty, 77
Parmenter, Doug, 44
Parton, Dolly, 33, 35
Passionflies, 50, 76, 81, 90, 123
Paul Thomas Productions, 136, 138, 140
Paul, Les, 22
Paulo's Restaurant, 100, 209
Paulos, 117
PDQ Records, 17
Peaches, 187
Pearl Jam, 146, 183
Peckinpaw, Sam, 200
Pegheads, 114
Pegram, Rick, 171
Pennington Street, 75, 211
People, 11
People Magazine, 34
Pepin, Art, 66
Pepper, Jessica, 116
Peppermint Lounge, 183
Perkins Studio, 152
Perkins, Carl, 88, 89
Perkins, Steve, 152
Perrodin, Mark, 69, 81
Perry, Al, 90, 92, 114, 116, 136, 146, 152, 157, 165, 168, 179, 185, 191, 195
Perryman, Lloyd, 51
Persian Gulf, 60
Pet The Fish, 179
Petkovsek, Mike, 174
Petty, Tom, 143
Philadelphia Pub, 209
Phoenix Firebirds, 170
Phoenix Symphony Orchestra, 107
Phy Bai Phor, 112
Pickens, Slim, 86
Pie Allen Neighborhood Association, 105
Pifer, Chris, 133
Pills, 186
Pima College Jazz Band, 67
Pima Community College, 14, 89, 163, 180, 181
Pima Community College Journalism Department, 214
Pima Community College Proscenium Theater, 165
Pima County Amateur Champion, 18
Pima County Fair, 62, 118

Pima County Fairgrounds, 61, 118
Pima County Health Department, 114
Pima Road, 207
Piman Indians, 119
Pink Cadillac Café, 75, 209
Pink'es, 209
Pioneer Days Celebration, 55
Pioneer Trio, 51
Pizza City, 49, 98, 152, 174
Plant, Robert, 165
Plastic Museum, 161, 171, 193
Plaza Bar, 209
Plaza de Armas, 82
Plaza Hotel, 209
Plowman, Dick, 180
Plumer Avenue, 210
Poco Loco, 209
Podglarski, Rita, 185
Poetry Band, 10
Pollack Advertising, 152
Pollo Elastico, 24
Pollock, Terry, 152
Polymur Records, 193, 194
Poppies, 112
Porter, Rick, 113
Porter's House, 113, 209
Posies, 62
Post Time Pub, 208, 209
Postal History Foundation, 68
Power 1490 AM, 114
Prairie Rose, 132
Presely, Elvis, 178
Presidio de San Agustin del Tucson, 157
Presidio Theatre Company, 156
Presley, Elvis, 63, 74, 88, 89, 178
Preston, Billy, 104
Preston, Cass, 21, 27
Preston, Janet, 21
Price Club, 142
Primal Urge, 144
Prince Road, 207, 209
Privett, Tom, 146
Prodigy, 50
Professional Rodeo Cowboys' Association, 56
Project Choki, 126
Propaganda Child, 175, 176, 186
Prophecy, 138, 140
Prudence Strude, 22
Psycho Beat, 50
Psychotic Jester, 171, 174
Ptacek, Rainer, 212
Puckett, Gary, 89
Puckett, Scott, 99
Pueblo Inn, 206, 209, 210

Puku Puku Lounge and Taco Bar, 209
Pulse, 37, 76, 93, 103, 140, 145, 179, 185
Purim, Flora, 73
Purple Merkins, 116, 157
Putney's Street Pub, 209
Pyper, Hal, 12, 20

Q

Quality Inn, 113
Quick Draws, 66
Quincy's, 209
Quinn, Ron, 228
Quiros, Jay, 44

R

Radical 2, 50
Radio Ground Zero, 90
Radisson Suites, 206
Rails, 176
Rain Convention, 174, 179
Raina Corp., 169
Rainbow Moods, 71, 109
Rainer, 146
Rainer and Das Combo, 95
Raines, Steve, 84, 87, 88
Raitt, 183
Ramada Airport, 208
Ramada Inn, 101, 207
Ramone, Joey, 103
Ramones, 98, 103
Ramsey, Buck, 132
Ramsey, Mike, 38, 102
Rancho Del Rio, 149
Randall, Sean, 116
Randolph Tennis Center, 118
Randy Love, 29
Rascals, 89
Rather, Dan, 62
Ray, Rick, 120
RCA Records, 69, 70, 96, 149
Real Deal, 45, 120, 125, 147, 148, 173, 179, 184, 202, 204
Record World, 195
Red Cat Amber, 158, 159
Red Hot Chile Peppers, 146
Redd Kross, 62
Redding, 184
Redding, Otis, 146, 204
Redhouse-Hauer, Mary, 26
Reel, 209
Reel, James, 145
Reeve, Don, 89, 90, 123, 165
Reflection, 175
Reflex, 120
Reform School, 165
Reiber, Marlin, 24
Reinsmen, 42, 101, 132

Relatives, 124, 125, 128
Rembrandts, 140, 144
Remo, 64
Reno-Coley, Sally, 101, 105, 107
Replacements, 133
Resort Drive, 206, 207
Revolting Cocks, 64
Rex Allen Arizona Cowboy Museum, 86
Rex Allen Days, 86
Reynolds, Bob, 22
Reynolds, Gregg, 126
Reynolds, Shane, 154, 170
Rheaume, Joe, 172, 174
Rhoades, Spyder, 37
Rialto's, 209
Richards, Keith, 143
Richards, Rusty, 101, 132
Rick Porter's House, 101, 209
Rick's Oasis Club, 209
Riddle, Nelson, 33, 35
Riders In The Sky, 101, 132
Ridin' High, 132
Rigberg, Jodi, 45, 63, 64, 65, 77, 100, 109, 122, 133
Right Now, 175
Righteous Brothers, 39
Rincon High School, 81
Rind, Phil, 164
Ringling Sisters, 62
Riopelle, Jerry, 179
Ritz, 179
River Road, 21, 27
River Roses, 20, 62, 81
Riverboat Six, 66
Road Runner, 21
Roadhouse Hounds, 127, 185, 187
Roadhouse Magazine, 204
Roadrunner Restaurant and Lounge, 209
Roads, Dave, 195
Robbins, Bobby, 183
Roberts, Chuck, 130
Robinson, Arami, 110
Robinson, Smokey, 151
Rock, 130, 140, 144, 161, 164, 166, 167, 171, 174, 176, 186, 189, 193, 210
Rock Café, 186
Rock for Pot Tour, 1993, 164
Rock Island Café, 165, 166, 209
Rockefeller's, 209
Rockin' R Wranglers, 132
Rocking E Saloon, 209
Rocky Mountain Emmy Awards, 177
Rode Way Inn, 209
Rodenkirch, Dave, 110

Rodenkirch, Jeff, 178
Rodeo Jesus, 152, 157
Rodgers, Jimmie, 55
Rodriguez, Hector, 102, 124, 125, 128
Rodriguez, Raoul, 102
Roger Road, 208
Rogers, Jimmy, 190
Rogers, Roy, 51, 52
Rolling Stone Deutchland, 197
Rolling Stones, 28, 43, 72, 183, 190
Romeo Void, 138
Romero Road, 206, 211
Ronco's, 193
Ronstadt, Gilbert, 34
Ronstadt, Linda, 33, 34, 35, 38, 80, 102, 124, 147
Ronstadt, Mike, 34
Ronstadt, Pete, 34
Ronstadt, Ruthmary, 34
Ronstadt, Suzi, 34
Roots & Wings, 60
Rose, Peggy, 12, 16, 20, 21, 23, 27, 30
Rosenthal, Sandy, 212
Rosie's Cantina, 22
Ross, Ed, 67
Round Up Band, 21
Round Up Saloon, 15, 21, 83, 166, 169, 209
Rouse, Charlie, 13
Rowdies, 24, 50, 76
Roxanne, 138, 140
Royal Presidio of San Agustin del Tucson, 156
Royal Sun, 209
Rozy Coyote, 140, 144
Ruben and the Romantics, 183
Rubio, Stev, 192
Rug Monkeys, 50, 76, 99
Rugburns, 195
Ruley, Gene, 186
Rumourz, 174
Rundgren, Todd, 103
Runes Café, 14, 15, 17, 22, 37, 209
Rupp, Greg, 79, 116, 123
Rush, Joe, 76, 175, 179, 185, 196
Rush, Otis, 127, 191
Russell, Leon, 43, 104
Rust, 111
Rusty Lantern, 209
Ruthrauff Road, 207, 209, 210
Rye, Margie, 24, 50, 53, 58, 59, 61
Ryle, Davis, 83

S

S.A.L.O.C., 57

Sabino Canyon Road, 208
Sacramento Dixieland Jubilee International Festival, 67
Sacred Reich, 164
Saddle City Band, 39, 94, 152, 169, 175
Safeway, 82
Salazar, José, 10
Salpointe High School, 67, 102
Salt Mines, 171, 193, 194
Salt River Ramblers Band, 60
Salter, Don, 194
Sam and Dave, 184, 204
Sam Taylor Blues Band, 147, 148, 185
Sam Taylor Blues Band Featuring Heather Hardy, 183
Sam Taylor's House of Swing, 204
Samaniego House, 209
Samarai, Psam, 64
Sambo's Restaurant, 38
Sams, Will, 104
Samurai, Psam, 123
San Agustin, 156
San Agustin del Tucson, 156
San Cosme, 157
San Francisco Bar and Grill, 113, 209
San Xavier band, 156
San Xavier del Bac, 15, 119
San Xavier Mission Pageant, 15
Sanchez Restaurant, 52
Sand Rubies, 75, 140, 143, 144, 168, 176
Sandrubies, 69, 175, 186
Santa Claus, 52
Santa Cruz Plaza, 57
Santa Cruz River, 157
Santa Fe Bar and Grill, 209
Santa Rita Ballroom, 204
Sapphire of Ironwood, 81
Saruwatari, Yuki, 134, 137, 139, 141, 149, 153, 154, 158
Sather, Red, 66, 67, 68
Satta, Norbeat, 133
Saturday Night Live, 46
Saunders, Al, 66, 68
Savage, Lee Anne, 165, 174
Savant, 140, 179
Saw Mill Café, 209
Scared of Heights, 76
Schieffelin Hall, 66
Schimmel, Eric, 37
Schneider, 200
Schokett, Bruce, 195

School of Art Institute in Chicago, 130
schoolson, 157
Schroeder, Holly, 10
Schultz, Jim, 66
Scott Avenue, 208, 210
Scoville, Kenneth, 82
Screen Actors Guild, 198, 200
Seagull, Jonathan Livingston, 108
Sears & Roebuck, 50, 58
Seeger, Pete, 200
Selena, 118
Seminole Indians, 109
Semple, Scott, 119
Señora Sands, 209
Seraphin, 144
Serres, Mike, 178
Servais, Scott, 154
Sex Pistols, 14
Sgt. Pepper, 74
Sgt. Pepper's, 186, 209
Shackleford, Gary, 16
Shake, 72, 95
Shakespeare, William, 57
Shamble, 176
Shanka, Richard, 165
Shannon, 76
Shark's, 209
Shed, 210
Shelter Recording Studios, 43
Shelton, Ricky van, 83
Shenanigan's, 210
Sheraton El Conquistador, 207, 208, 210
Sheraton Pueblo Inn, 210
Shew, Bobby, 13
Shirley's, 210
Shok Hilary, 157, 165, 175
Shooters, 62, 93, 210
Shram, Kevin, 199
Si Jargo, 162, 164, 171
Si Jargo Band, 114
Sid Levy and the MVP's, 26
Sidewinder, 69, 75
Sidewinders, 15, 53, 69, 75, 81, 144, 175, 176, 186
Silver Room, 210
Silver Screen Lounge, 113, 210
Silverbell Road, 54, 208
Silvertone, 62
Simon Peter Easter Pageant, 18
Simple Minds, 133
Sin, Mike, 97
Sinatra, Nancy, 22
Singer, Brad, 145, 168
Sippin' Whiskey Band, 102, 172
Sister Glow, 138
Sites, Ernie, 132

Ski Valley Lodge, 210
Skin on Skin, 119
Skinner Brothers, 112
Skinner, Bob, 170
Skinner, Gary, 38, 111
Skinner, Rick, 38, 111, 112
Skinny Puppy, 64
Skolliwoll, 175
Skyclad Records, 29
Slick Willy, 157, 174
Slick, Grace, 107, 166
Slither, 84
Sloane, Ari, 14
Slutes, David, 69, 70, 75, 143, 144, 175, 186
Sly and the Family Stone, 178
Small Paul and Beat Street, 26
Smiles, 136
Smith, Dylan, 75, 78, 116
Smith, Edsel, 55
Smithereens, 118
Smithsonian collection, 57
Smithsonian Institution, 52
Smokey Robinson and the Turtles, 151
Smokey's, 210
Smuggler's Inn, 208
Sneak Joint Lounge, 101, 210
Sneak Joint West, 210
Sneaky Pete's, 210
Sneed, Adrienne, 170
Soehl, Mike, 14, 64
Solarium, 210
Soldados de Cuero, 15
Solem, Phil, 140
Solorzano, José, 126
Somerset Club, 84, 101, 166, 210
Sommerset Club, 22
Songdog Café, 44, 210
Songtower, 175
Sons of the Pioneers, 51, 101
Sons of the San Joaquin, 101, 132
Sons of the Western Plains, 77
Sorce, Joey, 30, 31
Souls at Zero, 164
Soumakian, Rich, 161, 193
Sound Factory, 29, 123
Soundings of the Planet, 90, 123
Sounds of Brazil, 152
South by Southwest, 70
South Forty, 210
Southbound Group, 21
Southern Arizona Light Opera Company, 18, 57
Southern Arizona Motorcycle and Music Festival, 171

Southwest Alternatives Institute, 2, 213
Southwest Folklore Center, 92
Southwest Music Center, 166
Spacefish, 175
Spalding, Milton, 96
Spaulding, Neil, 67
Specimen, 98
Speedway Blvd., 101, 166, 206, 207, 208, 209, 210, 211
Speedway Saloon, 210
Spencer, Tim, 51
Spin Doctors, 146
Spinnaker, 210
Spinning Jenny, 145
Splinter Bros. & Sisters Warehouse, 210
Sports Page Lounge, 210
Sports-A-Rama, 210
Spring Fling, 22, 62, 118, 192
Springate, Bob, 66, 67
Sprouse, Daniel, 103
Squeezy Snake Lounge, 22
Squires, Dave, 107
Sruti, 90
St. Agustin, 126
St. Agustine, 156
St. Agustine Cathedral, 156
St. Asylum, 50
St. Elizabeth of Hungary Clinic, 118
St. Francis in the Foothills, 109
St. Mary's Hospital, 74
Stacey, Cynthia, 71, 108
Stafford, Jim, 39
Stannage, Brenda, 179
Star Crunch, 168
Starks, Burney, 212
Starlight, 175
Starliters, 183
Starner, Tim, 175, 191
Starr, Dan, 10
Starr, Steve, 212
Starship, 166
State Theatre of Arizona, 48
Statesboro Blues Band, 3, 20, 127
Statman, Arthur, 13
Steakhouse, Sonoita, 112
Steel Pulse, 122, 188
Steele Memorial Cancer Center, 118
Steele, Kimberly, 87, 96
Steele, Veronica, 83
Stephenson, 15
Stetson Nightclub, 210
Stevens, Hiram, 135
Stevens, Phil, 90, 165, 175
Stewart, Gary, 39, 115

Stewart, Rod, 190
Stickponies, 157
Stiebrs, Rudy, 66, 67
Stingrays, 210
Stitt, Dave, 93
Stitt, Duncan, 94, 114, 199
stjukson, 157
Stokes, Terry, 62
Stone Avenue, 39, 75, 103, 166, 206, 207, 209, 211
Stone Giant, 136, 138, 140, 152
Stone Poneys, 81, 124
Stone Temple Pilots, 161
Stoutenburg, Robyn, 143
Stray Cat, 210
Street Gypsy, 30, 31
Street Pajama, 3, 152
Striker, Eric, 115
Strom, Brent, 170
Stuart, Dan, 157
Studdrifters, 114
Studebaker's, 210
Stumble Inn, 42, 210
Subterranean Blues Band, 127, 191
Sudbury, Beth, 212
Sullivan, Richard, 172, 176
Summerhaven, 208
Summerset Suite, 26
Summit Studios, 30, 173
Sumter Drive, 206
Sun Swan Studios, 76
Sun Tran, 57
Sundance East, 210
Sundance West, 210
Sundin, Michelle, 86
Sundome, 107
Sundowner, 210
Sunrise Drive, 206
Supremes, 115
Surge, 63
Sutri, 123
Svendsen, Clarence, 67
Swan Road, 208, 209, 210
Swan, Pete, 21, 67
Swans, 22
Sweaty Nipples, 176
Sweet, Rick, 170
Swing Inn Lounge, 40, 83, 210
Swing Shift, 105, 106
Swinney, Katy, 128
SXSW, 139
Sydloski, Mike, 17, 90, 123
Syds, 22
Symington, Fife, 65
Syracuse University, 149

T

T.J. Canyon Band, 21
Tack Room, 149, 150
Takoma Record, 81

Takoma/Chrysalis Records, 194
Tall Cotton, 40
Tammies, 151, 175, 185, 188
Tanner, Fred, 60
Tanque Verde Guest Ranch, 101
Tanque Verde Road, 67, 137, 206, 207, 208, 209, 210, 211
Tantrum, 140, 144
Tapp, Vicki, 32
Taylor Jayne's Raspberry, 158, 159
Taylor, Beatrice, 120
Taylor, Bobby, 3, 20, 42, 45, 103, 120, 125, 147, 173, 179, 184, 202, 204, 212
Taylor, Jacques, 45, 120, 179
Taylor, Johnny, 184, 204
Taylor, Karen, 45
Taylor, Sam, 3, 20, 45, 53, 56, 58, 59, 120, 147, 148, 152, 175, 182, 183, 185, 187, 202, 203, 204, 212
Taylor, Sandra, 45
Taylor, Scott, 99
T-Bone Walker, 184, 204
TCC, 24, 57
Teague, Craig, 138
Teene, 75
Telemundo, 26, 49, 130
Telluride Bluegrass Festival, 95
Temple of Music and Art, 49, 130, 156, 210
Ten Years After, 190
Tender Trap, 210
Tequila Mockingbird, 210
Tequila Willie's, 101
Terre, J.J., 139
Terry & Zeke's, 210
Terry & Zeke's Again, 210
Tester, Bill, 136, 139
Texas Rangers, 154
TFTM, 44
Thach, Shelly, 170, 174
Thacker, Joy, 112
The High Sierra Jazz Band, 67
The Rock, 192
Thee Samples, 179
Theloneus Monk, 13
Thin Men, 133
Thing, 22
Thomas, Martin, 151
Thomas, Mickey, 166
Thompson, Bill, 177
Thompson, Hank, 39
Thompson, John, 72, 80, 89, 95

Thornydale Road, 207
Three Dog Night, 77, 78, 151
Threshing Floor, 133, 171
Tia Elena, 210
Timbreline Music, 195
Tin Ear Cocktail Lounge, 66, 210
Tinney, Craig, 44
Tinsley, Jim Bob, 132
Tiny Tim, 183
Tiny's Saloon, 21, 43, 210
Tjader, Carl, 186
Toad the Wet Sprocket, 183
Tohono O'odham Veterans Band, 163
Tom Petty and the Heartbreakers, 143
Tompkins, Richard, 72
Toole Avenue, 207
Tosh, Peter, 188
Tovi's Hoof & Horn, 21, 93, 210
Townsend, Mike, 93, 94
Townsend, Pete, 74
Toxic Ranch Records, 20, 50, 130, 133
Tracey, Ron, 62, 112
Trailmix, 132
Transatlantic Management, 98, 103, 129, 139, 165, 175
Transatlantic Management', 136
Travers, Mary, 34
Traxx, 130
Trenaine, Liz, 44
Trend, 115
Treuman, Bill, 68
Treumann, Manny, 66
Triangle, 123
Triple A, 170
Triple C Chuckwagon Lounge, 51, 210
Triple-A, 155
Trolley's, 210
Tropical Inn, 66
Trudy Fair, 132
Trujillo, Logan, 172, 174
Truth, 50, 76
TSO, 57
TSO Classic Concerts, 19
TSOL, 90
Tubac, 82
Tucker, Scooter, 170
Tucker, Tanya, 39
Tucson Amateur Championship, 184
Tucson Area Music Award, 197
Tucson Area Music Awards, 179
Tucson Arizona Boys Chorus, 105

Tucson Arts District, 81
Tucson Blonde, 159
Tucson Blues Society, 26, 89
Tucson Blvd., 207, 208, 210
Tucson Cablevision, 186
Tucson Chronicles, 213
Tucson City Amateur Champion, 18
Tucson City Council, 180
Tucson Classics, 62, 65, 118
Tucson Community Cable, 103
Tucson Community Center, 55, 57, 60, 74
Tucson Convention Center, 18, 24, 33, 56, 57
Tucson Desert Dancers, 39
Tucson Festival Society, 92
Tucson Festival, 1990, 15
Tucson Folk Festival, 44, 198
Tucson Friends of Traditional Music, 44
Tucson Fumbles, 210
Tucson Garden, 138, 140, 144, 146, 210
Tucson Garden Rock n' Roll Revival, 136
Tucson Gem & Mineral Show, 57
Tucson Girls Ranch, 55
Tucson International Mariachi Conference, 62
Tucson Jazz Orchestra, 26, 152
Tucson Jazz Society, 26, 75, 82, 152
Tucson Kitchen Musician's Association, 44
Tucson Lifestyle, 137
Tucson Mardi Gras of 1988, 26
Tucson McGraw's, 210
Tucson Meet Yourself, 82, 92, 163
Tucson Mountain Park,, 42
Tucson Museum of Art, 15
Tucson Museum of Art Historic Block, 15
Tucson Museum of Art Plaza of the Pioneers, 26
Tucson Musician's Compilation, 39, 50, 53
Tucson Musician's Showcase, 44
Tucson Nightlife, 50, 53, 58, 59, 61
Tucson Paging, 117, 130
Tucson Parks Foundation, 118

Tucson Police Department, 180
Tucson Public Libraries, 175
Tucson Public Market, 141
Tucson Rodeo, 56
Tucson Rodeo Breakfast, 55
Tucson Rodeo Grounds, 56
Tucson Rodeo Parade, 56
Tucson Symphony Orchestra, 12, 19, 57
Tucson Teen, 3, 213, 214
Tucson Toros, 154, 170, 174, 177
Tucson Tracks, 115
Tucson Unified School District, 67
Tucson Warehouse And Transfer, 75, 210
Tucson Weekly, 45, 185, 197
Tucson Y.W.C.A., 213
Tucson, Arizona Boys Chorus, 65
Tucson, history of, 82
Turbulence, 174
Turner, Ike, 183
Turner, Ike and Tina, 178
Turner, Jamie, 41
Turner, Joe, 184, 204
Turner, Tina, 151
Turpin, James, 14, 64
Turpin, Steve, 14, 64
Turtles, 178
Tutt, Terie, 63, 162
Twelve Tribes Reggae Shop, 47, 110, 122
Twin Peaks, 16, 28, 210
Twister, 24, 100
Two Pesos, 79, 121
Tyler, Richard, 150
Tyndall Avenue, 22, 207, 208, 210

U

U & the Risk, 140, 144, 145, 146
U.P.S., 152, 157
U.P.S., see Useless Pieces of Shit, 195
Udall, Morris, 86
UFO Lighting, 151
Uncle Dave Jeffrey, 152
Uncle Henry's Original Kentucky Mountaineers, 51
Uncle Steambag, 114
Underbelly, 168
Undone, 176
Unger, Julie, 162
Unicorn, 210
University Blvd., 44, 206, 208, 209

University Medical Center, 68
University of Arizona, 14, 15, 17, 18, 44, 57, 60, 62, 69, 88, 89, 91, 104, 114, 118, 137, 141, 149, 153, 158, 177, 178, 179, 186, 191, 192, 194, 195, 197, 213, 214
University of Arizona Cellar, 17, 46, 64, 138, 210
University of Arizona College of Medicine, 68
University of Arizona Department of Journalism, 181
University of Arizona Department of Theatre Arts, 57
University of Arizona Library, 92
University of Arizona Library Special Collections, 213
University of Arizona Medical Center, 118
University of Arizona Southwest Folklore Center, 163
University of Arizona Spring Fling, 22, 62, 118
University of Arizona Student Programs, 168
University of Arizona Student Union Cellar, 14
University of California Berkeley, 135
Unwinder, 210
Uribe, Tony, 127, 172, 176, 187
Useless Pieces of Shit, see U.P.S., 195
Users of the Wicked Gravity, 64, 123

V

Vactor, David, 150
Vactor, Drew, 149
Vagabundo, 101, 210
Valdez, Daniel, 34
Valencia Road, 206, 208, 210
Valencia, Valerie, 146
Valenzuela, Mitzi, 36, 37, 41
Van Dusen, Charlie, 20
Van Gogh's Italian Restaurant, 210
Vancouver Canadians, 155
Vanyon Tree, 210

Vasilé European Hair Salon, 164
Vaughn, Stevie Ray, 146, 183
Velardi, Glen, 185
Velvet Underground, 22
Ventures, 17
Veres, Dave, 170
Veterans' Memorial Hospital, 54
Vibrations, 28
Vibrations 5, 46
Victoria's, 210
Virtual Reality, 181
Viscount Suites, 210, 211
Visionary Blues Band, 119
Vista's, 210
Vital Signs, 136
Volunteer Center, 118
Vosu, Jason, 105, 106
Votang, 17, 123
Vox, Eric, 97, 98

W

W.C. in the Fields, 210
Wa:k, 15
Wagner, Michael, 161, 193
Wagon Tracks Records, 43
Wagon Wheel, 210
Wagoner, Bob, 101
Waits, Tom, 81
Wakatani, Eric, 123
Walker, Danny, 22
Walker, Jerry Jeff, 43
Walker, Mike, 47
Walker, T-Bone, 184, 204
Walker, Tom, 185
Wall of Voodoo, 79
Wall, Donne, 170
Wallace & Ladmo Show, 177
Wallace's, P.L., 169
Waller, Matt, 133
Walsh, Joe, 66
Walton, Karl, 63, 162
Wang, Nancy, 113
Warhol, Andy, 22
Warner, Steve, 83
Warren, Dale, 51
Warren, Selina, 63, 162
Washington, Grover Jr., 37
Washtub Jerry, 132
Watchel, Waddy, 143
Water, John, 22
WAVE, 37
Way Station, 140, 146, 151
Wayne, John, 83
Weapon X, 114
Webb, Dave, 83
Webb, Wanda, 83, 169
Webb, Wanda and Dave, 15
Weird Harold's, 210
Wells, Richard, 164

West University Neighborhood Association, 105
West, Rocky, 38
Western Association Festival of 1991, 101
Western Electric, 95
Western Music Association, 42, 52, 55
Western Music Festival, 42, 55, 104, 132
Western Railway Museum, 153
Western Way Circle, 209
Westfall, Eric, 92
Westin La Paloma, 88, 206, 207
Westward Look, 20, 26, 166, 208, 210
Westwood Studios, 133
Wetmore Road, 210
Whiskey Brides, 41
Whiskey's, 24, 211
White House, 105
White Knuckles Studios, 123
White Rabbit, 123
White, Bukka, 194
White, Chad, 173
White, Lavinia, 93, 130, 212

White, Michael, 69, 173
Whitney's, 211
Whittaker, Ray, 16
Who, 53
Who's Who in the West, 55
Wiggins, William, 174
Wilber's, 211
Wild Knights, 185
Wild, Wild West, 83, 95, 211
Wildcat House, 180, 211
Wildcat's Rock Café, 211
Wilde, Danny, 140
Wilder, Janos, 134
Wildfire, 40
Willcox, 86
Williams, Bill, 66
Williams, Jack, 86
Williams, Tennessee, 57
Wilmot Road, 27, 206, 208, 209, 210
Wilson, Ann, 165
Wilson, Nancy, 125
Windy Cities Bar and Grill, 128, 187, 211
Wink, 102
Winterhaven, 52
Wise Monkey, 175
Witkovic, Troy, 177
Witz, Katy, 125
WLS-AM, 86

Wolff, Paul, 98
WomanKraft, 90
Wonder Woman, 124
Wong's, 211
Wood, Jack, 13
Wooden Ball, 186
Wooden Nickel, 66
Woods, Albert, 152
Wooly Tooth, 186
Wooten, Howard, 37
Workshop Music and Sound, 20, 81, 152, 179
Wozniak, Michael, 44
WREX Records, 24, 130, 133
Writer's Room Recording Studio, 199
Wrye, Margie, see Rye, Margie
Wykle, Kara, 92

Y

Yaqui Matachin Dancers, 15
Yardbirds, 81, 190
Yaste, Lance, 104
Yates, Charley, 36, 38, 39
Yes, 115
Young Management, 196
Young, Neil, 72, 143

Young, Paul, 195, 212
Young, Pauline, 179, 196
Youth Alternatives, 213, 214
Youth Awareness Press, 213, 214
Youth Services Bureau, 213
Ysadora, 140
Yuma Beach, 76
Yuma Joe's Blues Band, 114

Z

Z Club, 114, 211
Zalicky, Al, 186
Zavala, Catherine, 151
Zebbhi Niyah, 122
Zia Records, 133, 139, 145, 152, 168, 173, 175
Zia Records 4th Arizona Compilation, 145
Zielinski, Nedra, 65, 76, 80, 82, 86, 92
Zip's Records, 17, 168, 172, 195
Zucker, Robert, 2, 25, 181, 204, 213, 214
ZZ Top, 72

Publishers

Robert Zucker, Entertainment Magazine

Tucson native **Robert Edward Zucker**, born in the mid-1950s, has been publishing for nearly four decades. He launched several Tucson, Arizona tabloid newspapers and authored dozens of manuscripts that are now being printed and digitized.

While publishing over monthly 200 newspaper editions, between 1978 and 1994, Robert also organized numerous local entertainment events, concerts, movie screenings and community projects. Originally hired by the Tucson YWCA in 1977, Robert developed *Youth Alternatives* (1978-1979), the first newspaper for Tucson teenagers and continued the publication as *Youth Awareness Press* (1979-1981). The newspaper was later titled as the *Tucson Teen* (1981-1990) after the original funding sources ended for the non-profit project. The *Magazine* (1982-1985) and the *Entertainment Magazine* (1985-1994) newspapers published for an older audience with a focus on local entertainment and national celebrities.

In January 1995, the Internet version of the *Entertainment Magazine On Line* (EMOL.org) was launched as one of the first Arizona publications to have a web presence. Robert spent a dozen years teaching desktop publishing and web publishing at the University of Arizona Department of Journalism (now School of Journalism) and launched the UA Journalism Department web site (1995). He spent eight years at Pima Community College as an instructor and adviser for the *Aztec Press*, the college newspaper. At Pima, he also developed an Internet journalism lab and the online version of the *Aztec Press* (1998).

Official Websites: http://emol.org/ and http://Robert-Zucker.com

Jon Rosen, *Newsreal*

Jonathan L is an American radio presenter, programmer, and entertainment media publisher who has lived in Berlin, Germany for the past four years. He published the *Newsreal*, an alternative Tucson, Arizona monthly music publication from the 1970s until October 1985. His radio career began in Tucson in 1982 at **KLPX-FM** with a show "**Virgin Vinyl**" which predates Alternative radio. He left Tucson in 1986 to start up Alternative radio station KEYX-FM.

Jonathan L organized his first large music festival for alternative station KUKQ in Phoenix, Arizona in 1989, years before the launch of festivals like Lollapalooza and the KROQ Weenie Roasts. For this reason, he is often called the "father of all radio festivals." In 2005, he returned form Los Angeles to create "Lopsided World Of L" which ran on Saturday mornings and Sunday evenings on KUPD-FM until he moved to Germany in 2010. The "Lopsided World of L" is produced and presented internationally every week by Jonathan L from his flat in Berlin, Germany. Now in it's 9th year, the "Lopsided World of L" is broadcast across the planet from Los Angeles, Phoenix, Berlin, Athens, Greece, Gothenburg, Sweden, and Brasov, Romania.

Official Website: http://www.jlradio.com

To Purchase Copies

Order Online:
- Amazon.com
- Barnes & Noble
- EMOL.org
- EntertainTucson.com

Purchase in Tucson, Arizona:
- Antigone Books, 411 N. 4th Avenue
- Hotel Congress, 311 E. Congress
- Mostly Books, 6208 E. Speedway
- Summit Hut, 7745 N. Oracle & 5251 E. Speedway
- Oracle Inn Steakhouse, 305 E. American Avenue, Oracle

Titles from BZB Publishing, Inc.

Available now in print:
"Entertaining Tucson Across the Decades, Volume I: 1950s-1985," by Robert E. Zucker
"Entertaining Tucson Across the Decades, Volume II: 1986-1989," by Robert E. Zucker
"Entertaining Tucson Across the Decades, Volume III: 1990s," by Robert E. Zucker
"Entertaining Tucson Highlights of Volumes I-III: 1950s-1990s," by Robert E. Zucker
"Treasures of the Santa Catalina Mountains: Legends & History," by Robert E. Zucker
"Traveling Show," by Robert E. Zucker

"Searching for Arizona's Buried Treasures," by Ron Quinn
"Mysterious Disappearances and Other Strange Tales," by Ron Quinn
"The Canyon of Gold, Buffalo Bill Cody and the Legendary Iron Door Mine Treasures," by Flint Carter

Other titles in preparation:
"The Kabbalah Wheel," by Robert E. Zucker
"From Print to Pixels," by Robert E. Zucker
"Twilight of Consciousness," by Robert E. Zucker
"Ballads of the Santa Catalina Mountains," by Gary Holdcroft (CD)
"The Miner's Story," a conversation with William "Flint" Carter (CD)

For more information, purchase titles directly, or to contact publisher:
BZB Publishing, Inc.
P.O. Box 91317
Tucson, Arizona 85752-1317 USA
520-623-3733

Email: publisher@emol.org

"Entertaining Tucson Across the Decades": http://EntertainTucson.com
Entertainment Magazine: http://emol.org/
Robert Zucker: http://robert-zucker.com

LOCAL TUCSON AUTHORS

Robert Zucker

Newspaper publisher since 1978, former journalism instructor.

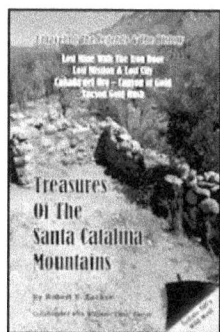

"Treasures of the Santa Catalina Mountains"
The Legends & History
By Robert E. Zucker
with Flint Carter
EMOL.org/treasurescatalinas

ISBN: 97819390500052 • 434 Pgs. • $30

"Entertaining Tucson Across the Decades"
3 Volumes 1950-2000's
Thousands of Local Musicians,
Interviews and Photos
By Robert E. Zucker
EntertainTucson.com

V1: ISBN:9781939050069 • 310 Pgs. • $20
V2: ISBN: 9781939050076 • 222 Pgs. • $15
V3: ISBN: 9781939050090 • 228 Pgs. • $15

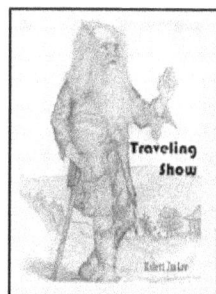

"Traveling Show"
Life's Journey in Poetry
By Robert E. Zucker
Robert-Zucker.com

ISBN: 97919390500038 • 229 Pgs. • $15

Published locally by
BZB Publishing, Inc.

Ron Quinn

Adventurer, prospector and treasure hunter.

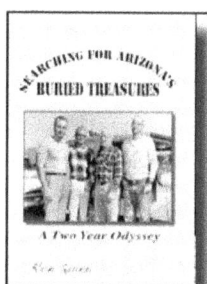

"Searching for Arizona's Buried Treasures"
82-lbs Gold Found near Tubac!
By Ron Quinn
EMOL.org/arizonatreasures

ISBN: 9781939050403 • 303 Pgs. • $19.99

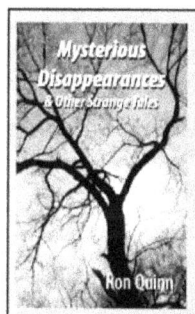

"Mysterious Disappearances"
Collection of Strange Tales
By Ron Quinn
EMOL.org/mysteriousdisappearances

ISBN: 9781939050045 • 202 Pgs. • $14.99

Flint Carter

Seasoned local prospector and treasure hunter.

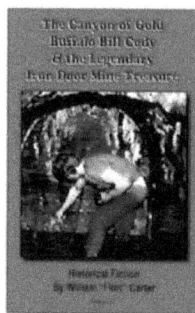

"Canyon of Gold"
Historical Fiction
By William "Flint" Carter
EMOL.org/mflintcarter

ISBN: 9781939050120 • 228 Pgs. • $20

Available at Amazon.com, Summit Hut, Mostly Books, Antigone's, Club Congress & Oracle Inn

BZB Publishing • P.O. Box 91317 • Tucson Arizona 85752 • (520) 623-3733 • publisher@emol.org

www.ingramcontent.com/pod-product-compliance
Lightning Source LLC
Chambersburg PA
CBHW081659270326
41933CB00017B/3221